ACES IN COMBAT

Books by Eric Hammel

---

76 Hours: The Invasion of Tarawa (with John E. Lane)
Chosin: Heroic Ordeal of the Korean War
The Root: The Marines in Beirut
Ace!: A Marine Night-Fighter Pilot in World War II (with R. Bruce Porter)
Duel for the Golan (with Jerry Asher)
Guadalcanal: Starvation Island
Guadalcanal: The Carrier Battles
Guadalcanal: Decision At Sea
Munda Trail: The New Georgia Campaign
The Jolly Rogers (with Tom Blackburn)
Khe Sanh: Siege in the Clouds
First Across the Rhine (with David E. Pergrin)
Lima-6: A Marine Company Commander in Vietnam (with Richard D. Camp)
Ambush Valley
Fire in the Streets: The Battle for Hue
Aces Against Japan
Aces Against Germany
Six Days in June
Air War Europa: Chronology
Aces Against Japan II
Carrier Clash
Aces At War
Air War Pacific: Chronology

ACES IN COMBAT

The American Aces Speak

Volume V

Eric Hammel

Pacifica Press

Manufactured in the United States of America.

Typography by Words To Go, Inc., Pacifica, California

ISBN 0-935553-28-2

Library of Congress Cataloging-in-Publication Data

Aces in combat / [compiled by] Eric Hammel
p. cm. — (The American aces speak ; v. 5)
First person battle narratives by American fighter aces serving in World War II.
Includes bibliographical reference and index.
ISBN 0-935553-28-2 (alk. paper)
1. World War, 1939–1945—Aerial operations, American. 2. World War, 1939–1945—Personal narratives, American. 3. Korean War, 1950–1953—Aerial operations. 4. Korean War, 1950–1953—Personal narratives, American. 5. United States. Army Air Forces—Biography. 6. United States. Air Force—Biography. 7. Fighter pilots—United States—Biography. I. Hammel, Eric M.. II. Series: Hammel, Eric M. American aces speak ; v. 5.
D790.H254 1992 vol. 5
359.4'00973 s—dc21
[940.54'4973] 98-4265
CIP

For Steve Burnstein,
the best friend a guy ever had

Contents

Glossary and Guide to Abbreviations

A-20 USAAF Douglas (Havoc) light bomber
A5M IJN Mitsubishi Type 96 (Claude) fighter
A6M IJN Mitsubishi Type 0 (Zero, Zeke, Hap, Hamp) fighter
A-24 USAAF Douglas (Dauntless) light attack bomber (same as SBD)
A-36 USAAF North American (Apache) ground-support fighter (early P-51 variant)
AA Antiaircraft
ack-ack Antiaircraft gunfire
AD USN Douglas (Skyraider) carrier attack bomber
Airacobra USAAF Bell P-39 or P-400 fighter
API Armor-piercing incendiary (bullet)
AT-6 USAAF North American (Texan) advanced trainer
B-17 USAAF Boeing (Flying Fortress) four-engine heavy bomber
B-24 USAAF Consolidated (Liberator) four-engine heavy bomber
B-25 USAAF North American (Mitchell) twin-engine medium bomber
B-26 USAAF Martin (Marauder) twin-engine medium bomber
B-29 USAAF Boeing (Superfortress) four-engine very heavy bomber

B6N IJN Nakajima (Jill) carrier torpedo/level bomber
Betty IJN Mitsubishi Type 1 (G4M) twin-engine medium bomber
Bf-109 German Messerschmitt fighter
Bogey Unidentified aircraft
Buffalo USN/USMC Brewster F2A carrier fighter
Buster Emergency speed
C-47 USAAF Douglas (Skytrain) twin-engine troop carrier/cargo transport
C-54 USAAF Douglas (Skymaster) four-engine transport
C-87 USAAF Consolidated (Liberator) four-engine transport (B-24 variant)
C6N IJN Nakajima (Myrt) carrier reconnaissance plane
CAP Combat air patrol
Claude IJN Mitsubishi Type 96 (A5M) fighter
CO Commanding officer
Corsair USN/USMC Vought F4U carrier fighter
CPT Civilian Pilot Training program
D4Y IJN Yokosuka Type 2 (Judy) carrier dive-bomber
Dauntless USN/USMC Douglas SBD carrier scout/dive-bomber
Devastator USN Douglas TBD torpedo bomber
Do-217 German Dornier twin-engine medium bomber
E13A IJN Aichi (Jake) float reconnaissance plane
F-6 USAAF North American (Mustang) photo-reconnaissance fighter (P-51 variant)
F-80 USAF Lockheed (Shooting Star) jet fighter-bomber
F-84 USAF Republic (Thunderjet) jet fighter-bomber
F-86 USAF North American (Sabre) jet interceptor
F1M IJN Mitsubishi Type 0 (Pete) float reconnaissance biplane
F2A USN/USMC Brewster (Buffalo) carrier fighter
F4F USN/USMC Grumman (Wildcat) carrier fighter
F4U USN/USMC Vought (Corsair) carrier fighter
F6F USN Grumman (Hellcat) carrier fighter
F9F USN/USMC Grumman (Banshee) carrier jet interceptor
FDO Fighter direction officer
Fi-156 German Fiesler reconnaissance plane

Flak Antiaircraft gunfire (from ***F****lieger* ***A****bwher* ***K****annon*)
Flying Tigers Nickname for the Chinese Air Force's American Volunteer Group (AVG)
Frances IJN Yokosuka P1Y twin-engine medium bomber
FW-190 German Focke-Wulf fighter
G Force of gravity (x 1)
G.50 Italian Fiat fighter
G3M IJN Mitsubishi (Nell) twin-engine medium bomber
G4M IJN Mitsubishi Type 1 (Betty) twin-engine medium bomber
GI Government Issue (refers to American servicemen)
H6K IJN Kawanishi (Mavis) four-engine long-range maritime patrol bomber
He-111 German Heinkel twin-engine medium bomber
He-177 German Heinkel twin-engine heavy bomber
Hamp Variant of IJN A6M Zero fighter
Hellcat USN Grumman F6F carrier fighter
Helldiver USN Curtiss SB2C carrier scout/dive bomber
HVAR High-veolocity aerial rocket
IFF Identification Friend or Foe (radio device)
(jg) junior grade
Jake IJN E13A float-reconnaissance plane
Jill IJN Yokosuka B6N carrier torpedo/level bomber
Ju-52 German Junkers trimotor transport
Ju-87 German Junkers (Stuka) dive-bomber
Ju-88 German Junkers twin-engine light bomber/dive-bomber
Ju-188 German Junkers twin-engine medium bomber
Judy IJN Yokosuka Type 2 (D4Y) carrier scout/dive bomber
kamikaze Refers to Japanese suicide aircraft
Ki-27 IJA Nakajima Type 97 (Nate) fighter
Ki-43 IJA Nakajima Type 1 (Oscar) fighter
Ki-44 IJA Nakajima Type 2 (Tojo) fighter
Ki-45 IJA Nakajima Type 2 (Nick) twin-engine fighter
Ki-57 IJA Mitsubishi (Topsy) twin-engine transport
Ki-61 IJA Kawasaki Type 3 (Tony) fighter
Kingfisher USN Vought (OS2U) observation-scout floatplane

Lancaster British Avro 683 four-engine heavy bomber
Liberator USAAF Consolidated B-24 four-engine heavy bomber
Lightning USAAF Lockheed P-38 twin-engine fighter
LSO Landing signal officer
LST Landing Ship, Tank
Luftwaffe German Air Force
Mach Speed of sound
Mae West Inflatable life vest
Mavis IJN Kawanishi H6K four-engine long-range maritime patrol bomber
Mc.202 Italian Macchi fighter
Me-108 German Messerchimitt communications plane
Me-110 German Messerschmitt twin-engine heavy fighter/night fighter
Me-210 German Messerschmitt twin-engine heavy fighter (Me-110 variant)
Me-410 German Messerschmitt twin-engine heavy fighter (Me-110 variant)
Me-262 German Messerschmitt twin-jet fighter
MEW Microwave Early Warning ground-control radar
MiG-15 Soviet-built jet fighter
Mitchell USAAF North American B-25 twin-engine medium bomber
Mosquito British de Havilland D.H.98 twin-engine two-seat bomber/fighter-bomber/night fighter
Mustang USAAF/USAF North American P-51 fighter; RAF/RCAF North American ground-cooperation fighter
Myrt IJN Nakajima (C6N) carrier reconnaissance plane
Nate IJA Nakajima Ki-27 fighter
Nell IJN Mitsubishi G3M twin-engine medium bomber
Nick IJA Nakajima Type 2 (Ki-45) twin-engine fighter
OS2U USN Vought (Kingfisher) observation-scout floatplane
Oscar IJA Nakajima Type 1 (Ki-43) fighter
OTU Operational Training Unit
P-36 USAAC Curtiss (Hawk) fighter

P-38 USAAF Lockheed (Lightning) twin-engine fighter
P-39 USAAF Bell (Airacobra) fighter/fighter-bomber
P-40 USAAF Curtiss (Warhawk) fighter
P-43 USAAC Republic (Lancer) fighter
P-47 USAAF Republic (Thunderbolt) fighter
P-51/F-51 USAAF/USAF North American (Mustang) fighter/fighter-bomber
P-61 USAAF Northrop (Black Widow) twin-engine night fighter
P-63 USAAF Bell (King Cobra) fighter
P-400 USAAF Bell (Airacobra) export variant fighter/fighter-bomber
P1Y IJN Yokosuka (Frances) twin-engine medium bomber
Pete IJN Mitsubishi Type 0 (F1M) float reconnaissance biplane
POW Prisoner of war
R4D USN/USMC Douglas (Dakota) twin-engine passenger/cargo plane (same as C-47)
RAF Royal Air Force
RCAF Royal Canadian Air Force
ROTC Reserve Officer Training Corps
RP-63 USAAF Bell (King Cobra) target fighter
RPM Revolutions per minute
R&R Rest and recuperation
Sabre USAF North American F-86 jet interceptor
SB2C USN Curtiss (Helldiver) carrier scout/dive-bomber
SBD USN Douglas (Dauntless) carrier scout/dive-bomber
Shooting Star USAAF/USAF Lockheed F-80 jet fighter-bomber
Spitfire British-built Supermarine fighter
Stuka German Junkers Ju-87 dive-bomber
TBD USN Douglas (Devastator) torpedo bomber
Thunderbolt USAAF Republic P-47 fighter
Tojo IJA Nakajima Type 2 (Ki-44) fighter
Tony IJA Kawasaki Type 3 (Ki-61) fighter
Topsy IJA Mitsubishi Ki-57 twin-engine transport
USAAC United States Army Air Corps
USAAF United States Army Air Forces

USMC United States Marine Corps
USN United States Navy
USS United States Ship
V-2 German sub-orbital ballistic ground-to-ground missile
VB USN bombing squadron
VBF USN fighter-bomber squadron
VF USN fighter squadron
VF(N) USN night fighter squadron
VHF Very high frequency (radio)
VMF USMC fighter squadron
VT USN torpedo squadron
W-34 German Junkers light transport
Wehrmacht German armed forces
Wildcat USN/USMC Grumman F4F or General Motors FM carrier fighter
Yak-3 Soviet-built Yakovlev fighter
Yak-9 Soviet-built Yakovlev fighter
YE/ZB USN aircraft carrier directional radio homing beacon (also known as YE)
Zeke IJN Mitsubishi Type 0 (A6M) carrier fighter
Zero IJN Mitsubishi Type 0 (A6M) carrier fighter

PART I

In Combat Over East Asia and the Pacific

THE FIRST STUMBLING STEP

Lieutenant ROGER MEHLE, USN
VF-6 (USS *Enterprise)*
Marshall Islands—February 1, 1942

Roger William Mehle was born in Cincinnati, Ohio, on October 16, 1915. He graduated from the United States Naval Academy in June 1937 and served aboard the battleship USS New Mexico *for two years before being selected to undergo flight training. He earned his wings at Pensacola Naval Air Station in June 1939. In July, Lieutenant (jg) Mehle underwent carrier landing qualifications as a member of USS* Saratoga's *Fighting Squadron 3 (VF-3), and in late 1940 he was assigned to VF-6, a newly re-equipped Grumman F4F Wildcat unit stationed aboard the USS* Enterprise. *He was aboard the carrier with his squadron, making for Pearl Harbor from Wake Island, on the morning of December 7, 1941.*

Fighting Squadron 6, a unit of Air Group 6 commanded by Lieutenant Commander Wade McClusky, was embarked in the USS *Enterprise,* CV-6. On the morning of February 1, 1942, following a scary predawn rendezvous off the starboard bow of the ship, our tensions were, in fact, somewhat eased as Wade led five of us to 10,000 feet and headed toward our assigned target area, Wotje Atoll in the Marshall Islands, only about 50 miles from the ship.

Eased tensions? Well, only minimally. We were headed into *combat!* The enemy was going to try to *kill* us! Could we possibly hurt him with the two 100-pound bombs slung beneath the stubby wings of our six F4F Wildcats, or with four .50-caliber machine guns per plane that were so prone to jamming? Probably not, but they surely could hurt us! Stomachs were knotted and mouths were dry.

The fact is that VF-6 and the rest of Air Group 6 were woefully unprepared in all respects for that "raid" on the Marshall Islands. Together with a similar raid by the USS *Saratoga's* Air Group 3 against targets in the Gilbert Islands, this was the first, stumbling step in the grand offensive in the Pacific that led us to Tokyo Bay in September 1945.

During the summer of 1941, Air Group 6—the *Enterprise* Air Group—was primarily based ashore at Ford Island in Pearl Harbor, because the Navy's operating funds were so very limited. To our frustration, each working day was over at 1300 and flying was very limited. We were aware that there was some growing problem with the Japanese, but despite the occasional runway exercise during so-called alerts, we in VF-6 thought it was all one big continuing exercise to keep our spirits up. If not—if our leaders felt we would really be in a war with Japan—why were we not permitted a lot more flying hours, more shipboard experience, and especially more ammunition for our guns?

It was not until very late in November 1941—a week or so before December 7—when, in deep radio silence and secrecy, after recovering our air group and a Marine fighter squadron, the ship headed west toward Wake Island. For the first time since I had joined VF-6, we flew our F4F-3As with a full loads of .50-caliber ammunition—2,400 rounds, instead of the 144 rounds that were invariably loaded for gunnery exercises against towed target sleeves. Those extra bullets added up to more than 1,000 pounds of extra weight. As a result, the F4F's nimbleness was greatly penalized; it climbed slower, responded more sluggishly, and used up more fuel faster than we were used to.

One other very severe problem was brought to the attention of Wade McCluskey and me by Lieutenant Jim Gray, the VF-6 flight officer, when he pointed out that our aircraft had neither modern self-sealing fuel tanks nor armor behind the pilot's seat. I was the squadron engineer, and both Wade and Jim prevailed on me to fix at least the armor problem. My chief mechanic and I devised a stop-gap remedy. The chief procured from the ship's engineers quarter-inch boilerplate from which we cut patterns suitable for installation behind each cockpit seat. I personally was not in favor of adding another 100 pounds of weight to the already overloaded fighters, but naturally Wade and Jim prevailed.

At dawn on February 1, 1942, I was with Wade McCluskey and the four other pilots in our division, closing on Wotje, a tiny dot in the sea 8,000 feet below us that was becoming more defined as the sun slowly rose. Wade had said in our pre-takeoff briefing before that we would go in high, open out in line, push over, and dive steep and fast on any targets we could find on the airfield or in the atoll. That way, antiaircraft fire probably wouldn't touch us. We would drop one of our 100-pound bombs on any likely targets we spotted as we pushed over. That was the extent of our target planning because photo intelligence of enemy installations in the atoll wasn't available to us. If we didn't encounter enemy fighters, we would climb back up to 7,000 or 8,000 feet and dive again to drop our second bomb. We would be dropping a total of twelve 100-pound bombs; then we would return triumphantly to the ship.

When we passed over the airfield for the first run, ground fire was negligible; we had caught the Japanese by surprise. On the second bomb run, however, we received moderate to intense fire from guns on the island and aboard ships in the lagoon. Puffs from exploding heavy antiaircraft shells were all around. But Wade seemed to be right—steep and fast was the way to go. Get in, get out! I pulled out low over my drop point and heaved a sigh of relief as I started to climb. Then I looked to my left and was startled to see, only about three feet from where I sat, a large hole clear through my wing root! What was that this about "probably won't get hurt?"

My third dive, a strafing pass over the airfield, was steeper and faster than the first two. No more holes appeared in my F4F that time.

Lieutenant Jim Gray must have had some kind of premonition when he insisted upon the installation of armored seat backs before the Marshalls raid. As we all discovered upon returning to the ship from our various missions, his flight of F4Fs had run into some opposition in the air over their target, Taroa Island in Maloelap Atoll. The fuselage of Jim's F4F was peppered with many holes, and there were numerous 7.7mm bullets plastered against the armor plate he had been so anxious to have installed. They were lodged squarely behind his back.

So that was the way things developed between December 7, 1941, and February 1, 1942. We learned we would be striking a blow of revenge sometime in late December, and at the time the news struck many different chords in each of us—elation, pride, courage, and of course a touch of dread. Thankfully, our first puny efforts against the Marshall and Gilbert islands were to be magnified thousands of times over as the next three-and-a-half years rolled victoriously by!

Later that afternoon, a small number of Japanese aircraft struck back at the Enterprise. *Roger Mehle happened to be on the flight deck, in his F4F's cockpit, when the action began, and he was able to get aloft in time to intercept, damage, and ultimately shoot down an Imperial Navy Aichi E13A Jake float reconnaissance plane. An hour later, Mehle and two other VF-6 pilots shot down a Mitsubishi G3A Nell twin-engine bomber that had just attacked and missed the* Enterprise *with its bombs. On February 24, 1942, Mehle and two other VF-6 F4F pilots shot down a Kawanishi H6K Mavis four-engine patrol bomber just off Wake Island.*

Shortly after a series of raids on Japanese-held island bases in late February and early March 1942, Lieutenant Commander Wade McCluskey was made the Air Group 6 commander, Lieutenant Jim Gray assumed command of VF-6, and Lieutenant Roger Mehle fleeted up to squadron executive officer. Following the Battle of Midway, Mehle and other senior combat veterans returned to the United States to train new pilots.

In early 1944, Lieutenant Commander Roger Mehle's Light Carrier Air Group 28 joined the USS Monterey *for a combat tour that included numerous strikes and battles across the Central Pacific, the Philippines, Okinawa, and Formosa. On June 11, 1944, Mehle shot down two Impe-*

rial Navy Mitsubishi A6M Zero fighters in the Mariana Islands; and on June 19, during the "Marianas Turkey Shoot," he achieved ace status when he downed a pair of Nakajima B6N Jill torpedo bombers.

Following World War II, Roger Mehle rose steadily through the naval aviation ranks. His final combat command, as a rear admiral, was off Vietnam in 1967, directing Task Force 77, the Attack Carrier Striking Force.

Rear Admiral Roger Mehle passed away in 1997.

DECISION AT MIDWAY*

Lieutenant JIM GRAY, USN
VF-6 (USS *Enterprise*)
Midway—June 4, 1942

James Seton Gray, Jr., was born in Milwaukee on February 1, 1914. In 1930, at sixteen years of age, he became the youngest licensed pilot in the United States.

Jim Gray graduated from the Naval Academy in the Class of 1936, served two obligatory years aboard ship, and fulfilled a life-long ambition when he was accepted for naval flight training in 1938. By December 7, 1941, Lieutenant Gray was the flight officer with Fighting Squadron (VF) 6 aboard the USS Enterprise.

During the carrier raid against the Japanese base on Taroa in the Marshall Islands' Maloelap Atoll on February 1, 1942—his twenty-eighth birthday—Lieutenant Gray missed by only a few minutes becoming the very first U.S. Navy fighter pilot to down a Japanese airplane. Instead, he became the second Navy pilot—and the first future Navy ace—to score victories in World War II when he shot down two Imperial Navy Mitsubishi A5M Claude fighters over Taroa. He took part in other daring early carrier raids in February and March 1942.

On June 4, 1942, Lieutenant Jim Gray took part in the decisive action of the Battle of Midway as squadron commander of VF-6 and leader of a ten-plane flight of VF-6 Grumman F4F Wildcat fighters

---

* This article was written by Captain James Gray shortly before his retirement from the Navy in late 1965. It is used with permission of his family.

assigned to protect the slow, vulnerable, outmoded Douglas TBD Devastator torpedo planes of Torpedo Squadron (VT) 6, also based aboard the Enterprise. *Something went wrong for the VF-6 escorts and the VT-6 TBDs during this crucial mission, and Jim Gray received most of the blame meted out by chroniclers of the great carrier battle. In about 1965, toward the end of his naval career, Gray finally broke a two-decade silence to respond to what he felt was unwarranted criticism of his decisions by several historians. The following is his response, edited for clarity and style; included is a slightly abridged passage from a book about the Midway battle.*

Among the records of varying historical importance which repose in the United States Naval Academy Museum at Annapolis is "The War Record of Fighting Squadron Six." This is a diary-type document in which the squadron's duty officers summed up each day's activities during the seven months of World War II on and subsequent to December 7, 1941. Fighting-6 was embarked in the USS *Enterprise.* Since the War Record was informally maintained and not a required item by the instructions from higher authority then in effect, this document found its way to the museum rather than to the National Archives.

It is unfortunate that battle reports and messages in the record do so little to explain the "why" of decisions or actions taken in the heat of battle or under the yoke of great responsibility. Great men who played prominent parts in the writing of history are able to recast the details in later years through the publication of their memoirs. Less important men who through circumstance made a small appearance upon one of the great stages of history are less fortunate. As commanding officer of Fighting Squadron 6 at the Battle of Midway, it was my privilege to play a small part.

There were many, many factors which would seem to have absolutely no bearing on the action of June 4, 1942, which served to influence decisions taken on that day. Early training in aviation, previous experiences in combat, and the Battle of the Coral Sea less than a month earlier were such factors. It will presently become evident that it is appropriate to consider some of these before reviewing in detail the part played by Fighting-6 as escort to the initial *Enterprise* strike group at the

Battle of Midway. Neither these nor the squadron's War Record were considered by . . . numerous authors or students of the battle.

In his excellent book, *The Big E,* Commander Edward P. Stafford makes the following statements concerning the initial action on June 4, 1942:

> After breakfast, . . . Lem Massey [the Torpedo Squadron 6 executive officer] and [the operations officer] Art Ely conferred with Jim Gray. It was agreed that Gray would keep his fighters high to preserve the altitude advantage he needed against the agile Zeros, and, at the same time, provide protection for the *[Enterprise]* dive-bombers. Ely's radio call, "Come on down, Jim," would be the signal that the torpedo planes needed help and Gray's fighters would dive to the attack. . . .
>
> At 1110, Jim Gray caught sight of the enemy carriers. He looked below him for the torpedo planes and saw the tiny wide-winged wedges disappear into a cloud, headed for the target. This tactic, he remembered, had been used at Coral Sea, where the Devastators of the *Yorktown* and *Lexington* had successfully used cloud cover in making their approaches.
>
> The flight of fighters armed their guns and flew on toward the enemy, awaiting Art Ely's call to action.
>
> It never came.
>
> While two torpedo squadrons [VT-6 and VT-8] were being slaughtered by the Zeros and the AA down among the enemy ships, Jim Gray circled with ten fighters four miles overhead. Between the scattered clouds he could see the curling wakes and flashing guns of a fleet under air attack. Some, at least, of the frantic radio transmissions made by the torpedo pilots must have filtered into his radio, which was tuned to Ely's frequency. But he did not receive the prearranged distress signal—and he had a dual responsibility. In a decision which has been a matter of bitter controversy within naval aviation ever since, Gray elected to keep his fighters high, preserving their altitude advantage, in order to cover [the *Enterprise]* dive-bombers in their approach.

♦

[*Editor's Note:* Stafford, Commander Edward P., USN. *The Big E.* New York: Ballantine Books, 1974. In the original hardcover edition of this book, released by Random House in 1962, Stafford asserted that Gray spoke at breakfast directly with the VT-6 commander, Lieutenant Commander Gene Lindsay, rather than with Massey and Ely. Gray's original 1965 article quoted from the offending passages appearing in the 1962 edition, but the excerpts shown here are from the 1974 edition, into which Gray's version of the breakfast meeting was incorporated. Factual changes aside, Stafford left in the reference to a "bitter controversy," and indeed there has been one—among Midway buffs—despite the fact that the record was long ago set straight to the satisfaction of the principals involved and most Midway chroniclers following on the corrected Stafford account. It is the "bitter controversy" that we attempt to dispel here. There is no such thing.]

If there is "bitter controversy in naval aviation ever since," let it be known that the controversy is between those who know the facts of the matter and those who don't. Suffice to say, Captain George D. Murray, commanding officer of the USS *Enterprise,* and Lieutenant Commander Wade McClusky, the Air Group 6 commander, never questioned any decision made by any of their flight commanders. Later that year, when he reported at Pensacola as chief of Naval Air Training, Rear Admiral Murray ordered me to serve as squadron commander of the fighter training squadron there.

But this is ahead of our story. Let us go back to Milwaukee County Airport in 1929, before it was known as General Mitchell Field. It was there that I learned to fly as a flight student under the late "Speed" Holman (with whose Laird biplane he was first to win the Thompson Trophy Race three times), the late Stan La Parle, and Frank Ernst (who later became senior pilot at Northwest Airlines). Part and parcel of the fundamentals which these pioneers drove home to their students was, "Only a fool runs out of gas in an airplane." This was stressed as forcefully as, "Don't lose flying speed." On navigation training flights at Pensacola years later, it was given the same weight. Much later, over a fleet engagement at Midway, these words were to play a part in my decision to remain at altitude for reasons which will soon be apparent.

The introduction of the F4F-4 Wildcat into Fighting-6 took place after the Marcus Island raid in March 1942. It was an event that provoked from the pilots howls of protest over the F4Fs excessive weight. This was in contrast to simultaneous expressions of pleasure at having received for the first time a fully combat-ready fighter. Until April 1942, we had fought in the F4F-3A, which lacked self-sealing fuel tanks and armor plate. It was thanks only to homemade armor fashioned from boiler plate obtained from the *Enterprise* engine room and installed behind our seats that several of us had returned safely from the Marshalls strike in thoroughly perforated airplanes. In that action we learned that we were no match for the Zero in maneuverability. It was only when the Zeros had pulled up in front of our guns after completing firing runs on us that we had been able to make some kills.

We tried to improvise additional gasoline capacity in the F4F-4, since the additional weight (nearly 8,000 pounds versus the 7,400 pounds with which we flew in a fully combat-loaded F4F-3A) seriously reduced our range. The record for April 22, 1942 reads, "Fighting Six is now working on a monstrosity to put more gas in an F4F-4. Okay if it weighed nothing full."

Our fears concerning fuel limitation were not without foundation. On June 4, 1942, the day of the Midway battle, Machinist W. H. Warden landed in the water, out of gas, although he had been airborne well under three hours on a combat air patrol over *Enterprise* that involved nothing more than circling overhead. The escort fighters on the initial strike had been airborne longer than Warden by the time they were recovered at 1250 on the day of the battle. That fuel was a major problem was further corroborated by the fact that the Fighting-8 escort group under Lieutenant Commander Pat Mitchell failed to head for home soon enough, and the entire flight ran out of fuel and landed in the water.

There is a factor concerning the proper use of fighters that is appropriate to mention here.

On December 7, 1941, the following entry was made in the War Record. ". . . No planes launched to attack the Japanese planes rendezvousing over Barbers Point [Oahu]. At 0830, all fighters were available, engines running, and pilots in planes (fully armed) . . . the order was given to launch the four-plane combat air patrol and to send the rest of the fighters down Number-1 elevator. Maintained combat air patrol over ship until sunset."

Since we were in the cockpits of our planes with radios turned on, just south of Oahu, we could hear the frantic messages of men under mortal attack as our Air Group 6 dive-bombers, launched but a few minutes before, stumbled with no warning of any kind into the middle of the Japanese strike on Pearl Harbor. We knew that there were Japanese aircraft to be countered and we wanted to go after them.

Our skipper, Lieutenant Commander Wade McClusky, asked Captain Murray and Rear Admiral William Halsey to launch us for what we hoped would be a field day. The admiral reminded us that these fighters were for the defense of our own fleet, and this is what they would be used for. We were bitter, and we had difficulty sharing the admiral's view, but history has left no question that the admiral made the correct decision.

The following excerpts from the War Record indicate exactly how unhappy we had been at not getting into action over Pearl: "22 December 1941. Everyone seems to feel it's the war between the two yellow races. Wake was attacked this morning and probably surrendered with *Saratoga* but 700 miles away and us steaming around in circles east of the 180th [meridian]"; or "23 December 1941. Wake is gone, Singapore, Hong Kong, and Manila are all seriously threatened. We still haven't dared to stick our necks in to fight."

When we were over the Japanese fleet at Midway, our ten aircraft were the major slice of the *Enterprise's* protection; and Admiral Halsey's advice that these aircraft were meant primarily to defend the fleet added considerable weight to my belief that this fighter unit must not run short of fuel.

On May 28, we were joined by a pilot who had participated in the Battle of the Coral Sea. We spent many hours trying to learn in detail what had happened there. This pilot, Ensign William Wileman by name, drove home several points which greatly influenced our plan of action at Midway.

Wileman told us that every time one of our fighters had gotten off by himself and had tried to mix it up with the Japanese Zeros, he was either lost or badly shot up. Lieutenant Dick Bull, one of my classmates at Annapolis and at Pensacola, (who was very experienced because he had been flying privately before he entered the Academy in 1932) was last seen alive chasing after a pair of Zeros between the clouds. At the Coral Sea, it was the fighters and the dive-bombers as they reached their push-over points that had taken the losses. The torpedo planes had flown in using cloud cover to make their attacks and returned practically unscathed. The *Lexington* torpedo planes attacked their target (which was later identified as the carrier *Shokaku)* through a hole in the clouds.

During our years of training together in the *Enterprise* Air Group, we had considered the proper tactics to attack a fleet. Without an external bomb load, the fighter was considered almost useless against a major ship, except when strafing a carrier with a full deckload of aircraft. No bombs were carried by the fighters at Midway.

Most of the ships of the Japanese fleet at Midway were screened from us by clouds. Through thin patches we could occasionally see the wakes of some of the ships, and the one carrier that we could see in the clear did not have planes on deck. We could see no airborne aircraft at all. Had the dive-bombers shown up the need to refuel required that we return to *Enterprise,* we should have gone down for the purpose of spreading the AA fire and to guard the dive-bombers' tails from any Zeros that might come in on them as they arrived at the push-over point. On June 6, we used this tactic successfully when Fighting-6 strafed accompanying destroyers as the dive-bombers plastered a heavy cruiser.

These then are some of the ingredients which played a part in our actions of June 4, 1942. We may now consider the actual sequence of events as the vivid memories are called upon to record them for the first time since the squadron "Narrative of Events" (which is in the archives) was prepared by me as commanding officer.

Lieutenant Commander Gene Lindsey, the Torpedo-6 commanding officer, had cracked up coming aboard when he flew out from Ford Island a few days earlier to head for Midway. He had been the first plane to land, and we were all seriously jolted when we saw him go over the side as we circled waiting for our turn. Gene had made a slow approach and fell off in a stall as he came over the ramp. He and his crew were rescued, but he had been badly cut about the face and badly shaken up. He was left pretty much to himself to rest and repair as we steamed to our date with history. My conference concerning the procedure to be followed in escorting the torpedo planes was with Lieutenant Art Ely, the operations officer. I never saw Gene Lindsey from the time of his crackup until the Midway launch, save to mention in the mess how pleased we were about his successful rescue.

Art and Lem Massey, the Torpedo-6 exec, concurred that we should put the fighters high for the benefit of the dive-bombers, since at the Coral Sea action it was pretty much proved that U.S. fighters had to have altitude over the Zero to be of any use at all. The subject of possible cloud cover never came up. Art was to say "Come on down, Jim" in the event he thought he needed help.

There are enough war stories on the shelves to cover adequately the pre-battle thoughts and actions of men who may not see another sunrise after the next. Most of these were written by men who lived this experience. Still, we have yet to see one which could describe the activities of Air Group 6 on any "strike night" or on the night before the Battle of Midway.

These pilots were a a group of keenly trained professionals who for the most part had spent a year or more working together for just this chance to make a major score against the Japanese. There were no religious services so far as memory serves. We were too busy. Remembering how several of us had lost out on sure kills in previous actions when nothing happened as triggers were pressed, we loaded our guns bullet by bullet with loving care and checked our firing circuits. No dirty airplanes ever flew from the *Enterprise* in those days. Plane captains took pride in keeping their aircraft gleaming and sleek. Many bought wax with their own money to outdo the others. Charts and plotting boards were cleaned and prepared for the morning's data. By the time all of the preliminaries were in hand, most pilots were too exhausted to do more than turn in and go quickly to sleep. It is doubtful that there were any atheists in *Enterprise* on the night of June 3, 1942. The prayers that were routine from all of us were, perhaps, a little more intense.

At breakfast the next day, the small talk was hardly different from any other morning. "One-eyed sandwiches" were an *Enterprise* favorite, and that's what most of us had: a slice of toast holed to accommodate an egg, which is fried in butter therein until the egg is "over medium" and the toast golden brown. Collins, the chief wardroom steward, was gifted in being able to keep a large number of constantly starving aviators happy with his offerings of good food. If one of our wives could do the one-eye as well, we never identified her.

Until launch at 1000, all our activity was a repeat of the same things we'd done over a hundred times before.

June 4, 1942, was a warm, rather damp, hazy day with many patches of low cloud. After takeoff, we made our standard rendezvous, and on getting over the low cumulus it became a clear, beautiful day. Our flight joined without difficulty into five two-plane sections. We started our long climb immediately on join-up, getting about halfway to our desired altitude of about 22,000 feet by the time the torpedo planes were formed.

A formation of TBDs was seen at this time to be joined up and headed for the enemy. Since they were without fighter escort, we took station over them and continued to climb. We had a considerable speed advantage, so it was necessary to **S**-turn back and forth, even in the climb, in order to keep the torpedo planes in sight. It was impossible to tell one torpedo outfit from another at altitude, so it actually turned out later that it was Torpedo-8 over which we flew, since they had fifteen planes in formation (Torpedo-6 was able to get off only fourteen), and they flew a beeline to the Japanese fleet. For a while, we tried to cover another outfit on diverging course, but it was too far behind us to continue. We learned later that Torpedo-6 made a big dogleg to the southwest, overshooting the Japanese fleet by an estimated fifty miles, then searched to the northwest, and finally attacked in a northeasterly direction. This added three sides of a square to their approach path.

The foregoing accounts for my not having heard anything from Art Ely. Our torpedo planes didn't arrive at the target until well after we had reached the limit of our fuel safety margin and were hightailing it for home.

We had little difficulty in following the torpedo planes below us. The low scud was above them, but less than a quarter of the sky was overcast until we arrived in the area, where we were expecting the Zeros to come diving out of the sun at any moment.

As we neared our estimated time of arrival in the vicinity of the fleet, we continued to **S**-turn, as much to keep from being ambushed as to see our torpedo planes. Then, as if in an answer to our prayers, a huge area of solid overcast was noted ahead to the west. Once the torpedo planes were safely under the overcast, they could use the clouds for cover, and we could concentrate on keeping the area sanitized for the dive-bombers.

We watched the torpedo planes disappear under that solid sheet of cloud, and at our altitude there was precious little we could do for them thereafter. We maintained course until Lieutenant (jg) Jack Kelley came on the air with "There they are, at one o'clock, down, Skipper." We thought he meant aircraft, and aboard my plane the guns were recharged in order to ensure that the two dummy rounds with which each belt was led had been worked out in favor of live rounds. We could see the Japanese fleet.

There is no question that all of us knew we were "on" in the world's center ring that day. Seeing the white feathers of ships' wakes at high speed at the far edge of the overcast, and realizing that there, for the first time in plain sight, were the Japanese who had been knocking hell out of us for seven months, was a sensation not many men know in a lifetime. Our necks were working overtime as our eyes searched every sector for Wade McClusky and the *Enterprise* dive-bombers—and for the highly respected Zeros.

For some time we had been flying a dead-reckoning course, because the torpedo aircraft were no longer with us. We closed on the Japanese fleet until we were just outside their antiaircraft range, which was easily determined by bursts which were let go at our flight for the purpose of determining just this from their point of view. We entered a gentle left turn in order to try to spot the dive-bombers.

While we were in this turn, the Zeros were slaughtering our torpedo planes under the cloud layer beneath us. Our radios were working perfectly on this flight, and it can be said that Torpedo-8 went to glory with teeth tightly clenched and hands on triggers and throttles. There wasn't one peep from any of them during their run in. Jack Kelley later said he heard someone mention Zeros, but that was it.

We completed a few circles while making trial radio calls without success to the group commander. We were receiving the YE radio direction homing signal from the *Enterprise* loud and clear, so we weren't the least bit concerned with navigation.

We tried to call the ship to report our YE sector as an aid to the others, but our transmitters wouldn't cover the distance. We could hear the *Enterprise,* but she couldn't hear us. Eventually, attention went in a routine manner to the gas gauge.

The jolt one receives upon noting that, from a completely unsuspected source, there is now a critical problem was mine at that moment. Fuel was at about half of what we had been used to having at the completion of some two hours of flying. The problem now became one of whether or not to make a strafing dive on the carrier we could see clear of the clouds. If the SBDs were to arrive, mixing it up with the Zeros—other than a firing pass—was out of the question. In a dogfight, throttles are "two-blocked" at full and propeller revolutions are at high RPMs. Under this kind of demand, gasoline disappears as though there is a hole in the tank. We simply were now without that higher capability. And we faced another problem with the YE homing system. Because the YE was line-of-sight, we could hear *Enterprise* at altitude, but we would lose it down low. These, too, were considerations which were going through my mind as we circled.

Returning from the Marcus strike some months before, I had missed the ship by but a few miles because it was hidden in a rain squall. Only because Admiral Halsey broke radio silence less than 1,000 miles from Tokyo to bring me in did the Air Group 6 roster still include my name. None of us cared to get that low on fuel ever again.

Since there would be no margin for error were we to get down low at this distance, the sensible thing to do was to get on back for more fuel—or so it seemed at the time. After what seemed an eternity of waiting for the SBDs, we headed for the *Enterprise.* We landed aboard just a few minutes later because the return flight was "down hill" all the way. We had been airborne about three hours—some planes more than that, some less, since the leader hit the deck at recovery time and not everyone got aboard on the first pass.

It wasn't until after sunset and our last combat air patrol was on deck that we heard the details of the day's work (we all made at least three flights that day). When news reached us that the torpedo boys had been nearly wiped out, the shock was as total as that which one would receive from learning of a death in his immediate family. These were shipmates and dear friends of many years. To lose so many in a single day was devastating. But we were too tired and too busy to do more than feel the pang of an aching heart. The Battle of Midway continued through June 6, and Fighting-6 was very much involved in the entire action.

Some weeks later, we were headed for home aboard the USS *Mount Vernon.* Ensign George Gay, Torpedo-8's only survivor, was aboard, and so naturally we asked him how the Japanese could have been so successful when there was so much cloud cover about. He conceded that with the fighter tactics we emplpoyed at the time, there was very little we could have done between the overcast at 800 feet and the water. It was from Gay that we learned that Lieutenant Commander John Waldron, the Torpedo-8 commanding officer, had led a "book"-style attack on the Japanese, deploying from a "vee of vees" to line abreast and barreling in at full throttle on the deck. Unfortunately, full throttle in the TBD wasn't too much over 100 knots. This meant that the very maneuverable Japanese fighters had just enough room to make high-side approaches, picking off the single torpedo planes one at a time, for a grand slam. Gay admitted that had they remained at cloud level, they probably could have gotten close in before being knocked down, but with the torpedoes then in inventory the maximum drop altitude was something under 100 feet. One way or the other, because they had to come down low to drop, our torpedo planes would have "bought it" that day.

It was at Midway that Lieutenant Commander Jimmy Thach, the Fighting-3 commanding officer, used the "Thach Weave," which he had devised, to keep himself and his flight in business when he was under fire by Zeros at low altitude. This consisted of keeping another plane or section in view off to one side so that each could watch the tail of the other, and then weave over to shoot off any violators. Jimmy and Fighting-3 had all they could do to get out of there with their own necks, much less help out with the torpedo planes. His weave was like the latter-day angle-deck carrier—so simple in concept that all of us wondered why we hadn't thought of it long before. Thanks to this tactic, and with the solidly built "brick outhouse" Grummans, the Zeros never again bested U.S. Navy fighters in World War II.

Sunday morning quarterbacks are as active after a sea fight as for any football game. Although the commanding officer and nearly every member of Fighting-6 was decorated for his part in the Battle of Midway, there were those who made it clear that we could have done better.

The foregoing is our story, and while it is unfortunate for us that the spotlight of history burned less brightly in the actions before Midway and after, particularly in 1944 and 1945, when we were knocking hell out of them, only with the benefit of foresight equal to hindsight could we have acted more wisely than we did. Without question, we should have immediately pushed over to strafe Japanese ships by way of creating a diversion to help our torpedo people. Since we believed the Zeros in our area to be at altitude, hunting for our dive-bombers, we had no inkling of the picture down below until it was all over.

All of us feel deeply for the days of living which our shipmates missed and the years of sadness which their loss brought to those dear to them.

Later, at Pensacola, we were too busy to direct our thoughts anywhere but to the future. At Barin Field, we would often do more than 2,000 hours of flying in a twenty-four-hour period. The squadron worked an "eight-day week"– every eighth day off. This meant that the senior people never had a day off. Even so, our thoughts did go back to Midway and "If I had only known . . ."

The Navy needed fighter pilots—thousands of them—in 1942–43. Training duty was naval aviation's highest priority—with one exception: In December 1943, night fighter volunteers were needed to stop Japanese fliers whose tactics had shifted to the darkness. As much to get some rest as to get another shot at the ones who got away, I went back to the *Enterprise* and tried my utmost to make payment in full for any debt I may have owed the gallant torpedo pilots of the Battle of Midway.

On the afternoon of June 6, 1942, during the final actions of the Midway Battle, Lieutenant Jim Gray shot down a single-float seaplane at sea near the U.S. fleet. Following his tour training new carrier pilots—during which he authored the fighter pilot's "bible"—Commander Gray formed VF(N)-78, which he led in combat before assuming command of VF-20 aboard the Enterprise. *While commanding VF(N)-78, Jim Gray shot down an Imperial Navy G4M Betty twin-engine bomber between Okinawa and Formosa on October 11, 1944. He achieved ace status when, on October 24, 1944, just before the Battle of Leyte Gulf, he brought down a Kawanishi H6K Mavis long-range patrol bomber near the U.S. fleet. And, as the VF-20 commanding officer, he shot down an Imperial Army Nakajima Ki-43 Oscar fighter off Luzon on December 16, 1944. At war's end, he was in command of Fleet Carrier Air Group 3.*

In the early 1950s, Commander Gray headed the Navy's all-weather program and authored its first manual, and later he oversaw the Navy's nuclear-weapons planning for the Atlantic Fleet. He retired from the Navy in late 1965 with the rank of captain.

NIGHT DUEL

1st Lieutenant JOE GRIFFIN, USAAF
75th Fighter Squadron, 23d Fighter Group
Kweilin, China—November 23, 1942

Joseph Henry Griffin was born in Pauls Valley, Oklahoma, on November 18, 1917.

I first got hooked on flying when I got to ride in a Ford trimotor airplane in Pauls Valley. After that, I took instructions and had several flights in the Piper Cub. My next opportunity to fly was in Norfolk, Virginia. I enrolled in the Civilian Pilot Training program at the William and Mary's Extension in Norfolk, and it was there that I received my private pilot license.

I applied to the Navy for flying school but was turned down, because I needed to have two full years of college credits, and I lacked one-half of a credit. I returned to Pauls Valley and took a correspondence course for that half-credit. Since I had already been turned down by the Navy, I applied to the Army for a flying cadet position, and I was accepted.

I was assigned to Class 41-H and started my Primary training in San Diego. From there, I received my Basic training at Moffett Field, California, and my Advanced training at Mather Field, also in California. I graduated from Mather as a second lieutenant on October 31, 1941, and was assigned to the 51st Pursuit Group's 16th Pursuit Squadron, which was stationed at March Field, California. I was a fighter pilot.

While at March Field, I flew the AT-6s and checked out in the P-36 and the P-40. I even got in a little gunnery, strafing ground targets. The day after Pearl Harbor, my squadron was transferred to Mines Field (later renamed Los Angles International Airport). We were assigned to protect our area of Southern California and fly coastal patrol looking for enemy submarines.

On December 31, 1941, the 51st Group received orders to report to the San Francisco port of embarkation on January 11, 1942, for transfer overseas. Because I had very little flying time in the P-40, the group commander decided to leave me in the States and had me transferred to the 49th Pursuit Group, which was based at the San Diego Naval Air Station.

I put the time I was with the 49th Group to good use and checked out in both the Republic P-43 Lancer and the Lockheed P-38 Lightning. During this time, we were flying coastal patrol looking for subs. We had several alerts but never sighted the enemy.

I volunteered at every opportunity for an overseas assignment. On the third try I was successful, and on May 15, 1942, I was ordered to proceed to New York City for deployment overseas. We flew on a China Clipper flying boat to Natal, Brazil. Then we flew across the ocean to Africa, where we took a British Lancaster bomber, converted for passengers, to Cairo. We then flew the old "Gooney Bird" [C-47] into India, and then across the Hump [Himalaya Mountains] to Kunming, China.

I was in China from June 1942 to June 1943. I had the opportunity to fly for several weeks with the American Volunteer Group (Flying Tigers), under the command of Colonel Claire Chennault. When that outfit was disbanded on July 4, 1942, I was formally assigned to the 75th Fighter Squadron in the 23rd Fighter Group, which was activated the same day.

On the night of November 23, 1942, we had a squadron party. Since the Japanese had been quite active in our area, three of us were not allowed to attend and instead had to remain on alert at the field. After dark, we received a report from the Chinese warning net that Japanese planes were heading in our direction at an unknown altitude. When the net reported that they were close enough to reach us in fifteen minutes, we scrambled.

We didn't know their altitude, so each of us climbed to a different altitude. First Lieutenant John Lombard stayed the lowest, at 2,000 feet;

Major Hal Pike climbed to 5,000 feet; and I climbed to 10,000 feet. We were sure that by being at different altitudes we had a good chance of spotting the enemy airplanes.

Lombard saw them first and called us down to his altitude. As I started diving, I saw the tracers from John's guns. He set one of the bombers on fire and it crashed. He moved over behind another bomber, but before he could start shooting, the gunner hit his P-40 and set it on fire, and he had to bail out.

Hal Pike was next to attack the bombers. He was successful in shooting one down.

Having dived from 10,000 feet, I was flying at a very high speed, and I almost overran one of the bombers. Because it was very dark, with little, if any, light from a waning moon, it was very difficult to see the bomber. But I could see the exhaust flames from its two engines and got in a short burst before I had to pull up to avoid a collision. I must have damaged him with that first burst, because he slowed down so much that I couldn't fly slow enough to get behind him.

The bomber went down on the deck, following a light-colored road that wound down a valley with hills on both sides. I started making side quartering passes at the bomber from each side. I would line up the reticule of my gun sight ahead of the bomber and start firing, knowing that he would fly through my bullets. Although the tracer bullets from my six .50-caliber guns completely blinded me, I was certain that he was flying through my bullets. At the end of each firing pass, I would be heading directly into the low hills flanking the valley, so I had to give my engine full throttle in order to climb above them, then make turn tightly to make another quartering firing pass.

On several of my passes, I saw tracers coming at me from the bomber, and on two of my passes I felt bullets striking my airplane. The Japanese gunner was very good; I could see his tracers coming straight at me, and at the last second they would curve back of me. I couldn't get out of range of his guns for fear that I might loose sight of the bomber.

After each pass, I hoped to see the bomber either crash or catch on fire. After several passes, I was even hoping I would loose sight of him, because this was a duel, and I knew I would either shoot him down or he would do the same to me. The churning in my stomach was urging me to lose sight of him.

On my final pass, all but one of my guns quit firing. As I pulled up and recharged the guns, the bomber flew behind a small hill and disappeared. I spent about five minutes looking for him without any luck. I was very fortunate this happened where it did, because I was at the end of the road that he had been following.

I didn't have the foggiest notion where I was, but I was able to follow the road back to Kweilin. When I got there, I had to land on a 20-foot-wide taxi strip lighted on each side by lanterns—eleven bombs had hit our runway and put it out of commission. That was the first time that I had landed a P-40 at night, and, to say the least, I was very nervous. When I got out of my plane, my knees buckled on me and it took several minutes before I could stand.

I had fired 1,400 rounds of ammunition and had been hit three times in the rear of the engine section and once in the tail. The front of my plane was covered with oil from the bomber.

Using a map, I was able to show the operations officer where I had last seen the bomber. At daybreak, he sent a crew out to the place marked on the map and that's where they found the bomber. They said there wasn't a square foot of the plane that didn't have a bullet hole in it.

The bomber's pilot was the only one of his three-man crew that survived the crash. He was captured by the Chinese and brought to our base. He seemed like a decent sort of a chap, so I gave him my cigarettes. I was later told that the guards confiscated the cigarettes when I left. I doubt the pilot survived his captivity, because most Chinese felt lots of hatred toward the Japanese. The only previous contact the guards had had with the Japanese had been to helplessly watch Japanese aircraft bomb and strafe their villages and countrymen.

I met General Chennault the next day, and he congratulated me on my victory. I later learned that our group commander, Colonel Bob Scott, had recommended that I be awarded the Silver Star for my action that night. The recommendation was approved by General Chennault and forwarded to General Joseph Stilwell, who disapproved it.

While flying with the 75th Fighter Squadron, I also destroyed two Zeros in aerial combat, one on April 28, 1943, near Kunming and the other on May 2, near Hengyang.

I returned to the United States in June 1943 and activated the 393d Fighter Squadron, in the 367th Fighter Group, as squadron commanding officer. I trained my outfit in P-39s. Just before we deployed to the European Theater, I was transferred to group headquarters as operations officer and was sent with an advance echelon to the Ninth Air Force in England to check out our new base and make certain it was ready for our group.

The 367th Fighter Group was assigned to the Ninth Air Force and equipped with P-38s. Our mission was bomber escort and close support of our army. I participated in the Normandy invasion, during which I flew numerous top-cover missions for the invasion fleet. During this tour, in aerial combat, I destroyed one Messerchmitt Bf-109 on June 17, 1944, near Evreaux, France; two Focke-Wulf FW-190s on August 23, 1944, also near Evreaux; and one FW-190 on August 25, 1944, over Chastres Airdrome. I also destroyed one Junkers Ju-52 transport on the ground.

I flew 150 combat missions in the P-40s, P-43s, P-47s, and P-38s. During my career I flew nearly fifty different types of airplanes. I retired from the Air Force in 1970 as a full colonel.

ACE THE HARD WAY

Captain EFFIE PIERCE, USMC
VMF-121
Vella Lavella area—January 15, 1943

Francis Edwin Pierce, Jr., the son of a Marine officer, was born at the Philadelphia Navy Yard on March 10, 1918, and raised at several military bases in the United States and abroad. Pierce graduated from high school in Coronado, California, attended San Diego State College for two years and Pasadena Junior College for two more. While in school, he ran the mile and two-mile races on the track teams, but his favorite activity in college was the Civilian Pilot Training (CPT) course. He also attended a Marine Corps platoon leaders' class during summer breaks.

Effie Pierce left college in 1940 and went to work for Consolidated Aircraft, where he found himself "handing nuts and bolts to the guys putting B-24s together." In April of that year, he went on active duty with the Marine Corps as a private first class and attended the platoon leaders' class at the San Diego Marine Corps Recruit Depot.

Pierce qualified as an aviation cadet in April 1941. He began flight training at Corpus Christi, Texas, as part of the first class of 150 cadets to attend the course at the then-new base. Shortly before receiving his wings, 2d Lieutenant Effie Pierce was named regimental commander of the more than two thousand cadets who were by then being trained at Corpus.

Next, he was attached to an advanced carrier training unit at San Diego, where he flew Brewster F2A Buffalo fighters. In March 1942, he was transferred to the Pacific to fly Grumman F4F Wildcat fighters on combat patrols in the vicinity of Palmyra Island, which along with other Central Pacific outposts were subject to frequent attacks by Japanese bombers based at Tarawa and other atolls in the Gilbert Islands.

Captain Pierce joined the veteran VMF-121 at Espirito Santo in the fall of 1942 and received special training before moving up to Guadalcanal shortly before Christmas. On Christmas Day, Pierce flew his first combat strike, a raid against Munda Field in which fourteen Japanese planes were destroyed on the ground.

In the eighteen days that followed, VMF-121 F4F pilots flew regular patrol and escort hops. But on January 12, Pierce ran into the first Japanese aircraft he had ever seen in the air while escorting SBD dive-bombers on a strike in the area of New Georgia and Santa Isabel islands. One of the four escorting Wildcats was shot down on the first pass, but the remaining three pilots got ten Japanese planes. Pierce was credited with two confirmed kills and one probable.

On January 15, 1943, twelve VMF-121 F4Fs were escorting sixteen Marine SBD dive-bombers on a strike against a flotilla of Japanese destroyers in the central Solomons. I was flying section lead on Captain Hunter Reinburg, my high-school classmate who was also the son of a Marine officer. The dive-bombers were at about 15,000 feet, there were eight F4Fs about 1,000 feet above them, and four F4Fs were on the right side of the formation. The fighters were supposed to strafe Munda Field on the way back to Guadalcanal.

We found the Japanese ships in the Slot (New Georgia Sound) about an hour after we formed up over Guadalcanal. The SBDs attacked while the F4Fs covered them. I saw one of the destroyers get blown up, and a couple of others got a good going over, but then twenty-four Zeros moved in on us, and my attention was distracted from the dive-bombers. I spotted the enemy planes first and warned the other pilots that they were at 9 o'clock high. When I first saw them, the silver-colored Zeros were following one another in a long line, rolling and stunting in order to scare us with their airmanship. They did that quite often, but to no avail.

My biggest distraction was a Zero that came up under me on the first pass. He shot my plane full of holes. I felt shrapnel from a 20mm cannon shell enter both my legs behind the knees, and a 7.7mm machine-gun bullet struck my left calf. I also saw two holes open up in my left wing; I could have crawled through either of them.

As soon as the 7.7mm slug and 20mm shrapnel hit me, I let go of the stick and grabbed both my legs. But I immediately saw a Zero pulling up directly in front of my gun sight, so I grabbed at the stick again. The Zero pilot must have figured I was knocked out, because he made a perfect target. I kept saying "You damn fool, you damn fool" as I opened up on him, aiming for the cockpit and engine. He was a cold turkey. My guns were boresighted for 450 yards, but he was only about 50 yards away when I fired a short burst at zero deflection. I don't think he ever knew what hit him; he just blew up right there in front of me. As near as I can tell, this Zero was the second of two that had shot me up from below.

Even with a vein cut in my right leg, shrapnel wounds in my left leg, and a bullet hole in my left calf, and with my Wildcat's left wing so perforated with holes that portions of it looked like a huge sieve, I somehow managed to keep flying. I quickly took the belt off my trousers and tied it around my left leg to stop the bleeding as much as possible. Then I pulled out both shoelaces and used them to fashion a tourniquet above my right knee. I thought about pulling out for base, but I figured if I tried to fly back by myself, the Zeros would have shot me down for sure.

Both legs were numb, but I could move them enough to operate the rudder controls. In fact, I was just getting the hang of it when another Zero flew in, about 300 feet above and right in front of me. I nosed up, fired a short burst, and saw him catch fire and crash.

While this was going on, the other pilots were active, too. Most of the Zeros had disappeared, either shot down or just scared away.

Hunter Reinburg got on the tail of one Zero that was trying to circle around us, but Hunter was out of ammunition by then, so I radioed that I was going in. I made one pass, missed, and went back again. I fired a 30-degree deflection shot from his left side from only about fifty yards away. The Zero burst into flames that time, and we saw him crash into the water at a 50-degree angle.

We started back toward Guadalcanal at 12,000 feet, but I was having trouble with my plane. If I allowed the engine-manifold pressure to get under 30 inches, the holes in my Wildcat's left wing caused that wing to lose its lift, so I had to fly full right tab all the way back to Guadalcanal and, because my Wildcat's air-speed indicator was shot away, Hunter flew alongside to check my speed. The bleeding in my legs was down to just some oozing, but I had to loosen the tourniquet from time to time, and that caused some heavy blood loss.

When we were back over the field and had descended from 12,000 to 6,000 feet, I let my wheels down to see whether the plane could fly slow enough for a landing. It wanted to spin left, so I flew out over the water, where I spotted one of our destroyers, and started to bail out. My legs were useless, however, so I had to pull myself out of the cockpit with my arms and position myself over the wing of the plane. I let go, missing the elevator and rudder. I started to pull on the D-ring to release the parachute, I said to myself that I sure hoped whoever had packed the 'chute had done a good job.

I blacked out when the parachute canopy opened, but I came to almost instantly, swinging nicely beneath the canopy. I still had the D-ring in my hand, and the first thing I did was to draw back my arm to throw it away. Then I thought it would make a good souvenir, so I held onto it. I still have the ring.

We had heard that the sharks in the area were fierce. It was said that the people on Savo Island, near where I was coming down, fed their dead to the sharks, and that the sharks hung around there, looking for their next meal.

The destroyer crew saw the parachute open. The ship came to a stop near where I was going to land in the water, and a small boat was lowered away to pick me up. I was aboard the destroyer after only eight minutes in the water. No sharks were attracted by the blood I lost in the water.

Pieces of shrapnel were extracted from my legs in the destroyer's sick bay, I was given a pair of crutches, and the skipper fed me the first steak dinner I had had in eighteen months. I was sent to the base hospital for observation. Later, I was transferred to a hospital on Espirito Santo, and then to another hospital in New Zealand. I was operated on four times. After two months of treatment, I was released and returned to flight status, rejoining VMF-121 without taking sick leave. In June 1943, I went on my second combat tour. On June 3, 1943, I shot down two Imperial Navy G4M Betty bombers while covering the landing on Rendova.

Captain Effie Pierce was credited with three victories for the January 15 battle—enough to make ace status. He was also awarded a Navy Cross for heroism, but he maintains that he stayed in the fight out of sheer necessity.

After leave and a promotion, Pierce was given command of VMF-214 while it was being reformed in the United States following a stellar South Pacific tour. But Pierce, who was intent on returning to combat, soon arranged to serve as Major Hunter Reinburg's executive officer when Reinburg led VMF-121 back to war for the invasion of Peleliu. VMF-121 met no Japanese aircraft this time out, but the squadron saw plenty of dangerous action bombing and strafing targets on bypassed Japanese bases in the Palau Islands.

Major Effie Pierce left the Marine Corps in 1954 to work in private industry.

STRIP ALERT

1st Lieutenant DICK SUEHR, USAAF
39th Fighter Squadron, 35th Fighter Group
Port Moresby Area—April 12, 1943

Richard Charles Suehr was born one of ten children in Crafton, Pennsylvania, on May 4, 1917. He attended Marquette University as a premed student and was a member of the wrestling team for four years. Upon graduation from Marquette in early 1941, Suehr enlisted in the

Army Air Corps Flying Cadet program. He earned his silver wings and gold second lieutenant's bars on October 31, 1941.

On December 25, 1941, 2d Lieutenant Suehr sailed from California to Australia with a group of pilots, maintenance personnel, and crated Curtiss P-40 fighters originally bound for the Philippines. On February 15, 1942, Lieutenant Suehr was with a small group of P-40s on the way from Australia to Java when he was forced down in the north Australian jungle. It took him ten days of hiking and swimming to get close enough to civilization to be rescued. As a result of this harrowing experience, Suehr missed out on a combat baptism over Java, but he was amply compensated when, with the 35th Fighter Group's 39th Fighter Squadron, he was ordered to Port Moresby, New Guinea, to fly the inferior Bell P-39 Airacobra against the vastly superior Imperial Navy Zero fighter and vastly more experienced Imperial Navy fighter pilots. Dick Suehr not only survived this first New Guinea combat tour, he downed a Zero over Morobe New Guinea, on June 9, 1942.

After transitioning to P-38s in late 1942, the 39th Fighter Squadron was recommitted to battle over New Guinea, and on January 6, 1943, 1st Lieutenant Dick Suehr downed an Imperial Army Nakajima Ki-43 Oscar fighter near Gasmata, New Britain. Two days later, he shot down a pair of Imperial Navy Zeros (and probably downed a third) over Lae, New Guinea.

On April 12, 1943, I was a fighter pilot in the 39th Fighter Squadron, flying P-38s from Port Moresby's Fourteen-Mile Strip. Very early in the morning, word was received that the Japanese were going to strike our base at Milne Bay, so most of our squadron's aircraft took off at 0605 hours to assist in the defense. At 0930 hours, the six of us who were left at Fourteen-Mile Strip were on strip alert when we were ordered to scramble because what was thought by our radar people to be a Japanese reconnaissance plane was making its way to Port Moresby.

We took off and climbed to 25,000 feet using maximum power. When we were advised that Japanese aircraft were coming in at 27,000 feet, we climbed to 30,000. By the time we got there, it was about 0955 hours. On the way, we were advised that we would be intercepting the main bomber fleet, which had not gone to Milne Bay after all. The ground controller vectored my flight into position, but by then we had seen the Japanese and were proceeding on our own.

There were 110 aircraft in the Japanese formation—an estimated fourty-five twin-engine Betty bombers and the rest Zero fighters. When we first saw them, they were ahead of us, flying from the direction of the Owen Stanley mountain range, from northeast to southwest, directly toward the Port Moresby military complex—airstrips, storage area, and the dock. The bombers seemed to be one large formation flying in three vees of about fifteen bombers in each vee. They were covered by fighters above and to the sides.

As soon as we saw the enemy, we dropped our fuel tanks and proceeded on course to intercept. We were right over Port Moresby and they were about ready to drop their bombs, so we ran in and made a pass at them. The bombers stayed on course, but the fighter pilots saw us as we rolled into our dives, and a number of them gave pursuit.

I had full power on as I went into a leftward dive. My objective was to try to divert the bombers from their target. I went right through the bomber formation, shooting at them as I went. I was not aiming at any specific aircraft; I was spraying them to get as many hits on as many of them as I could. Nevertheless, I did not see any hits during this attack.

Well, as I went through the enemy formation of bombers, the fighters caught on to my tail. I was doing about 575 to 600 miles per hour. I only had one other person with me, and that was my wingman, 1st Lieutenant Harvey Clymer; the other P-38s were trailing because they could not keep up with us. The Zeros came after us, but we were going much faster and there was no way they could stop us. Harvey even shot down one of the Zeros at this particular time.

I was diving so fast that when I tried to pull out of the dive, the darn airplane just kept going straight down. I had been flying the P-38 in combat for eight months, but this was the first time I was unable to pull out of a dive. I instinctively rolled in trim, cut power, and pulled the control column back. But all that didn't help; I was still going straight down toward the water. I put my feet on the instrument panel and pulled back on the yoke, but, again, nothing happened: I was still heading straight for the water! At that point, I said my prayers, because I figured this was it.

Then, as I hit the heavy lower air, the airplane made a 180-degree turn and started climbing. By the time I rolled out the extra trim and added power, I was right back up to 25,000 feet—and right in the middle of the Japanese. I shot as best as I could and dived out of there. I made a shallow dive this time, so I wouldn't get myself into trouble.

I pulled out of the shallow dive and looked around. I was all by myself. I followed the course the bombers had been taking and overtook one of them, a straggler. I came straight up behind it, and from about 20 degrees off the tail, fired three short bursts. I observed strikes on the fuselage, wing section, and left engine, which began trailing smoke. The bomber lost altitude and crashed right into a hillside.

My flight was up there alone when the bombers came; but just as they were leaving, our airplanes that had been up at Milne Bay came back and got into the fight. At the same time, the 40th Fighter Squadron, which was still equipped with P-39s and which had remained in the Port Moresby area, also engaged the enemy. Altogether, we ended up with twenty-seven victories and, as far as I could tell, there was no damage to any of the facilities at Port Moresby.

While we were up there in the fight, the Australian antiaircraft guns at Port Moresby were blasting away at the bombers. A few days later, I went over and talked to the Australians; I told them that I'd seen their bursts and that they had done a real good job. They were very happy to hear that. I'm not sure they really did much good, but they were given credit for one of the bombers.

The Betty I shot down on April 12 was my fifth victory, so I felt real proud of myself. This was the last raid the Japanese made on Port Moresby while I was there, and I don't think they made any more, because it was a very costly raid.

The problem I had had pulling out of my dive was caused by compressibility, which I had never heard of despite my eight months' flying experience in P-38s. It was a problem unique to P-38s and was caused by the way air traveled over the large engine nacelles during high-speed dives from high altitude, where the air is thinner. Because no air was able to hit them, control surfaces in the wings and tail were inoperable. A number of our P-38 pilots were killed when they couldn't pull out of such dives. My instinctive response, rolling in as much trim as I could, was the right thing to do.

♦

Dick Suehr returned to the United States in May 1943 and was married during his post-combat leave. He took up duties Stateside until he rotated back to the Pacific in November 1944. While serving in the Philippines, he ditched his P-38 and swam twelve hours before reaching an uninhabited island. After three days alone on the island, Suehr was rescued by Filipino guerrillas, with whom he lived for the next six weeks. He eventually returned to his unit and flew combat missions until the war ended. He remained in the service after the war and retired in 1968 with the rank of lieutenant colonel.

INTERCEPTION OVER ORO BAY

Flight Officer SAMMY PIERCE, USAAF
8th Fighter Squadron, 49th Fighter Group
Near Oro Bay, New Guinea—May 14, 1943

Sammy Alpheus Pierce was born on August 21, 1921, in Ayden, North Carolina, and grew up on a nearby farm. He boxed and played football and baseball, first in high school, then at North Carolina State University, which he attended in 1938 and 1939. He was also a member of the Army ROTC during his two years at NSU.

Pierce had joined the North Carolina National Guard in 1939 and, when the Guard was federalized in August 1940 he was given the choice of being inducted for national service or being discharged to remain in college. He chose to be inducted and stay with his National Guard unit, but he soon obtained permission to be discharged so he could reenlist in the Army Air Corps. He was accepted for pilot training as an enlisted man in 1941 and graduated from flight school as a sergeant pilot on September 6 1942.

Next, Staff Sergeant Pierce was assigned to the 20th Pursuit Group, with which he flew a total of thirty-four hours in P-39s and P-40s before shipping out to the Southwest Pacific Area in November 1942. In December he was assigned to the 49th Fighter Group's 8th Fighter Squadron, by then a veteran P-40 unit. In March 1943, Flight Officer Pierce dropped his first bomb of the war on the Japanese airfield at Lae, New Guinea, during the Battle of the Bismarck Sea—but he had yet to fire his guns at another airplane. That came on April 11, 1943, while attacking a force of Imperial Navy G4M Betty twin-engine medium bombers escorted by Zero fighters. In that action, Pierce was credited with a Zero fighter definitely shot down and a Betty bomber probably shot down.

Of all the missions I flew in World War II, the most difficult was probably an interception of twenty-seven Bettys with a cover of approximately forty Zero fighters. It took place on May 14, 1943. At the time, the 49th Fighter Group was flying P-40Es out of the strip at Dobodura, New Guinea, which was inland just five or six miles southwest of Buna and twelve to fifteen miles north-northwest of Oro Bay.

The 8th Fighter Squadron had sixteen airplanes on alert that day, and the 7th and 9th Fighter squadrons each probably had the same number available. My position in our flight was wingman for the flight leader, 1st Lieutenant Ernie Harris. Second Lieutenant Bob Howard was the element leader, and 2d Lieutenant Bitsy Grant was his wingman.

At about 1030 hours, the group was scrambled to intercept an incoming formation of Betty bombers and Zero escorts. We all took off and climbed at our maximum rate of about 2,500 feet per minute, At about 10,000 feet, Bitsy's propeller went out on him and he returned to Dobodura. The rest of us continued on and up, bound for 27,000 feet, which about as high as our P-40s could go. As we climbed, our four flights spread out in search formation on a line running from northwest to southeast. We assumed this formation because our radar at the time could only give us the altitude and approximate location of enemy airplanes.

By about 1045 hours, we had reached approximately 20,000 feet and were in the vicinity of Oro Bay when we picked up the bomber formation. The Bettys were flying in a large vee composed of three nine-plane vees that were each composed of a vee of three three-plane vees. We were still about fifteen miles from meeting them, so we continued to climb on a course that would put us to the left of their formation with an altitude advantage of about 6,000 feet. At that point, their fighters would be at least 2,000 feet higher than us, but there was nothing we could do about that, because we would reach our maximum altitude when we got in position over the bombers.

When we were in position, Ernie half-rolled to his left and began an overhead pass, picking up the lead Betty in their formation as his target. I rolled in behind Ernie and picked up the leader of their second flight as my target.

My guns were boresighted to converge at 300 yards, so I started firing at a range of 1,500 feet. I was going straight down and firing when my windshield started to freeze over. My field of vision was restricted, but I managed to keep my target in sight long enough to fire a second burst at it; at the same time, I was trying to clear the windshield. I didn't have any room left to try to pull out of my dive and stay above the Bettys, so I continued the dive and rolled to the right just enough to go between the two planes on my target's wings. As I pulled out of the dive and continued to clear the frost off my canopy, I saw several large pieces falling away from the Betty I had shot at.

I pulled out of the dive at about 12,000 feet and fooled with the cockpit heater until it started to clear the canopy. Then I looked around to try to relocate Ernie Harris and Bob Howard. I found them; they were approximately 5,000 feet above me and off to my right.

As I climbed on a course to join up with Ernie and Bob, I noticed that a Japanese fighter was chasing Bob. The Zero was at Bob's 6 o'clock. That put the Zero about 3,000 feet above me, at about my 10 o'clock. In an effort to at least shoot in front of the Zero to make the pilot break off his firing pass on Bob, I pulled my gunsight up above the rudder of Bob's P-40 and fired. The Japanese pilot was probably as surprised as I was when my bullets hit him in the right wing root and cockpit area. The Zero fell off in a slight diving left turn. I didn't think I'd done much damage, so I followed him down to try to get another shot. At around 7,000 feet, I got a straight-on shot at his underside, and I fired a short burst. The Zero remained in the slow diving turn until it hit the water.

I was at 2,000 feet when I started climbing again to try to locate any friendly fighters I could find. If I couldn't, I decided I would return to base.

I had climbed to about 15,000 feet on a southwesterly course when I saw one of the Bettys coming toward me on a northeasterly heading. It was about 2,000 feet below me and all alone. The left engine was smoking. I made a diving turn to the right and fired at it from about 1,000 feet. I saw some hits behind the cockpit and bomb-bay areas that didn't seem to do much damage, so I pulled around in a climbing turn to the right to a position above, to the right, and slightly ahead of him. I then rolled into a diving turn to the left, rolled out at an angle of about 10 degrees, and fired again. This time I had a better lead, and I saw hits in the forward portion of the plane that knocked out the smoking engine—or, maybe, the engine quit from prior damage. Nevertheless, the Betty still seemed to be under control, so I made another pass in which my guns stopped firing. The Betty was losing altitude pretty fast, but it still seemed to be under control. I didn't stay around to see what happened—I had no guns—but I feel sure the pilot had to ditch.

I couldn't find the other two members of my flight—or any other friendly fighters—so I turned back to the southwest and started climbing on course back to Dobodura. I reached an altitude of about 16,000 feet and, as I leveled off, I observed a Japanese fighter a thousand feet or so above me, going in the opposite direction. I had no ammunition left, so I hoped fervently that the pilot wouldn't see me. I also nosed down slightly to gain as much airspeed as possible in the event he did see me and came after me. He did.

I knew that the Japanese pilots normally wouldn't meet us in gun range when we were head-on to them, so I turned enough to meet him head-on. When he was within my gun range, I pulled the nose up to meet him directly head-on. Sure enough, he made a sharp climbing turn to his left. I immediately made a diving turn to my left (his right), rolled out, got enough of a lead so he wouldn't be able to catch me, and—after I was sure the Zero was gone—continued in a shallow descent to Dobodura at normal cruise speed.

I was given credit for the Betty bomber from the first overhead pass and the Zeke fighter I shot off Bob Howard's tail, but the straggling Betty bomber was listed as a probable. In all, during that one action, P-40 pilots from the 49th Fighter Group shot down eleven Betty bombers and nine Zero fighters. Our attack caused the Bettys to jettison their bombs before they reached their target—shipping and the harbor in Oro Bay.

Following more action and promotion to commissioned rank, Sammy Pierce was injured during a bailout at night in the rugged New Guinea bush. He eventually made his way to friendly lines, but he was hospital-

ized in Australia and sent back to the United States in May 1944. In the space of a few months, he was assigned as a P-51 instructor, served at the Army Air Forces Test Pilot School, and served again as a P-51 instructor. In October 1944, 1st Lieutenant Pierce was reassigned to the 8th Fighter Squadron as operations officer.

While flying a P-38 on December 26, 1944, Sammy Pierce shot down an Imperial Army Ki-44 Tojo fighter and four *Imperial Navy Zero fighters over Clark Field, Luzon, bringing his score to seven confirmed victories. He never got a shot at another Japanese airplane in the war.*

Captain Sammy Pierce returned to the United States in late 1945 and remained in the service. He retired as a lieutenant colonel in 1963 and worked in private industry until 1986.

NO FUEL TO SPARE*

Lieutenant (jg) VERNON GRAHAM, USN
VF-11
Russell Islands Area—June 12, 1943

Vernon E. Graham was born in Rocky Ford, Colorado, on September 13, 1919. He enlisted in the Naval Aviation Cadet program in October 1940; was called to active service to train at Corpus Christi, Texas, in June 1941; and received his wings and commission in June 1942.

In August 1942, after undergoing carrier training, Ensign Graham was assigned to VF-11, a new unit equipped with Grumman F4F Wildcat fighters. In May 1943, VF-11 began a land-based tour of duty on Guadalcanal.

When I climbed into my Grumman Wildcat on the morning of June 12, 1943, I felt it was just another of those routine jobs. My buddies later told me they felt the same way. I had never fired at a Japanese plane, because I never had met a Zero or had an opportunity to get on the tail of one. The Zeros simply hadn't come our way, or, seeing us first, had cleared out. For weeks we'd been sitting up there, itching for some real

* Based on an "as told to" story by Tom Bailey and appearing in *True Magazine* in 1943.

action, and nothing had happened. Strafing flying fields is not exactly what you'd call unexciting, yet when the Japanese stayed down there in their holes, it wasn't much fun. Shooting up barges is something like shooting fish. Then suddenly it came!

"Approximately thirty-five Japs at twenty-five thousand, heading this way," the voice from base said in my earphones. He then gave us the location reported by the F4U Corsair fighters that were on patrol duty that morning. The F4Us were Marine planes. "Intercept if you have sufficient gas," the voice went on. "Use your own judgment."

I looked at my gas gauge. My tanks were low, and I doubted I'd have enough fuel left to climb to 25,000 feet and still get home. Two of the four VF-11 division leaders checked their gas supply and reported back that it would be impossible for them to intercept.

I looked across at Lieutenant William Leonard, the leader of my division, and got his nod. That meant that he was going up, gas or no gas. I checked my gauge again and nodded back. A second check had convinced me that I'd get up there all right, with maybe a little to spare. So would the others, but we would all be in the same boat. Maybe we'd have enough gas to get back, and maybe not. But if we got up there, we'd at least have a shot at those Japanese. We could pitch into them for a few minutes and then head for base.

I hand-signaled my wingman, Lieutenant (jg) Robert Gilbert, and the two divisions began climbing. The sun was overhead, which made it difficult to spot the enemy aircraft. But they were up there somewhere, and if our gas supply lasted, we'd find them.

Suddenly I saw one of the other pilots point upward, and then I spotted them, circling, diving, and whirling about like dragonflies. Those four Marine F4Us on patrol had pitched into the Japanese, who were circling cautiously, watching for an advantage. Those thirty-five Zero pilots were so busy trying to get a sneak blow at the Marines that they apparently didn't see us coming up to meet them.

The dogfight had our Marines in the center with better than an eight-to-one advantage for the Zeros. But we were eight strong, which would—if we got to them—make it twelve to thirty-five, a figure that had come to be considered more or less equal, in view of the air battles of that time.

Lieutenant (jg) Claude Ivie's Wildcat was on my right and a little ahead of me. As we came into the fight, one of the Japanese whipped over on Claude's tail and let go a short burst. The Zero then did a slow roll, after which the pilot fired another burst. Nothing happened to the Wildcat: It absorbed the Japanese lead like a sponge. Still another roll. I couldn't understand that. Of course, I had yet to fire my first shot in aerial combat, and that slow roll might, so far as I knew, be part of the Japanese strategy. If so, however, my instructors had forgotten to mention it.

The rolling Zero next went into a short dive and came up facing me at about 250 yards. I was still puzzled by his actions when I realized he was heading straight for me. I had to do something about it. In all those months I had waited for a chance at a Japanese plane, I had thought of the thousand-and-one things that might happen, and right now one of those possibilities had become a stark reality. It was up to me to kill or be killed. This was it.

Suddenly I was dead on him, and I let go. The Zero seemed to shudder a little as it swept by, and when I looked back it had nosed down into a dive. A moment later, it was spinning dizzily with flame and smoke pouring from it. I had finished off the first one in less time that it takes to tell about it. It had seemed much easier than I had thought it would be. Yet had the scales of chance been tipped slightly to the Zero's favor, it could have been my plane spinning so crazily toward the water.

I now had time for a brief look around to size up the situation. I saw another Zero falling, with smoke trailing out of it, but I had been too occupied with my own troubles to see who shot it down. Another Zero was just below and a little ahead of me. The pilot saw me at the same time I spotted him, and he came up to meet me. If anyone ever tells you a Zero can't maneuver, he simply hasn't seen one in action, for my adversary was in position and facing me at about 500 yards before I could blink an eye. Then I got the surprise of my life. He rolled over on his back and flew straight at me upside down. I had been puzzled by the first Zero's slow roll, the reason for which I hadn't yet figured out. Now this one was showing me something real nifty in aerial maneuvering. At the moment, I wondered if he was trying to protect himself by exposing his belly to my guns instead of his topside. But there was no time to ponder this or anything else; I had to do something, and do it quickly. When two fighter planes are hustling at each other at tremendous speeds, 250 yards is no distance at all. I fired a short burst into that exposed belly. The plane never completely righted itself again. It flashed by below me and kept right on going down, down, down. That familiar trail of smoke marked its plunge seaward.

I wonder how many fighter pilots have ever had my experience of meeting two enemy screwballs in one day. They were the first Japanese I had ever encountered. Both had maneuvered crazily, as if they were trying to show me something new.

Way off to my left, another Zero spiraled down, burning like a cracker box. Circling high above him were a couple of Wildcats and an F4U. The Japanese had widened the circle now. Apparently they had found it unprofitable to come in too close. Two more were going down in flames off to the right. It was fairly raining Zeros, but the fight was by no means over. Those Japanese fighters had gas, and ours didn't. I realized all of this a second later.

Another Zero was suddenly coming at me at about 500 yards, its guns ablaze. I headed straight toward it and opened up. It kept on coming. It seemed we would crash head-on in a split second. I had heard how a Japanese pilot will frequently commit suicide by flying straight into an enemy ship if he can't get it any other way. I pulled up—or, rather, started to pull up—and let him pass under me, but suddenly his ship simply went all to pieces. One wing exploded, and I flew through a shower of plane splinter and parts. An object which could have been the Zero's motor lurched past me. A moment later, I saw the other wing and part of the fuselage whirling crazily toward the water. That was number three.

As I came out of the shower of Zero parts I looked ahead and around to see what next was coming at me. For the moment, I was in the clear. Surely, old Lady Luck was riding with me that day.

Then came number four. He was after one on my boys—I think it was Bob Gilbert, who had just sent a Japanese pilot to a flaming death. Gilbert had been busy disposing of his Zero and apparently hadn't seen the other one slide down on his tail. I banked my Wildcat and made a side run on the Zero. The pilot didn't see me coming, or if he did he paid no attention. I came in close and cut loose. Then something happened internally, and that Zero burst into flames that completely enveloped it. The Japanese fighter dropped like a blazing torch.

At that moment, I wasn't sure how many I had shot down. I hadn't thought about counting them. It was all happening in minutes. I was trying to get as many as I could before my gas supply ran out. Then I was going to try and coast into the landing strip in the Russell Islands. The fight was swift. I hadn't had time to think of anything but my gas supply. There hadn't been an opportunity to look at the gauge until now. One look, and I knew I was just about through. According to the gauge, there wasn't a drop left, but my motor was still running. It was only a question of minutes now, perhaps seconds.

Just then, an F4U roared by with a Zero on its tail. I pulled up in time to fire a spray of bullets at the Zero as it flashed by. I didn't know whether I had hit him or not. And then I was all through. I was out of the fight for keeps, for my motor began missing. It took me a moment or so to get my bearings, then I went into a dive, hoping to give that Wildcat enough momentum to carry me to the landing strip in the Russell Islands. I was high and might have a chance to make it.

I had heard that the Japanese would pitch into a man out of control or too disabled to continue the fight, and this proved to be true. The moment the Japanese realized something was wrong, they closed in for the kill. I couldn't turn and fight them, and they took advantage of it. Two swooped down on my tail, and my chances of making that landing strip were sliced to almost nothing. I had flattened out and was about to go into another dive when a Marine plane came to my rescue. He swooped onto those Zeros' tails and pulled out. Right behind him came another F4U. Finding the F4Us on their tails, the Zero pilots dropped me like a hot potato and started running.

In the clear once more, I looked back and saw that the other fellows had pulled out too and were going to try and make the strip. There wasn't enough gas in the eight Wildcats to fill a cigar lighter. The landing strip at the Russell Islands was still a long way off. From some recess, the motor drew a little more fuel. This helped me gain some speed and distance, which was fortunate, for without this added lift, I wouldn't have made it. Some of the other fellows were not so fortunate.

I didn't know that one of my wheels had been partly shot away and was no good for landing. When I saw that I was going to make it and let down the wheels and landing flaps, there was no indication that I was heading for trouble. As luck would have it, I struck a soft spot on the runway. The weakened wheel crumpled, and my plane flipped over. My head struck something, and I knew no more until I awakened hours later in the hospital. They told me I had fractured my skull and broken a collar bone but was otherwise unhurt.

The whole action was hazy to me then, and I tried not to think about it. I didn't think much about it until sometime later, when Captain Kenneth Ford of the Marine Corps came to see me. I didn't know him then. He said, "Nice shooting, fellow. Thanks a lot." I still didn't know what it was all about. "I was in the F4U you helped out in that scrap," he said. "The one with a Jap on its tail."

I nodded vaguely. "What happened to that Jap?" I asked.

"What happened to him? Why, you got him. Didn't you know?" It was then that I learned that the last Zero at which I had sprayed a double burst of bullets had also gone down in flames. I had shot down five in one mission.

Lieutenant Bill Leonard was credited with downing two Zeros, which brought him to five victories; Lieutenant (jg) Robert Gilbert shot down three Zeros; Lieutenant (jg) Teddy Hull shot down two; and Lieutenant Kenneth Viall and Ensign Claude Ivie each got one. Our Navy fliers had participated in fourteen victories, and not one man was lost; but Ensign Lowell Slagle was wounded by a bullet in his rump, and he barely escaped worse injury when a 20mm shell exploded between his parachute and the back of his seat. Claude Ivie ran out of fuel before reaching the Russell Islands, but he made a good water landing and was rescued shortly thereafter. Marine F4U Corsair pilots taking part in this action were credited with six kills and four probables.

Lieutenant (jg) Vernon Graham was awarded a Navy Cross for downing five Japanese aircraft in a single action.

Following his return to the United States with VF-11 in January 1943, Lieutenant Vernon Graham spent the remainder of the war training new fighter pilots. He left the Navy in October 1945 and eventually went into teaching and school administration in California after earning degrees at the University of Colorado and Stanford University.

TAIL SHOTS

2d Lieutenant ROGER CONANT, USMC
VMF-215
Kahili Airdrome—August 25, 1943

Arthur Roger Conant was born on October 21, 1918, in Crystal Falls, Michigan, and raised in Wisconsin. While attending the University of Wisconsin, from which he graduated in 1941, Conant took the first part of the Civilian Pilot Training program, so it was natural for him to enlist in one of the flying services. He selected the Navy's Aviation Cadet program, which he completed at Corpus Christi, Texas, in August 1942. He opted for a Marine Corps commission and, following the completion of his training, 2d Lieutenant Conant was sent to photographic school. He was then assigned to VMF-215, which was forming at Goleta, California, preparatory to shipping out overseas. Conant, who had accumulated 321 flight hours since entering the CPT, had never flown an F4U Corsair, but he was able to get in one familiarization hop—just 1.1 hours—before VMF-215 left for Hawaii to complete its training syllabus. In Hawaii, and later at Midway, training was rigorous, and Conant got in more than a hundredfcfx flight hours in the Corsair.

On my first combat contact, I flew wing on Major Bob Owens, the squadron commander, while covering the landing operation at Vella Lavella. I flew a very good formation on Bob; I probably never moved out from him more than ten or fifteen feet. All my attention was focused on flying formation, and I didn't look around at all. I do remember seeing the flash of a Zero's wingtip out of the corner of my eye one time, but I really don't remember much about the operation, because I was flying close wing on Bob.

I kind of learned from that experience that I wasn't going to do anybody any good flying that close on my leader. I hadn't been protecting Bob, and I wasn't doing any good for myself. As a result, on subsequent operations, I loosened up. I didn't just fall back on my leader, I cut in on the corners, and I found I was able to of keep an eye on Bob without flying a real tight formation. That worked out pretty good.

My next enemy contact after Vella Lavella was a mission flying close cover on XIII Bomber Command B-24s to Kahili on August 25. Once again, I was flying wing on Bob Owens.

As soon as we arrived over the Kahili area, we had enemy fighters all over the place, but we managed to stay with the bombers. Once the B-24s dropped their bombs and headed home, they flew into the clouds. Since we couldn't fly cover for the bombers once they were in the clouds, we were free to engage the Japanese fighters.

That's when Bob Owens ran right into a covey of Zeros. As Bob went after the fighters, I would cut inside, picking them off as they tried to tail in behind him. Whenever a Japanese fighter went in after Bob, it would end up in front of me. Eventually, however, I got sucked back a little bit.

One airplane I shot at directly was an Imperial Army Kawasaki Ki-61 Tony that got on Bob's tail. Until then, Bob had been weaving back and forth, shooting at various airplanes, and I had been doing the same thing. It was more or less one continuous fight. When the Tony went after Bob, I was 200 to 300 yards behind him and closing. The Tony seemed to have had an initial altitude advantage—he was going faster than Bob, and closing. I was dead behind the Tony, about 500 feet, and there was no deflection. I had the throttle firewalled, and I didn't have to maneuver at all. I was gaining on the Tony, but not fast enough. I had to open fire at a pretty good range. I think I fired one continuous burst, probably for ten seconds. It's hard to fire short bursts when the guy is right in your sights. Our guns were boresighted at 600 feet, so he was right at my optimum impact point.

I hit the Tony; I hit him good! I didn't see the shells hitting him, but I saw the results. No flames, no explosion; he just tumbled ass over teakettle. I knocked off his drop tank. It was kind of pillow-shaped. It flew right past me. He definitely went down, but I lost sight of him as I was trying to catch up to Bob. As the Tony rolled over, I went right over him.

As I raced after Bob, I saw a Zeke coming in on the right side. He was after Bob, but then he saw me coming and pulled up. I pulled up after him and fired, and I hit him pretty good, too. It was another tail shot, from which you can hardly ever miss. The airplane didn't blow up, but there was an explosion on his right wingtip.

Bob and I had fired an awful lot in that dogfight. When I had started shooting at that last Zeke, all my guns were working. But they slowly petered out as they ran out of ammunition. Finally, I had only one gun firing, but I had already scored significant hits on the Zeke. He went down. I didn't see him go in, but the kill was confirmed by someone else. In fact, both airplanes I had shot down were confirmed; someone saw them hit the water.

After I shot down the Zeke, Bob pulled up into the clouds. I tried to get up in the clouds, too, but I couldn't make it. I was too far behind and ended up kind of hanging on my propeller, trying to get into those clouds. But along came a Zeke on my port side, about 30 degrees off my tail. I could see the smoke coming off his wings: *gunfire!* I knew I wasn't going to get up into those clouds in time, and the Zeke was going to get me if I didn't do something. So I just jammed the stick forward and headed straight down at a pretty good clip. I went down 5,000 or 10,000 feet and got enough speed to get away from the Zeke. Who wants to stay in a dogfight when you don't have any ammunition?

I often shot off all my ammunition. I probably used it all up on twenty-five of my missions. Someone had figured out that every .50-caliber bullet cost the American taxpayer about ten cents. My feeling was that all the bullets we didn't use were going to wind up rusting away on some tropical island after the war. So I figured I'd give the taxpayer his money's worth.

In addition to the Tony and Zero (and two Zero probables) he was awarded for the August 25, 1943, melee, 2d Lieutenant Roger Conant shot down a Zero near Vella Lavella on August 30, and single Zeros over Rabaul on January 14, January 18, and January 22, 1944.

Upon his return to the United States following more than 100 combat missions with VMF-215, Captain Roger Conant applied for night-fighter training, but the war ended while he was en route to the war zone with a new night-fighter squadron. He left the service at the end of the war but was called back in 1950. He served in Korea for a year, flying Grumman F9F Panther jet fighter-bombers and Douglas R4D flareships.

Released from active duty in 1952, Major Conant went to work as a test pilot for Douglas Aircraft and, later, as a project pilot with McDonnell-Douglas. He retired from the Marine Corps Reserves in 1953 with the rank of lieutenant colonel.

FAITH, DETERMINATION, AND A BIT OF IRISH LUCK

Captain CHARLIE SULLIVAN, USAAF
39th Fighter Squadron, 35th Fighter Group
New Guinea—September 20–October 20, 1943

Charles Peter Sullivan was born in Eureka, Illinois, on July 31, 1915. In February 1941, after graduating from Northwestern University with a degree in business administration, he enlisted in the Army Air Corps Flying Cadet program. He learned to fly at the Spartan School in Tulsa, Oklahoma; Randolph Field in San Antonio, Texas; and at Brooks Field in Brooks, Texas. Upon receiving his commission and pinning on his silver wings at Brooks Field on September 21, 1941, 2d Lieutenant Sullivan was transferred to Mitchell Field, New York. In January 1942, he was shipped to Australia and assigned to fly P-39s in combat with the 35th Fighter Group's 39th Fighter Squadron.

While flying a P-400 fighter (a P-39 export variant) near Port Moresby on June 17, 1942, 2d Lieutenant Charlie Sullivan scored his first aerial victory, a Japanese bomber. But it wasn't until after the 39th Fighter Squadron transitioned to P-38s that Charlie Sullivan began his steady climb to ace status: 1st Lieutenant Sullivan downed a Ki-43 near Gasmata, New Britain, on January 6, 1943; a Zero over Lae on March 3, 1943; a Zero probable over Huon Gulf on March 4; a Betty near Port Moresby on April 12; and, finally, a Ki-43 near Lae on July 26, 1943.

On September 20, 1943, I was flying one of sixteen 39th Fighter Squadron P-38s that were escorting V Bomber Command B-24s on a raid against the Japanese base at Wewak. I was leading a four-plane flight.

We were still south of Wewak, flying at 24,000 feet, when my plane developed engine trouble. I decided to return to Port Moresby, and I left the formation, but I had not gone far before the engine began running fine—so I turned back to rejoin my squadron. Then I looked into my rearview mirror and saw an unmistakable image: that of a Japanese fighter in firing position. He was so close I didn't bother to look over my shoulder and I didn't have time to be afraid!

Instinctively, I shoved the P-38 into a violent dive, dropping my auxiliary gasoline tanks as I went. It was then that I felt the shudder of bullets striking my plane. He had hit my left engine, which began spraying oil that started a smoky fire. I raced for the clouds below at speeds of nearly 500 miles per hour. The plane shuddered and shook from the strain. I looked back. I was pulling away from the Japanese fighter, but he was still stalking me. Oil began to spray on my windshield, obscuring my vision. I thought about parachuting right then, but instead I cut off the flaming engine and feathered the propeller, which stopped the fan and turned the blades so they would cut through the air with minimum drag. The fire in the left engine went out and my windshield cleared—but the stalker was still with me.

At about 3,000 feet I entered fleecy clouds, but the clouds had gaps between them. I sailed through the first cloud, emerging into the clear, and saw that the stalker was still there. I went into a second cloud, then out into the clear air again. The stalker was still trailing me. To make matters worse, I was beginning to lose my precious dive speed now that I was on one engine. The third cloud loomed up. I needed to vary the program, or eventually he would nail me. So, while in the third cloud, I put my plane in a spiral and came out underneath the cloud, then flew beneath it for some time.

While I was in the third cloud, I thought about how clever it would be of me if I could circle around behind the stalker and shoot him down. But Wisdom said, "What if you miscalculate and come out right in front of him? Wisdom won! I quickly dismissed that idea. When I came into the clear again my pursuer was nowhere in sight. I had eluded him! Or perhaps he was low on gas and had turned for home.

I had radioed my squadron that I was hit and on fire, but the fire was now out and I was on a course for Port Moresby at 3,000 feet. But there were complications. With my left engine cut off, I had lost my plane's only generator, causing my batteries to give out. As a result, I lost radio contact with Port Moresby. I berated Lockheed and the Army Air Forces for not spending a little more money in order to put a generator on the right engine, too. For want of a nail . . .

As soon as I was certain I had lost the stalker, I began to think about the long flight home—at least two more hours in the air—and the necessity of climbing to at least 7,000 feet to get through a pass in the mountains. But this was not to be. The right engine began heating up and white smoke was soon trailing from it—most likely because of a Prestone leak in the coolant radiator. I decided to try the left engine again. Somehow I got it cranked up and running, so I feathered the right engine and shut it down. I flew for about five minutes before the left engine began to smoke again. So, with black smoke streaming from the left engine and white smoke streaming from the right, I decided I must either make a forced landing or bail out.

I had been flying over tall trees for some time and did not wish to parachute, as I had friends who had parachuted and landed in tall trees, with the result that they sustained everything from broken legs to broken backs. I elected to set the plane down if I could.

I was at the end of the road. Both engines were dead, the props were feathered, and I was sinking rapidly. As I lined up on an open area, I jettisoned the canopy, pulled down my goggles, and rode it in at about 130 miles per hour. The P-38 acted like a giant lawn mower, cutting off small trees, kunai grass, and brush.

I came to a screeching, sizzling halt. The engines sounded as if they would explode. In landing, I had hit my head on something in the cockpit; it split my cloth flying helmet and gave me a deep head wound. With blood pouring from my head, I thought I was mortally wounded, but the shock spared me some severe pain. It was only a scalp wound, which I quickly bound up. My right elbow was also hurt, but not seriously. I grabbed my parachute, survival pack, and the one-man raft in the seat; I was still wearing my Mae West inflatable life vest. I took off with hardly a backwards glance, for I feared the Japanese might have seen me come down and because the engines were so hot they might explode or start a fire.

I went down at high noon about 5 degrees, 30 minutes south of the Equator. The air was stifling and the silence oppressive in the kunai grass, which stood ten to twelve feet tall. A few moments earlier, I had been sailing along at about 180 to 200 miles per hour. Now I was on the ground, feeling lonely and sensing that I had been thrust back five hundred years in time. Home was nearly four hundred miles away. To the west were mountains, which I hoped to cross to an outpost mission and airstrip named Bena Bena.

It took me three or four hours to slice my way through the tall, swaying grass to the shelter of some trees, a distance of probably no more than seven hundred yards. I tried cutting the kunai with my machete, but it was futile, so I high-stepped and fell forward time and time again. I finally reached the trees and shade, but I was exhausted.

I found a bit of a clearing, where I cut up my parachute to make a tent and hammock of silk. Such luxury!

The first night in the jungle was terrifying, because of the strange noises and shrieks of birds and small animals. It later rained almost every night starting about 1600 hours, but I was spared that first night, the only night of my travels that it did not rain. I stayed the second day among the trees, peering out frequently toward my plane, which I could not see.

At the time, the Fifth Air Force's air-sea rescue efforts were meager, to say the least, especially in the interior of New Guinea. Rescue efforts on my behalf probably consisted in their entirety of instructions to all pilots: "Look for Sully somewhere down in the jungle." Indeed, they did look for me the next day—from about 25,000 feet, then went home and reported, "No sign of Sully." The following day the instructions were, "Don't forget about Sully; he's out there someplace." Flying once again at 25,000 feet, they did not see me. On the third day, the talk went to, "Too bad about ole Sully." And that's the way it actually happened!

I watched for rescue planes all day from below my canopy of trees. Then I ventured out to see what was around me. Water, which I had needed badly the previous afternoon, was hardly seventy-five yards from where I slept. It was so welcome! I filled my faithful little emergency drinking can (about one-pint capacity) and ate some of my chocolate bar. I was still a bit jumpy and watched closely for Japanese troops or natives.

I wasn't really frightened, but the jungle was new to me, so I felt I could not take chances. I was very lonely, but full of hope, and I wanted to get somewhere before my head injury gave me trouble. I put sulfa powder on the wound, which I bandaged with my field dressing.

I slept rather well the second night, but I frequently awoke to check noises. The moon was on the wane but still quite large.

On the third day, I decided I was gaining nothing staying where I was. I thought of my trip ahead and optimistically concluded I could be home in four or five days. Little did I comprehend the power of the jungle and the difficulties that lay ahead.

I hid the remnants of my parachute at the edge of the kunai grass and covered or otherwise obliterated most of my camp markings. Wisely or unwisely, I did not spread my chute above the top of the kunai—I reasoned that the Japanese had as much chance of seeing it as my friends did. I felt that I was truly on my own, because I didn't think the friendlies could pluck me out of the woods.

I gathered my possessions—the tent, the hammock, the one-man raft—took a heading of 135 degrees for Port Moresby, and bravely set off. When I crossed my drinking stream, I took off all my clothes and shoes to wade across the twelve-foot wide, four-foot deep run. On the other side, I dressed back up in my long-sleeved khaki shirt, long khaki trousers, woolen socks, ankle-top GI shoes, and cloth flying helmet. Then I took up my course of 135 degrees again. The going was much easier here than in the thick kunai grass; it was all trees, thickets, and some grass.

At about 0900 hours, I heard a radial-engine plane. I thought it was a Japanese fighter, which were mostly radial-engine aircraft, but it turned out to be an American single-engine A-24 dive bomber, with crew of a pilot and observer or gunner. I tried in vain to start a fire in the damp underbrush. I searched for my matches in my waterproof container, and came up with a good, old farmer-type match. But the kunai grass was too wet. Frantically, I searched for tracer ammunition for my trusty Colt .45-caliber automatic pistol. The A-24 was then only a quarter of a mile from me, flying at about 100 feet. It was so close, I could see the pilot and the observer, who had his canopy rolled forward in order to see better. Moments later, the A-24 was gone, out of sight. It was disappointing, but not overwhelmingly so. After all, this was only my third day down. So I struggled on.

The path was hard, but I found some trees that had been chopped down some time before. This greatly encouraged me. The path led to an abandoned grass hut—an exciting discovery! My thoughts raced from one idea to another. Was this just a way station for a native hunting party? When had people last been here? I found some discarded fish bones, but it did not appear that anyone had been in the hut for some time. I continued on, crossed another small stream, then came to another shelter on the bank of another stream. I crossed this stream and continued along the path, which was marked by crocodile footprints. Losing the trail where wild pigs had rooted up the path, I returned to the last stream, set up my hammock, cleared an area, and retired for the night. I always retired at sundown, because the dangers of wandering about in the dark jungle were apparent to me.

It began to rain about midnight, and the downpour continued all night. I was drenched and rose frequently to exercise by simulating skipping rope and shadowboxing until I was warm, then I went back to sleep. What an uncomfortable night it was.

I suspected there was a river nearby, so I elected to leave my hammock, Mae West, one-man raft, and box of .45-caliber ammunition at my camp while I searched for the river. I intended to come back and retrieve the heavy stuff. I blazed a trail as I went along, breaking off small branches and cutting into the bark of trees to leave marks. I found the river, but when I tried to retrace my steps to my camp, I became lost, confused, and bewildered. I could not recognize my trail-blazing effort.

The jungle closed in on me oppressively. I panicked. I wanted to run blindly away, anywhere—just run and run. It was a terrible, fearsome feeling that I had never experienced before or since. Somehow, faith and reason prevailed. I knelt down and prayed earnestly: “Mary, conceived without sin, pray for us who have recourse to thee. Never was it known that anyone who sought your help or intercession was left unaided.” Mary was listening and interceded with God. I stood up, now calm and confident. I resolved to take a compass course, which I believed would take me back to the river. I did not deviate from the course. In about twenty minutes, I was back at the river bank, but it was not the same spot here I had first come upon the river. The jungle had won. I was not about to try to find my heavy equipment.

Now my problem was getting across the river without my Mae West life vest or the raft. Undaunted, I looked for trees with which to build a raft. I began to flail at small trees with my twelve-inch machete, but the trees were tough and the job was arduous. I gave up that idea and began collecting limbs and logs from along the river bank. I tied seven or eight logs together with parachute cord and confidently set sail. It was not to be.

The logs were soaked through and the raft would not fully support me, so I just lay on it, half in and half out of the water. I drifted with the current, kicking my feet for a little extra stability. All seemed to be going well; at least I was still afloat. Then I came to a bend in the river where the current quickened, and I was swept against a muddy bank about four feet above the water level. The swift current swung my raft around and it hit me in the back. I lost the raft and, like the proverbial drowning man, I frantically grasped for anything around. I kept my pistol in my right hand and above the water all the time I was flailing. Then, Providence came to my aid! I saw a vine hanging down from the side of the bank, grabbed it, and steadied myself. The makeshift raft floated merrily on, disappearing downriver.

I surveyed my precarious position. I was in deep water, in the current, but the swift part of the current was narrow. I realized that if I shoved off from the bank, I would cross the swift current and soon be in shallow water. This I did, and after reaching the shallow, pebbly shore, I decided to wash my clothes. I had had enough for one day, so I prepared for night. Beneath a huge tree only a few feet from the river, I fashioned a little shelter, using sticks to support huge banana leaves that served as my roof. Then I booby-trapped my little area, using parachute cord as a cordon, hoping that any intruder would trip over my alarm system and awaken me. Branching into my river was a beautiful mountain stream, which I planned to explore the next day. Bridging the juncture of the river and the stream was a fallen tree, which I believed was used by the natives to cross the river.

It rained most of the night, but my tree and banana-roof shelter served me quite well. I was tired and slept soundly!

I awoke, ate the last square of my chocolate bar, looked to the east, and got ready to start up the mountain stream. There was a sand bank on the left of the stream that extended for a short distance and appeared to lend itself to easy walking. As I approached the sand bank, I was startled to see a solitary human footprint in the sand. Just one footprint. I looked on either side of the print for another footprint. There was none. It was baffling. I thought of when Robinson Crusoe discovered his man Friday's footprint in the sand.

The footprint was pointing up the mountain stream. In the distance I detected a clearing on the side of the mountain. We had been told that the natives girdled a tree near the base, so the tree would eventually die and fall over. It was in such clearings that the natives planted their gardens. The mountain stream seemed to lead in the direction of the clearing—hopefully, a garden tended by friendly natives.

We had had good luck with the coastal natives in the Port Moresby area. Indeed, several of my comrades in the 39th Fighter Squadron had been helped back to our camp by natives after being shot down. So up the middle of the sparkling stream I proceeded. The stream varied from knee- to waist-deep. The bottom was rocky and uneven, but I never fell.

After proceeding up the stream for about an hour, I began to shout periodically in the hope of attracting the attention of the "friendlies." About 0900, movement on the right bank caught my attention. I stopped dead in my tracks. Gradually, the figure of a man appeared from behind the tree cover. He had a weapon, a spear or bow and arrow, which he lowered. I felt he had drawn a bead on me from behind his cover.

I raised my hand and waved, smiled, and tried to appear very friendly. Under such circumstances I could be *very* friendly, but at the same time, my right hand moved ever so close to my trusty .45, which was holstered on my right hip.

I advanced very cautiously, gun hand at the ready, smiling, and trying constantly to appear relaxed and friendly. I reached the bank, which was about three or four feet above the water. The native extended his hand and helped me up the bank. We went back into the trees a few feet, where on the ground lay a freshly killed wild pig. Nearby was a young native woman. My host indicated that I should sit down, which I did, and he proceeded to dress his pig.

He laid the pig on its back and chopped it open through the chest cavity with a stone axe. I noticed the woman had a bunch of ripe bananas in a fiber bag. I indicated by munching actions that I was hungry, and I pointed to her bananas. My host indicated to her to give me some bananas, and she gave me two or three, which were delicious. She was very shy and giggled a little, but my host was stern and businesslike as he continued with his task. I was fascinated when he sopped up blood from the pig's chest cavity with spongy leaves and then squeezed the blood into a three- or four-inch diameter bamboo tube. I was to see more of the bamboo tube later.

Soon the dressing of the pig was complete and it was obvious we were ready to depart the area. I then saw New Guinea chivalry at its best. My host—I was to learn later that his name was Tootaroo—loaded the pig on the shoulders of his mate, gathered his spear, bow, and arrows, and headed for the stream.

Very shortly we were at the bank of the stream. Tootaroo took the pig from the woman's back and she got down into the water. Then Tootaroo loaded the pig on her back again. Next, he got down into the water, and I followed. We walked downstream for about fifteen minutes before coming to a path on the left side, where the bank was almost level with the water. Tootaroo and his mate started up the path, and I began to follow at a tactful and respectful distance. Suddenly, Tootaroo turned to me and pointed emphatically back down the stream, whence I came. I protested and indicated by my motions that I wished to continue with them. He shook his head angrily and again pointed downstream. By sign language it came out: "Go back downstream." I said, "No, I go with you," and he replied, "No, you don't." To which I responded, "Yes, I do!" After a couple of these exchanges, he simply turned away and started up the path. I hesitated, then followed. I expected him to turn on me again, but he did not, though it was obvious he did not want me to come along.

Quietly, we plodded on for perhaps thirty minutes before Tootaroo stopped and began to shout as if to warn someone ahead that he was bringing a stranger home for dinner. My heart sank. What should I do? I considered my options: either leave them and go back to the known loneliness of the jungle, or continue with them to an unknown but at least human company. I reasoned that if I left them, they would still know I was out there, someplace. The thought of more food and what I hoped were friendly natives won the debate. Apprehensively, I followed.

Shortly, we arrived at a small, level clearing. There were old campfire remains and a strange-looking stick placed in the fork of a short vertical stick that had stuck upright into the ground.

Tootaroo started a fire and cooked some pig meat in a cylindrical earthen vessel. He later placed some whole bananas in the ashes and baked them. In about a half hour, my feast was ready. Bananas have never tasted so good. Meantime, I was aware that little dark faces were beginning to appear from behind the bushes and foliage. Soon the faces materialized into bodies of men, women, and children. They approached me cautiously. Still on my best behavior, I smiled and did nothing to excite them. They were curious about all my possessions and poked at my pockets. One youth was particularly curious and wanted to see everything in my pockets, which were loaded with compasses, parachute cord, ammunition, and a small can. The can was similar to a sardine can and had contained my field bandage. The bandage was now wrapped about my head and tied under my chin. I had my cloth flying helmet, split in the crash-landing, perched on my head with my flying goggles still attached. I sensed that the curious boy was a little retarded, but he looked happy and his companions appeared most tolerant of him. I must have been a bedraggled-looking curiosity. More and more natives began to appear and disappear, seeming to bring back a whole new audience each time. Twice, men who were obviously chiefs arrived to look me over from a comfortable distance.

The chiefs wore beaded bands around their foreheads and all the men appeared to have little sticks in their noses and ears. The men's hair was different from the bushy hair-style of the Port Moresby-area natives; it was twisted into many small, tight braids. Each time a chief or newcomer arrived or left, I was frightened. For all I knew, they would bring Japanese soldiers.

The afternoon passed this way. I was the new sideshow in town.

During the early part of the afternoon, I tried to determine the meaning of the strange sticks, the older fire, and a small shelter that was open on all sides. It was obvious someone had camped here before. I pointed to the shelter, fire, and sticks and, by sign language, questioned the natives.

One man held up three fingers and pointed to me, as if to say that three men like me had been there. I made signs: did they go that way (toward suspected Japanese-held areas), or did they go that way (toward Australian- or American-held territory)? The native pointed down at the ground! Now there was a discomfiting thought: the three like me had not left the area; they had died or had been killed!

As twilight approached, the audience, never more than ten at a time, had dwindled to five or six people. By implicit invitation, I accompanied

Tootaroo, his mate, and several others into a nearby area containing two thatch-covered huts. I concluded that they did not consider me a threat, so were taking me in for the night.

It was an interesting family affair. Actually, I believe these were two families of three men in all, including one chief, Tootaroo, and a new acquaintance named Sego, plus two women—Tootaroo's mate, Sego's mate, and three or four children. The other natives I had seen during the day apparently lived elsewhere.

The women prepared dinner: more pig, yams baked in the ashes, and lima-type beans cooked in blood. They also got out the bamboo tube that contained the blood from the dead pig's chest cavity. After putting some herbs or leaves in, they held the tube over the open fire. Presently, when the mixture was bubbling nicely, they proceeded to shake the contents into their hands and ate it with great gusto. As we sat around the campfire circle, I was served food on a huge banana leaf. Occasionally, a dog tried to run through the circle to get a morsel of food.

Eventually, we arrived at names for the major players. I explained I was Charlie, which they thought was pretty funny. Tootaroo was the native I had found with the pig, Sego was an another young man with a mate and a boy of five or six, and the chief was either Lulawai or "Headaman."

It was a pleasant, light-hearted, jovial evening. After dinner, we were joined by other natives from the area.

I tried to explain my presence among them. I simulated a plane (a *balus* in their language) flying high in the sky with engine sputtering, then crashing to the ground. I made signs to show me crashing forward in the cockpit and injuring my head. Strangely enough, my story got through, except to my dismay they all laughed when I pointed to my head. Then one native took over and retold my story in his native tongue, accompanied by appropriate gestures. Again, they all laughed at the crash-landing and my injured head. Perhaps they laughed in relief that the mighty flying *balus* was indeed vulnerable.

They had a pet emu or cassawary, which was cute but nonetheless a pest. It circled the group around the fire, came up behind me, and began pecking my back. I tolerantly pushed it away a couple of times, but it was persistent. So I backhanded it with my right hand, knocking it back a bit. My hosts loved that; they laughed merrily. Everything seemed so congenial and friendly.

When it became dark, the women and children went inside a rectangular thatched hut while the men remained near the fire with me. At length, they gave me a small hollow log to sleep in or on. It was about four feet long, and wide enough for even a very heavyset person. I lay near the fire in my log, with my right hand placed comfortingly near my holstered .45. I was alert for any strange behavior or action, but it became apparent to me I had nothing to fear.

Occasionally, during the night, one or another of the men stirred and replenished the fire. It was obvious that they had to keep the fire burning. I suspect they started fires by friction or sparks from stones. I awoke each time the fire preserver got up to tend the fire.

The night passed without incident. At dawn, the small village began to stir. It appeared that Sego's mate, their son, and Headaman were planning to travel. Perhaps I wanted to go with them? I made signs about departing, hoping to convey the idea that I wished for a plan or route to go home. They seemed to get the idea and mentioned several places or names of people. I copied these on the back of my map. There were such names as Masaro, Lowy Kowy, and Bena Bena.

I tried to write the words phonetically, then repeated them back to Sego. I had heard of Bena Bena, which I knew was somewhere across the mountain range from my suspected location. It occured to me that a relay system to get me home could be arranged. The names I had been given were locations or contacts along the way. This sounded encouraging, for earlier that morning I had had the sinking feeling that I would not be able to escape the area and perhaps have to spend my life in the jungle wilds. That was a sobering thought, but the more we exchanged signs, the more hopeful I became. Not wishing to waste time, I signed, "We go." Strangely enough, they were ready also, so we turned to leave the village. I suspected then that Sego, his family, and Headaman were actually returning to their own village, located some distance away.

Before we left, I gave Tootaroo the small field-dressing can as a farewell gift. He received it stoically. Not too impressed, I thought.

Shortly after we left Tootaroo's home, we began a rather arduous climb. I thought I was in fair shape, but I began to tire. At one point, about an hour after starting out, Headaman approached me and signed that he wanted my big machete knife. I thought he was leaving us for good and simply desired a souvenir, so I shook my head "No!" He disappeared into the trees, but he returned in about twenty minutes with freshly cut stalks of sugar cane, which we sucked on for a time. It was delicious and refreshing. I felt a bit of remorse at not giving him the knife to cut the cane for all of us.

We started on again, and in about another hour we all stopped when Sego pointed out a small pitfall in the path that had been covered with light branches and leaves. It appeared to be a security measure for a nearby village. Thoughtfully, they detoured me around it, and shortly we stopped again as they shouted a warning to unseen natives that they were bringing in a stranger.

In a few minutes, we arrived at the top of a lightly forested ridge. It was about noon and a most pleasant day, sunny and nice. A few locals came out to look me over, and the overall atmosphere was relaxed. When we arrived in the village, Sego cooked some food, which was unremarkable in comparison to the feast I had had the night before.

It seemed to be a lazy day. I decided to rest, perhaps share another meal with them, and depart early in the morning for that faraway place called Port Moresby. The villagers left me alone, except for Sego's little son, an alert and happy child. I tried to amuse him as best I could as I took off my shirt so I could better enjoy the pleasant sunshine. I also cleaned my .45. At Tootaroo's village, I had made signs for something with which to wipe my gun, and my idea got through. I had been rewarded with fibers impregnated with lard or some other grease, which I now used. I was constantly amazed and pleased at how effective sign language could be when you really worked at it.

I was enjoying myself, but my idyllic afternoon came to an abrupt end. Sego came and led me to meet two new natives, and it was as if a cool wind and dark clouds permeated the scene. Suddenly, I had a sense of impending danger. However, I tried to seem confident and cheerful as by sign language I indicated how I hoped to be relayed over the hills to friendly territory.

The obvious leader of these two visitors was named Aidee, but Aidee's partner did not give his name, so I named him "Grinning One" or

"Grinny." Facetiously, I thought he had cut cards early in the afternoon for my knife and won. I did not like his attitude and distrusted both of them.

Standing toe to toe in the clearing, Sego and Aidee had a violent argument. Finally, Aidee grabbed two spears and thrust them violently into the ground as he appeared to read Sego the riot act. And Sego obviously acquiesced to whatever Aidee wanted of him.

I was standing nearby throughout the argument, and I felt compelled to say something to ease the tension. In what I hoped was a light-hearted manner, I said, "What is the matter, Sego, did you take his spears?" Of course, I knew that the natives did not understand my words or care about my opinion. I was later to conclude that my ultimate fate was the subject of the argument, that Sego had tried to defend me, and lost. Sego appeared crestfallen as we all turned away from the scene of the argument.

As twilight approached, the waning moon came out, and the villagers began to prepare dinner. Gone was the hospitality and friendliness of the previous village. I wandered about, but no one asked me to eat with them, not even Sego. I walked up to one family campfire and made signs of eating. I was no longer hungry, but I wanted to see whether they would give me food. They handed me something, but did not ask me to sit down on the ground with them. I wandered away, not knowing what to do.

Aidee and Grinny suddenly appeared beside me and started a small fire. Nearby was a thatch-roof hut with a very small doorway. As I sat down near the fire, facing the rising moon, Aidee and Grinny took up positions on the other side of the fire and stared at me without showing any emotion. I felt I was being stalked!

To show my nonchalance, I sang every popular and college song I could think of. I was determined not to show fear or undue concern. Earlier in the day, Aidee had conveyed the idea that he had been to the coast, and he did seem to be a more worldly person than the others. As we sat around this fire, he pointed to the moon and indicated that I perhaps had arrived at the wrong time of the month and that perhaps he regretted it had worked out this way. These were only impressions, but the feeling that there was an impending threat was definitely there.

After I had exhausted my song repertoire, I suppose Aidee thought it was time to move on with his plan. He and Grinny rose and slowly approached me. They sat down on either side of me, so close that they brushed my sides. This was too close and threatening for me, so I immediately stood up. I believe they were about to attempt to overcome me. As I cast about for an idea to ease the tension or provide them with reason to leave, I again noted the nearby hut and crawled through the doorway, taking with me a little grass mat the natives had given me. I crouched just inside the doorway, hoping they would go away, but this was not to be.

Aidee and Grinny approached the doorway and Aidee reached inside to tug at my shoulder, a clear suggestion that I come out. Thinking that perhaps Aidee was simply envious of my attentions to Sego and his little boy, I stepped outside. Immediately, several natives, including Aidee and Grinny, closed in around me. They were carrying spears, bows, and arrows.

Without anyone actually jabbing me with a spear, I was prodded, not too subtly, along a path that led up a small incline. Soon we reached a circular hut—the execution chamber? Above the doorway I could make out in the dim light a stick device that reminded me of the stick symbol I had seen the day before, at the edge of Tootaroo's village. This symbol was a forked stick embedded in the ground with another stick placed across the fork. Whatever it was, I took it as a disturbing sign.

My escorts gestured that I go into the hut. I didn't see any alternative, so I bent down and entered. Four natives followed me in. One carried a fire brand and an empty—but ominous-looking—bamboo blood tube. My heart sank a little lower as all signs were most foreboding. I felt maneuvered, but no course of action came to mind. Hoping against hope that things would get better, I continued to play their game. The native with the fire brand started a small fire in the middle of the hut and another native handed me the grass mat again, suggesting by signs that I lie down and sleep, to which I replied aloud, "I always sleep sitting up." Simply responding aloud made me more confident, although I knew they understood little beyond what I could convey by means of my limited sign language.

I was about six feet from the door, wary, and sitting on my mat with my back against the wall. I realized I was in a very vulnerable position. If a melee ensued, they might block the door to prevent my escape, even if I shot some of them. When I pressed my hands against the bamboo wall at my back, I realized I could not easily break through it.

The room began to fill with smoke as there was no ceiling opening. Seizing on this situation, I began to cough and wave my arms to indicate the smoke was too much for me. A native stood up and began tearing a hole in the roof to let out excess smoke. Now or never, I thought, as this had created the diversion I needed.

From a crouching position, I bolted for the opening and came out of the hut just in front of the doorway. As I came out, I pulled my .45 automatic from its holster and chambered a round. The hammer was back, and the .45 was ready to fire. Then I slipped the safety switch on and dropped the .45 back in its holster.

As I stood and waited for their next move, more natives appeared, so I elected not to make a run for it. Those in the hut followed me out, bringing the bamboo tube and the fire brand with them.

Once again by common consent, we moved down the path away from my "execution chamber" to a rectangular hut with a porch extension that was open on three sides. There we stopped. I was escorted inside and again given my grass mat along with a firm indication to lie down. I took the mat and sat down, facing the interior of the enclosure with my back vulnerable to the outside darkness.

The men stacked their bows, arrows, and spears against a post and started up the fire. Once again, we eyed each other as we all sat on the ground. Some of the men decided to smoke or chew betel nut. They made some square motions with their arms, as if to say, "See, I have nothing to harm you with." They wanted me to see that they weren't making any overt moves. I let them smoke and chew. Most of the men who chewed took betel nut with some lime from a small gourd. They put a little lime on some betel leaves, chewed up a bit of betel nut and then spit it out in one hand. After looking at the mess, they would put the betel nut combination back in their mouths. The headman had a little fiber bag that contained a broken mirror. I suppose that made him the kingpin. He chewed with great dignity. After chewing for awhile he would reach into his bag and pull out the mirror. Then he would stick the mess out on his tongue and look at it to see if it was the right consistency or color. Because he had the mirror, he did not have to spit the betel mess into his hand.

Sego and his little boy were inside, too. The boy's job was to keep the fire going. It might have been sort of an initiation ritual for him. The boy was only about six years old and was clearly there against his wishes. He kept crying. Suddenly, Aidee took a brand from the fire and stuck it right in the child's face. The little boy stopped crying and kept up the fire real well after that. That didn't make me like Aidee any better.

The contingent inside the hut included Sego, his son, Grinny, Aidee, the headman, and a lookout who sat in the back of the hut. I could hear other natives rustling around outside the hut. I was afraid that if we sat there long enough, someone on the outside might strike me with a spear. If I could manage to move to the doorway of the hut, they would all be in front of me. I got up slowly, walked slowly toward the entrance, and sort of stooped over sideways by the doorway. I then took a fire brand and sort of flashed it in back of me to make sure that there was no one in back of the hut. My move placed all of them in front of me, so I was at least temporarily in command. Just to be sure, I took out the my .45 and placed it across my right thigh.

We sat there from about 2000 hours to about 2200. I threatened them with the strength of the Fifth Air Force: "The *balus* will come and boom-boom the hell out of your villages." But that didn't seem to bother them, though they did shrink down and repeat "boom-boom!" a few times. They didn't like the idea, but I guess they didn't really think the Air Force was going to get there.

Next, I thought I'd try a little religion on them, thinking that the missionaries might have contacted them. Since I was convinced they were going to kill me, I didn't see any reason not to be frank about it. So I said, "God wouldn't want you to kill me." I think I spoke pretty convincingly. Aidee, who apparently had been out to the coast, muttered a word that sounded something like "Lord." But after I had gotten all through, Aidee said, "No savvy talk." I answered, "You savvy this gun don't you?" and shook the .45 right in his face.

I sat there for over an hour with my gun trained on Aidee. The whole time, I snapped the safety on an off—*click, click, click*—to be sure he got the message. But this guy remained cool as a cucumber.

After a while, the home team began to get a little anxious. The headman got up and sort of stretched, as if to show that he was tired. Then he walked toward me, indicating that he wanted to go behind me into the hut. It was pretty obvious that, if he went back there, I would have two fronts to cover. He got real close to me and motioned again that he wanted to go inside. I swung the .45 around on him and shouted, "Sit down!" Well, he withered right down beside me, clearly frightened.

This standoff had been going on for hours. I was thinking, I'm in command—temporarily. If I can just get them in close, in sort of a semicircle, they won't shoot through their own people. I didn't know how I was going to get out of the hut, but I didn't want them to shoot me before I did. The headman played right into my hands. He crouched right down beside me, which made Grinny unhappy. I thought that Grinny was showing some fear, so I reached out with my left hand and motioned for him to come in a little closer to protect me on the right. But before he did, he looked at Aidee, who was sitting right in the middle, sort of head-on to me. Aidee blinked his eyes. I think that meant, Yeah, go ahead and humor him. Grinny moved a little closer but kept looking over his shoulder. He was sort of a sassy little guy, and I didn't like the way he grinned. So, with the gun in my right hand, I grabbed him by a shoulder with my left hand and sort of yanked him. The poor guy probably thought I was going to shoot him in the back, because he was really scared.

At this point, I established a priority list of how I was going to take care of them. They all understood "Number One." I said, "Aidee, I get you number one. Grinny, I get you number two. Headaman, I get you number three." I didn't go to number four, because I didn't think it would last that long. Then I waved the .45 and described what it would do to them. Aidee sort of believed it. It all sounded rather grim, but I had to keep talking to try to make the point. Aidee was the only one who had not shown a bit of fear, but his team had not shown much initiative.

Next, I motioned for Aidee to move to a position right in front of me. He was close enough that I could touch him with my left hand. I signaled, "Come in a little closer." He rose slightly and sat without moving forward. "No! Closer!" I said. I then reached out a little farther and motioned him in closer. I guess he thought I was off balance, for he came right out of his crouching position and lunged at me like a tiger. He threw me against the wall, but I came to my feet naturally. I had the gun in my right hand, but he grabbed both my wrists and pinned me back briefly. Somehow, I forced the gun down and shot him from a distance of about six inches—right through the chest. The shot blasted him clear across the room. A split-second later, the headman came at me from the left side. If he and Aidee had timed it a little better, they might have had me. The headman came in from my left and went for both my wrists. He got my left wrist and grappled for my right. I pulled my gun back and shot him in the chest from my left side, *WHAM! WHAM!* Two shots, one to Aidee and one to the headman, in the space of two seconds. It was practically all over. My grim prediction was almost true. I got number one, Aidee, skipped number two, Grinny, and got number three, the headman.

I still remember it like it was yesterday. I can picture the dull glow from the fire, my smoking .45, and me standing there in a crouched position, like it was Custer's Last Stand.

I thought they would come after me in waves, but they didn't. Instead, they ran off like a bunch of scalded dogs and left me alone. The headman staggered outside and died. I then realized that no one was left in the hut but me. I ran out to the left as fast as I could, in the same direction as the staggereing headman, and cut back and made an end run, like in football. I ran full tilt to the left, then back to the center, and then I tripped in the tall grass. This probably saved my life, because if I had not fallen, I would have been still running. I slithered down into a little depression.

Back at the village, the natives had lighted torches and were screaming and shouting. I could hear them answering from all the neighboring villages. I seemed to be surrounded by their war whoops. When the torches were lit, they started to come up the hill. After they found the two men I had shot, they had a mourning ceremony. They beat on the ground and wailed, sobbed, and shouted for about an hour. It was terrible to just lay there on the ground and listen. The mourning ceremony went on and on. I could see their shadows.

Although I am usually optimistic, I couldn't see how I would possibly get out of there alive. As I lay there motionless with the .45 in my right hand and a fresh clip with six bullets in my left hand, I pondered the chances of my leaving alive. I knew the natives would not be kind to me after I had killed two prominent members of their tribe.

I prayed some more: "Dear Virgin Mary, never was it known that anyone who sought thy help or intercession was left unaided. Inspired with that hope and confidence, I ask your intercession with God the Father, God the Son, and God the Holy Spirit." I prayed the Hail Mary, which ends with "Holy Mary, Mother of God, pray for us sinners now and at the hour of our death." The chilling thought hit me: *"Now and at the hour of our death" had become one and the same for me!*

What could I do? Should I save the last bullet for myself—a permanent solution to a temporary problem? I agonized over this decision. My faith and upbringing had taught me that suicide was wrong and the cowardly way out. But I dreaded torture. Then I remembered somewhere in Scripture it was said that God will not permit a person to be tempted beyond his will or capability to resist, and that even Christ was tempted. So I decided not to save the last bullet for myself, but to continue to fight to the end or escape alive. It was comforting when I realized I had weathered that trial of temptation.

After about an hour, the mourning ceremony stopped and the natives went down into the lower end of the camp. Everything got real quiet. No fires, no voices, nothing. It was as still as death. A little hope trickled through my veins, but at about 0200 the natives came alive again. Up the hill they strode, with torches held high. This time, the light seemed to penetrate my little hideout, and I thought surely they would see me. But they didn't. They went through the mourning ceremony again, beating sticks on the ground, and all of that. From the shadows, I spotted the figure of a woman coming toward me. It seemed as if she had guessed where I was. She walked straight toward me, closer and closer. I couldn't bring myself to shoot her, so I thought I would shoot at the ground, get up, and run. She got closer, now about two or three feet from me. I could have reached out, stretched a little, and touched her toes. She stood right over me, sobbing and wailing her heart out. After what seemed an eternity, she turned and walked back to the camp.

By 0400, everything became very quiet again. It was totally dark—no fires, no moon. Dawn was coming, and I knew I had to get out before first light. With a great deal of fear and trepidation, I stood up, fully expecting to become a human pin cushion. But nothing happened, so I took a couple of steps while thinking perhaps they wanted a moving target. Still nothing happened. Then I really began to feel that I might get out of there after all. I tip-toed across an open area and climbed over a couple of little stone walls. I made up my mind to head for Port Moresby.

I had two compasses. One was a luminous compass that I could read at night. Having two compasses was a great consolation, because you get to where you don't trust one compass. I ran the gauntlet, past two open huts, but nothing happened. After I got by those, I went down a path.

It was beginning to get light. As I looked down the valley, I could see that a couple of natives were hunting. I immediately withdrew off the path, but as I did I stepped on a twig. It snapped, and the sound reverberated like a shot across the valley. The two hunters just froze in their tracks, like a couple of hunting dogs on point. They just stared at the spot at which they had heard the noise. They couldn't see me, but they had me pinpointed. Then one of them dropped out of sight. I knew I had to get out of there quickly, because they were going to either circle around to investigate or go back to the village to get help. I pulled off the path and took off my shoes, because I felt they had betrayed me by the noise of stepping on the twigs. I hung them around my neck and started crawling.

I crawled all morning. I was in such a desperate frame of mind that I hid my shoes under some bushes because they were making a clumping sound. I put them in there neatly, like I was putting them in a closet or under a bed, as if I might come back for them later. I was determined to make it difficult for the natives to follow me. I would crawl for three minutes and listen for two minutes, then crawl again. I did this for about two hours. I figured that if they were getting close, I would hear them during my rest interval.

I got to a tiny mountain brook, which was clogged with bushes and fallen trees and had several waterfalls. Remembering Boy Scout training and lore, I walked in the water to hide my tracks. About mid-morning I reached a rushing mountain stream. It took me about a half hour to decide where to cross it so as not to leave footprints on the banks. After I crossed the stream, I took off, almost running to get away from the area. My feet felt like they were cut to ribbons. I put my sulfanilamide powder from my jungle kit on them to keep them from getting infected.

When it seemed certain that I had gotten safely away, I stopped to build a shelter. I rested there for a couple of days, then moved on, built another shelter, and rested again. I went on this way for about three weeks, and by then I was getting pretty weary. One time I built a big fire, hoping that someone from my squadron was still looking for me. I gathered a huge pile of logs and started a fire that burned all night, like a prairie fire. It must have burned off about half of New Guinea. In fact, I had to get down in a ditch to get away from the fire. The next day, I had to walk through miles of burned stubble.

One day, I saw a shadow on the path and then noticed a figure coming toward me. It was a native woman. As soon as she spotted me, she started running away like a deer. I took off after her, but she left me in the dust. I spent a very uncomfortable night in an abandoned hut. I'm sure the natives were also uncomfortable that night, knowing I was out there.

One of my few possessions was my toothbrush, which was a great consolation. I brushed my teeth, but I didn't have much to eat. I had a pamphlet that told about native foods, but it had gotten wet and the ink ran all over it, so I couldn't read it. However, I did eat some papayas and small bananas.

By then, I had been barefoot for about three weeks, but I put on my socks every night, because the insects drove me wild. Without my cloth helmet, mosquito head net, flying gloves, and socks I would have been in terrible shape.

One of my favorite respites each day was to climb a hill and try to figure out where I was. I wanted to get up into the mountains, but every time I got to the top of one mountain, there was just another mountain, another valley, and another mountain ahead. Finally, I left the mountains and went back down into the plains. On my way down, while contemplating the panorama and the beauties of New Guinea, I saw a glimmer of light a few miles away. It turned out to be a reflection from a small, conical hill. I walked toward it, and late in the afternoon I was able see some human figures up there. I didn't think they were natives, but I couldn't tell if they were Japanese, Americans, or Aussies.

I was so desperate by this time that I thought, even if they were Japanese, I might sneak into their camp at night and steal food. The next day I homed in on the camp. I saw someone wearing an Aussie hat, but even that didn't convince me. Maybe one of those tricky Japanese was wearing an Aussie hat. I sneaked up closer and closer until I was about thirty feet from them. It was like playing hide and seek, where you come out from hiding and jump up to scare the seeker. I was so close to them that it was almost embarrassing to jump out and say "Here I am!"

Finally, I came out from behind a tree and saw that they were indeed Aussies who had come down from their fortification for lunch. I just stood there and tried to think of something clever to say, but the only thing I could think of was, "Well, here's another one of those bloody Yanks." The Aussies didn't say anything; they just looked at me in disbelief. It was kind of awkward. Later, I learned that two weeks earlier, in a skirmish with the Japanese, they had lost a second lieutenant who was about my size and had the same color hair. That was why they were so surprised to see me. I was all bandaged up and looked so much like their lieutenant that they thought I was him, come back from the dead.

The Aussie soldiers gave me some food but warned me not to eat too much or I'd get sick. Well, I did eat too much and I did get real sick. However, after three weeks of not eating, you can't really eat *too* much.

The Aussies had a radio and asked if I wanted to send a message. Of course I wanted to let my squadron and the Fifth Air Force know that I was safe. I composed a very concise message: "Captain Sullivan, 39th Fighter Squadron, arrived at this point. Injury slight. Please advise." The next morning, there came a reply: "Captain Sullivan will proceed on when able." Some callous, headquarters type must have composed that thoughtless message, because no one in the 39th Fighter Squadron would have been so inconsiderate. I thought, "To hell with them; I'll stay here for the rest of the war; I'll never go back!" Then I decided that I had better return.

The Aussies offered to send a native back with me across the mountains. I thought it over and quickly decided against that plan. They also suggested I might go with one of their patrols, which was planning to cross the river, although there was some danger of running into the Japanese. I decided that I had had enough of the natives and that I would go with the Aussies.

I was with the Aussie patrol, in their camp, for two days. I felt guilty about eating their food, because everything they had came in on their backs. They had no air drops whatever, but had lugged all of their food and supplies over the mountains. The first night out, we saw a big fire.

The Aussies thought it might be the Japanese, who would sometimes advance behind the cover of a big fire. As the fire came toward us, I was afraid I had really gone from the frying pan into the fire, but it was much better to be with twenty other guys than to be out there by myself. The threat did not materialize. I don't know who started the fire.

The Aussies were awfully nice to me. They even carried my .45, which had become too heavy for me. They realized I was very weak. A couple of big Aussies on either side of me helped me along. Although they had said we wouldn't go too far, we walked about fifteen or twenty miles a day. Eventually, we got across the big river and soon arrived at a camp where there was a small observation plane. We had been walking for two days.

The pilot, Lieutenant Frederick, who wore glider wings, said to me, "Captain, I will save you a big walk if you'll get into my little airplane. We'll fly to another airstrip." I agreed and got in. It was a tandem arrangement, so I sat in the front and Lieutenant Frederick sat behind me. We didn't have any parachutes, and the plane didn't run very well. "It always runs better in the air," Frederick said. Famous last words, I thought. Somehow, we took off and flew for a bit. When we got up to about 1,500 feet, he asked if I wanted to fly. I said I would like to try. But when I took control, it felt like I was holding it up in the air with my bare hands, so I gave it back to him. Soon after that, I saw that while the throttle was advancing and advancing, the engine wasn't reacting. Then Frederick announced, "I think we have to turn back." But as he turned it back in a big chandelle, the plane began to lose power. We had been flying over some real tall trees for a long time and I knew first-hand what tall trees could do if you had to crash-land. Fortunately, the trees thinned out and the pilot made a pretty good crash-landing in an open area. But the plane had fixed gear, so when it hit the grass, it flipped over on its back.

I was hanging upside down by my seat belt, so I just pulled the buckle and fell about four feet to the ground. Frederick was very solicitous: "Are you all right? Thank God! I'm glad it wasn't the general." It turned out he had been flying an Aussie general around. I fired off three shots—the international emergency signal—waited, fired another three shots, and waited again. Nothing happened, so we walked back to camp.

The next day, a C-47 transport plane picked me up at the Dumpu airstrip. I spent the night at Nadzab and the next day, October 20, I was flown home to Fourteen-Mile Drome near Port Moresby, where a glorious welcome was put on by my squadron. I was back from a thirty-day mission!

During the welcome, one dear friend said, "I knew you would make it. Oh yeah, I'll bring back your razor in the morning."

I was on cloud nine. I sent a cablegram to my beloved wife, Mareelee, advising her to pay back the insurance money. Ironically, as I learned later, one insurance agent had indeed tried to begin payoff procedures, but Mareelee politely threw him out! I sent a wire to my dear friend, Captain Tommy Lynch, who was on leave in the States: "Bring back my boots, you vulture." Tom had taken my favorite flying boots home with him. Tom was killed later, so I never got my boots.

Malaria struck me, which deprived me of following up on a suggestion made by one of the Fifth Air Force generals that I lead a revenge mission against the natives. Actually, my plan was simply to drop supplies to my Aussie commando friends and cause the natives no further harm. I was to direct the mission from a B-25 covered by four P-40 fighters.

Before I left Brisbane, Australia, for the States, I was advised that General Douglas MacArthur wished to see me and possibly decorate me. My weakened condition and the questionable condition of my uniforms motivated me to decline.

After arriving home, I spent Thanksgiving with Mareelee and our families. Following welcome rest and recuperation, I was assigned to a replacement training unit in Santa Maria, California to teach combat skills in my favorite airplane, the P-38. I was even able to give Mareelee a piggyback ride in a P-38. She literally rode on my shoulders.

Charlie Sullivan remained in the service and retired after nearly thirty years on active duty with the rank of colonel in 1968. In 1973, he added "O'" to the family name. In September 1993, he learned that a pair of Australian aviation enthusiasts had located, almost to the day, the remains of the P-38 he crash-landed in the middle of nowhere a half-century earlier.

BURN OUT

Captain GEORGE CHANDLER, USAAF
339th Fighter Squadron, 347th Fighter Group
Rabaul—January 20, 1944

George Throckmorton Chandler was born on February 1, 1921, in Wichita, Kansas. In November 1941, he dropped out of the California Institute of Technology to enter the Army Flying Cadet program, and he earned his wings and commission at Luke Field, Arizona, in July 1942. Lieutenant Chandler briefly flew P-40s with the 15th Fighter Group in Hawaii and was then transferred to the V Fighter Command's 49th Fighter Group, which was then flying out of Port Moresby, New Guinea. In February 1943, 2d Lieutenant Chandler returned to Hawaii to join the 318th Fighter Squadron, but a little over a month later he was transferred to the Thirteenth Air Force. Chandler joined the 347th Fighter Group's 339th Fighter Squadron to undergo P-38 transition training on New Caledonia and went to Guadalcanal in June 1943.

Lieutenant George Chandler's scored his first aerial victory in his first aerial combat—on July 3, 1943, he shot down a Zero fighter near Rendova. On November 8, 1943, while covering the U.S. invasion force in Empress Augusta Bay, 1st Lieutenant Chandler shot down two Zeros in a wild melee.

On January 20, 1944, the 339th Fighter Squadron was flying P-38s off of Stirling Island in the Treasury Island group, near the southwest coast of Bougainville. That day, twelve P-38s were assigned to cover 42d Medium Bombardment Group B-25s as they went in to strafe and frag-bomb the airplanes on Rapopo Airfield in the Simpson Harbor area at Rabaul. At least a dozen Marine F4U Corsair fighters were also assigned to help us defend the B-25s against Japanese fighters.

The person writing the orders for the mission was not knowledgeable about P-38 fighter tactics and was probably responding to the pleas of the B-25 pilots, who wanted the fighters to stay right with them, rather than above and ahead of them. We protested that we could not defend the B-25s as well if we were practically flying formation with them, down low—we needed a little altitude and room to maneuver so we could attack the Zeros before they could get to the B-25s. At *any* altitude, a Zero could turn much faster than a P-38, so unless the P-38 had some room in which to maneuver vertically as well as horizontally, it was at a terrible disadvantage versus Zeros diving from a higher altitude. But our orders remained specific and exact: we were never to be more than 1,000 feet above the B-25s, and we were to stay right with them throughout the mission.

Fortunately for me and others, the Marines did not get these same stupid orders about how they had to fly the mission. Before the inevitable fight started, the F4Us pushed up and ahead of the bombers and were in the logical place for our fighters to be.

We crossed the coast at about 1,500 feet, flying more or less formation with the B-25s. We could see many, many Zeros in the air ahead of us, waiting for us. We dropped our external belly tanks, and I took my flight of four to full power to gain all the speed we could as we went into the fight.

A Zero positioned itself to attack our squadron commander, Major Hank Lawrence, so I decided to intercept him. As the Zero started its dive toward Hank, I looked around to clear myself from other Zeros. I spotted one Zero coming head-on at me from perhaps 500 feet above. I had at least 300 miles an hour airspeed at that point, so I did not think it was possible for that Zero to reverse course and successfully attack me. I marked him off. I could see no other Zeros in my vicinity, so I headed for the Zero that was attacking Hank Lawrence.

It set up beautifully. I could intercept the Zero before he could get to Hank. However, the Zero pilot saw this, too, and broke off his attack just as I was coming into very good gun range to blow him all to pieces. Right at that instant, I heard gunfire from directly behind me. The Zero I had discounted moments earlier was in the hands of an airman skillful enough to execute a split-S and time his attack perfectly. And there he was, hitting me from behind.

The first hits were 20mm explosive shells that ripped into the top of the left engine and shot off the intake manifold. At that moment, I was climbing at a 20- or 30-degree angle to intercept the Zero that was diving on Hank Lawrence. I instantly pushed the wheel forward, which kept the pursuing Zero from hitting me with more bullets. No fighter pilot, no matter how skilled, could do much hitting with negative Gs on. This was because, as the ammunition belts moved out of the trays, they rose up to the top of the gun compartment and kinked. This kinking could jam the guns if they were firing.

I quit taking additional hits as I dove away, but my left engine was one roaring mass of blue flame. The instant the intake manifold was blown off, the engine stopped putting out power, but the propeller continued to drive the engine and held the same 3,000 RPM that I had set for it. As a result, the internal supercharger was jamming about 50 inches of manifold pressure into the pressure carburetor, and the pressure carburetor was squirting the required amount of gasoline into the compressed air from the supercharger. It was this pressurized fuel and air that was feeding the roaring fire in the left engine nacelle. I can still remember how hot the radiant heat from that burning engine felt against the left side of my face, above the oxygen mask.

A raging fire of that intensity could burn through the fire wall and into the main fuel tanks in a very short time, so my first reaction was to bail out of this airplane before it exploded in one great big ball of flame. By then, I was approximately level from the initial climb and pushover, so I pulled the nose back up and rolled it over so I could simply drop out when I opened the canopy and released my seat belt and shoulder harness.

As I rolled over, I could see a little hilltop about 1,000 feet below me. There, a Japanese gun crew was firing a four-barrel antiaircraft gun. I could see the muzzle flashes. With that sight in mind, it didn't take long to say to myself, "George, if you bail out here, those SOBs will shoot you to pieces in the parachute. Or if they miss, they will certainly take you prisoner. You might as well stay in this airplane and see if you can get the fire out and go home."

So I did not pull the handle on the canopy release. Instead, I rolled the airplane over to level flight. It was flying beautifully with 100 percent power on the right engine, even though the left propeller was windmilling. I started feathering the left engine, to see if the fire would go out. I moved the left engine fuel selector valve on the floor to the Off position. At that moment, I thought about the mixture control being in the Auto Rich position, so I moved it to the Idle Cutoff position. Instantly, the fire was out, the propeller was coming to full feather position, and I was accelerating in level flight under good control.

Now my problem was how to exit from this fight and not get finished off by another Zero.

By this time, the first of the B-25s were coming off the target and heading back toward Treasury Island. I snuggled in close to one of them and, with full power on the right engine, I was able to keep up.

Very quickly, both the B-25 pilot and I could see a gun position on another hill, right straight ahead. I watched as the B-25 engaged in a gun duel with this antiaircraft position, which had the usual four guns, probably 20mm cannon, firing. Then I watched in horror as the B-25 slammed into the top of the hill, wiping out the gun position. The B-25 bounced once and, at a very steep upward angle, rolled over upside down, fell into the jungle, and blew up in a big ball of flame.

The stream of B-25s coming off the target was now spacing out a little more, and the bombers were going faster than I could fly on one engine, but I was still trying to stay with them.

Suddenly, I saw a Zero at about 3 o'clock high as it prepared to make a high-side attack on me. I was only about fifty feet off the treetops, so I turned right into his attack to make him steepen his dive to a point where he could not shoot at me *and* avoid flying into the jungle when he pulled out. He saw the danger, rolled left, and went out and made a right-hand turn, which would put him close to being on my tail. However, I was already turning left into his attack for a head-on pass at him.

The Zero pilot wasn't watching his own tail as he came at me, and it was with great joy that I watched a Marine Corsair explode that Zero in a big ball of flame. As the Corsair pilot went back up into the fight above, he executed a victory roll right over me. I have tried to find that Marine, but the Marine pilots on that mission who claimed Zeros were all killed later in the war, so there is no way to express a proper thank you.

I kept grinding along and soon was out over the ocean. Then it was a matter of the good engine taking me home. The flight took a couple of hours. When I arrived, a P-38, also flying on single engine, was landing ahead of me. The pilot came in too slow, and when he applied power to try to reach the field, he was below the single-engine minimum control speed. The P-38 flipped over and crashed into the water just off the end of the runway, killing the pilot.

I had to circle away from the runway approach so I could pump down the landing gear, because the primary hydraulic system was out. My landing was uneventful.

Captain George Chandler downed his fourth Zero over Rabaul on January 24, 1944, and scored his fifth and final aerial victory—another Zero—on February 5, also over Rabaul. Shortly thereafter, he returned to the United States and spent the rest of the war teaching fighter tactics in California. He left the service in January 1946 with the rank of major and went into the banking field in his native Kansas.

SCRAMBLE OVER NANNING

1st Lieutenant LYN MARSHALL, USAAF
26th Fighter Squadron, 51st Fighter Group
Nanning, China—April 5, 1944

Lyndon Owens Marshall was born on July 16, 1920, and raised in Watkins Glen, New York. He became interested in aviation as a child, and, after graduating from high school, he entered Roosevelt Aviation College in Mineola, Long Island. Upon graduating from Roosevelt as a licensed aircraft and engine mechanic, Marshall took a job with Pan American Airways, working at Long Island's La Guardia Airport as a mechanic for its Clipper seaplanes.

I was at work the day war was declared against Japan, December 7, 1941. P-40 fighter planes from nearby Mitchell Army Air Base were flying overhead. When I saw them, my mind was made up; I wanted to be a pilot. I couldn't afford to learn to fly, but if I joined the Air Corps, I could learn and it wouldn't cost me. The thought never occurred to me that I might be flying in combat against the enemy. I just wanted to learn to fly.

I enlisted in the Army Air Corps on January 14, 1942, and was assigned to the South East Training Command. I graduated with Class 42-J and received my wings and commission on November 10, 1942. Shortly after that, my girlfriend, Jane, and I got married.

Tactical training in P-40 fighter aircraft came next at Pinellas Army Air Base near St. Petersburg, Florida. Then I was sent to Miami, the departure base for overseas duty. As soon as I had ten hours of flight time in the P-40, I was placed on alert.

I left the United States on February 10, 1943, without knowing where I was being sent. I landed in Karachi on the west coast of India a few days later. I was a passenger on a C-87, a B-24 converted to carry passengers and freight. I was held in Karachi, where I put in flying time in P-40s until I was needed in the combat zone.

My next destination was Dinjan Army Air Base in the province of Assam, which is located in the northeast corner of India, at the foot of the Himalaya Mountains. I flew my P-40 from Karachi, across India, to Dinjan, arriving on May 1, 1943. I was assigned to the Tenth Air Force's 26th Fighter Squadron.

Dinjan was located in a jungle. It had a single asphalt landing strip. While there, I flew missions into Burma to bomb and strafe bridges and Japanese ground forces. Also while I was stationed at Dinjan, I experienced engine failure twice. Fortunately, both failures occurred near Dinjan. I lost one engine because of an oil-pressure problem while I was in a formation takeoff. I crashed off the end of the runway but walked away. The other engine failure occurred at 20,000 feet, while I was on patrol over the base. I managed to get down and make a deadstick landing. I also had my appendix removed while I was at Dinjan.

In October 1943, the 26th Fighter Squadron was reassigned and transferred to the Fourteenth Air Force. Actually, the squadron was reassigned to our parent group, the 51st, which had had its headquarters at Kunming, China, for some time.

I flew various missions from Kunming into enemy territory, including Haiphong and Hanoi in French Indochina, now known as Vietnam. While strafing ground targets during one of these missions, my engine was damaged, but I was able to reach a friendly airstrip.

In March 1944, twelve P-40s and pilots, including me, were ordered to deploy to a remote base, Yungning Army Air Base outside Nanning in

Kwangsi Province. The base was located in southeast China, about ninety miles from the Tonkin Gulf. Our primary purpose there was to hit Japanese shipping on its way to the Philippine Islands.

No matter where I was located, the types of missions I flew were the same—escorting bombers, bombing and strafing attacks, patrols, interceptions, and reconnaissance. On March 13, 1944, the mission was to escort B-25 medium bombers to Hainan Island. The weather turned out to be very, very bad. This mission should never have taken place. There were two groups of four bombers, each with four escort fighters.

Because of the weather, the fighters were forced to fly close to the mountain range on the way to the coast and join up with the bombers at the coastline. My flight of four fighters succeeded in joining the bomber flight we were to escort. The other group failed to join, however, and those fighters returned to base.

Both groups were supposed to fly dogleg patterns to Hainan Island to fool the Japanese radar as to our intentions. But the four unescorted bombers flew a direct course toward the island, thus alerting the Japanese, who were out looking for us when we arrived. And they found us. We were flying on the deck, close to the water, because of the bad weather. Without warning, Japanese fighters came at us out of the haze and rain. They sure caught us in a bad position. I was able to get in a quick burst from my six .50-caliber wing guns, which knocked down one Japanese fighter, a Ki-44 Tojo, before I escaped into the haze and rain of the storm. The Japanese won this battle as we lost two bombers with their crews and one P-40, whose pilot was saved. It makes me wonder what would have happened if the weather had been better.

On April 5, 1944, I was operations officer at Yungning Army Air Base. Lieutenant Colonel Louis Hughes, Jr., was commanding. There was a high overcast above the base; the ceiling was about 10,000 feet. Five available P-40s were on the field with standby pilots, including me, in case there was trouble while the rest of the planes and pilots were out on a mission. Early in the afternoon, the Chinese warning net informed us that thirty-two Japanese aircraft were approaching the base from the direction of Hainan Island. I immediately took off along with 2d Lieutenant Sam Brown, 1st Lieutenant Alexander Duncan, 2d Lieutenant Lloyd Mace, and 2d Lieutenant Allan Putnam. I was the flight leader.

We climbed to altitude in the general direction of the approaching

Japanese aircraft. It was important to gain as much altitude as possible in the short time we had before the Japanese arrived. We climbed through the overcast and had reached 18,000 feet when we received a radio message: "They are approaching the field." I radioed to my flight that we were going down. We started diving in the general direction of the airfield, even though we couldn't see the ground because of the overcast.

When the Japanese aircraft arrived in the area, they were just beneath the overcast, which was at approximately 10,000 feet. Because we were above the overcast, we couldnt see their formation, which meant that I couldn't make a decision as to how we would approach them. The fact that there were thirty-two Japanese planes involved meant there were probably at least two units—two formations.

We broke out of the overcast at 10,000 feet and at a speed of 500-plus miles per hour. And there they were, just below the overcast! We passed through their formation. I am sure they were as surprised as we were. At this time, Lieutenant Sam Brown, a member of the 16th Fighter Squadron who was temporarily assigned with the 26th Fighter Squadron, collided with a Japanese fighter and was killed.

We must have startled the hell out them, and we sure busted up their formation, but of course we were no longer in formation, either. There were Japanese planes—Ki-43 Oscars or Ki-44 Tojos—scattered in every direction. It all happened so quickly.

The speed we had built up during the dive was to our advantage, as we could use it during the early stage of the fight. A P-40 could not out-climb or turn inside most Japanese single-engine fighters, but a P-40 could out-dive all of them. While they were probably trying to recover position in their formation, I was pulling out of my dive and regaining precious altitude.

It seemed the Japanese planes were everywhere. No matter where I looked or turned my P-40, a Japanese plane was there. I was not looking for specific Japanese planes when I pulled up; I didn't have to, as a Japanese fighter was directly in front of me. I fired a short burst from all my guns, and he went down in flames. There was another one to my left. I pulled toward him and fired, and a short burst put him down in flames, too. As I pulled away, I spotted another Japanese fighter about 200 yards away, on the tail of one of the other P-40s. I took after and shot him down, too. Shortly after that, I saw one more above me, about a quarter-mile away. I pulled up toward him and hit him with accurate shooting. I *must* have hit him, because his engine started smoking. I didn't chase after him to confirm my kill, though, because I saw another Japanese fighter strafing the airfield.

I called the fighter whose engine I smoked a probable, and I wasted no time getting to the one strafing the airfield. As I closed on him, he pulled up very sharply. I was near enough to him to start shooting. It appeared that I hit him in the engine and cockpit; then the plane rolled over and crashed.

During my high school days I had learned to shoot clay pigeons while shooting trap and skeet. In order to break a clay pigeon, I learned to lead them—to shoot ahead of them the proper distance in order to hit and break them. During flight training, we were also taught to shoot skeet. The skills involved were necessary when shooting down enemy planes. Short bursts from my guns were all that was necessary to hit my targets. In most cases they were deflection shots. I believe that without this training, I wouldn't have done nearly as well in combat. Without the knowledge and skill, I would have wasted ammunition trying to follow tracer bullets to the target, and then the target probably would have gotten away.

As I turned away from my fourth kill and was attempting to regain altitude, I saw another Japanese fighter closing fast from dead ahead. We both opened fire, and as I turned from him, I saw what looked like a piece of his wing fly loose. I lost him then, so I claimed only a damaged airplane.

I was getting too close to the ground, and I felt it was necessary to regain as much altitude as possible. I'm not sure that was a smart decision, but I felt that, if I could get up higher without being chased, I could get back into the fight before the Japanese left. While I was attempting to regain altitude, however, three Japanese fighters got on my tail. I kept looking to my rear and maneuvered my plane whenever they fired at me to avoid getting hit. While in a fight such as this, the throttle was pushed all the way forward, beyond a gate on the throttle quadrant, in order to obtain absolute maximum manifold pressure. This position was called "War Emergency power." The airplane's motor was giving me all the power it could.

While I was climbing and concentrating to avoid getting hit by the Japanese 20mm and 7.7mm rounds, I gradually lost speed, and my plane lost what we call lift. The airplane was not going fast enough for the air to support it. When this happened, it was impossible to control the airplane. My P-40 immediately flipped over on its back and went into an inverted spin, falling toward the ground. I had experienced an inverted spin in a P-40 while in tactical training. When it happened, if the pilot pulled back on the throttle to reduce power, the chances were good that the plane would fall out of the inverted spin with its nose pointed down. It would then pick up speed and regain lift, and the pilot would again have control.

I don't know at what altitude I was at when all this occurred, but because of the circumstances, I neglected to reduce the power. I remember fighting the sloppy controls as I was spinning down. Somehow, I finally came out of the spin, but I don't know why. Did I unknowingly cut the throttle?

I recovered just over the treetops. To my amazement, there were no Japanese on my tail. I believe they thought they had shot me down. The situation was suddenly much less hectic, and I counted my blessings as I climbed to regain altitude. I didn't see anymore Japanese that afternoon.

After the fight, I called in the other pilots. Along with one or two others who had enough fuel, I flew cover over the air base until the other planes in the squadron returned from their mission. When I landed, I ended up in a ditch alongside the grass runway because the tire on my left landing gear had been shot out. My plane had many punctures, but none that would have put me down.

Sam Brown was killed in a mid-air collision; Alexander Duncan was credited with one destroyed and one probable; Lloyd Mace was credited with one destroyed; Allan Putnam was credited with two destroyed, one probable, and two damaged; and I was credited with four destroyed, one probable, and one damaged. Ground forces found Japanese aircraft to substantiate all the kill claims, plus one, which was awarded to Sam Brown. I was awarded the Distinguished Service Cross for my actions that day.

An interesting sidelight: the Japanese had been in the Nanning area for some time before our arrival. How they treated the residents, I don't know, but the people were sure happy we were there. The people of Nanning were so elated to the see the Japanese get whipped in this scrap that they wanted to show their appreciation. Thus, many, many of them, including the governing body of Nanning, came to the base to present a banner showing the date of the fight, a "Flying Tiger" scrapping with a Japanese plane, and Chinese characters expressing their thanks to us.

In a letter to my wife Jane dated April 11, 1944, I wrote,

> A few days after a fight with the Japs, at the end of a day, the four us were principals in a parade in Nanning. We stood on open flat-bed trucks with high-ranking Chinese Army officials and governing officials of the city and were driven through the streets. Crowds of people were lining both sides, and long strings of firecrackers hanging from the second and third stories of the buildings to the sidewalks were going off. There were thousands of them. Unbelievable. Pieces of firecrackers were flying in all directions, onto the trucks and people. We had to cover our faces to protect our eyes. Every narrow street we were on was crowded with people and blazing firecrackers.
>
> After the parade concluded, we were taken to a hotel where a banquet was being held. The walls of the hotel were decorated with many signs, such as, 'The American Pilots are brave,' and 'The American Air Force is a model for the Chinese Air Force.'
>
> Next was dinner and speeches using an interpreter. The 'Theater Guild' brought fruits to the base. They also put on a theater production for us. What a memorable experience."

Lyn Marshall flew a few more missions from Nanning. Early in May 1944, he was ordered to return to the 51st Fighter Group headquarters in Kunming, then led a flight of eight P-51s to Lingling Army Air Base to assist the 23d Fighter Group's 76th Fighter Squadron. After flying twenty-three missions from Lingling, he returned to Kunming to serve as assistant group operations officer.

Marshall returned to the United States in early August 1944, and, following leave, took several maintenance courses leading to assignment as director of maintenance at a B-29 base in Nebraska. At war's end, he opted for a discharge from active duty but joined Air Force Reserve, from which he retired in 1960 with the rank of major.

BLACK SUNDAY

1st Lieutenant CALVIN WIRE, USAAF
433d Fighter Squadron, 475th Fighter Group
New Guinea—April 16, 1944

Calvin Charles Wire was born on April 15, 1914, in Pittsburgh, Pennsylvania, and raised in the Los Angeles area. Determined to fly combat airplanes, unable to qualify for U.S. Army Air Corps flight training because of his age, and certain to be drafted within a month, Wire enlisted in the Royal Canadian Air Force's pilot-training program in November 1941. By April 1942, he had completed the ground phase of his RCAF flight training—just in time to take advantage of an offer for American-born RAF and RCAF pilots and cadets to transfer to the U.S. Army Air Forces.

As a U.S. Army Air Forces aviation cadet, Wire completed Primary flight training at King City, California, and Basic at Lemoore, California. He earned his wings and commission at Williams Field, Arizona, in February 1943, and went on to train in P-38s. In July, 2d Lieutenant Wire and several dozen other P-38 pilots were shipped to Brisbane, Australia, to help form the Fifth Air Force's new 475th Fighter Group.

Calvin Wire's first aerial victory was an A6M Zero fighter he shot down over Wewak, New Guinea, on September 2, 1943. In the same action, he probably downed a second Zero and damaged a third. On September 26, Wire shot down two Zeros, also over Wewak; and he achieved ace status on October 24, 1943, when he shot down two more Zeros over Rabaul.

On April 16, 1944, the 433d Fighter Squadron was flying from Nadzab Airdrome. Our mission that day was to escort V Bomber Command B-24s and B-25s to Hollandia. This was to be our seventh mission aimed at softening up the general area prior to the pending invasion by U.S. Army and Australian Army ground forces.

The weather reports for the two days leading up to the April 16 mission had been bad; there was even the possibility of a hurricane moving in. The meteorologist had strongly recommended that all flights be canceled, but the man in charge—General Douglas MacArthur—said, "The mission must go on as planned."

As usual, the bombers took off first, formed up, and headed for Hollandia. Some fifteen minutes later, the three squadrons of the 475th Fighter Group took off and headed out. We flew through the usual clouds and rain storms, and caught up with the bomber formations south of Wewak.

Normal procedure was to take off on our main tanks and, as soon as we had gained some altitude, switch to our belly tanks. As we closed in on the Hollandia area, Captain Richard Kimball, who was leading the 433d Squadron, called to tell us to switch to our internal tanks and then drop our belly tanks. I was flying a P-38L, which, besides the main and reserve tanks, had two small 45-gallon tanks in the wings, out near the tips. Where possible, it was best to use this gas first, so that the extra weight on the outside wings was reduced prior to entering into any violent maneuvers. It was just good sense.

I switched from my belly tanks to my outer wing tanks—and both engines died. I immediately switched back to my belly tanks and got the engine started again. This time, I switched only to the left outer wing tank, and the left engine stopped again. I switched back to the belly tank and tried again with the right tank. Same result. I then went to my main tanks with no problem. I called Captain Kimball and told him my problem, and he replied, "We might need all fuel we have, so take your wingman and head back home."

I called my wingman, 2d Lieutenant Mort Ryerson, and told him I had to "snafu," and that he was to come with me. At this time, I was back on my belly tanks to make sure I would have as much time in the air as possible.

We flew at about 12,000 to 13,000 feet between a solid overcast and lower broken clouds. We had no problems until we were south of Wewak and approaching the Owen Stanley mountain range, where we found ourselves looking into a solid wall of clouds from the ground to as high as we could see. I had had a number of missions in this general area before and knew that some of the mountains were 13,000 and 14,000 feet high, so we climbed to 20,000 feet, looking for an opening. No luck!

We then headed north and went down to 12,000 feet. Once again, we flew east to west along the wall of clouds in search of an opening. Nothing doing.

As we were heading back east once again, I saw a plane on our left and so we headed for it. It was a nice, big B-24, heading for home. I called Mort and, said, "We hit it lucky. This guy has a co-pilot, a navigator, and a radioman. Let's latch on and follow him home." We snuggled in close on his right wing, and he rocked his right wing to let us know that we were welcome. Then we headed into that awful wall of clouds. We kept tucked in for about fifteen minutes, when, all of sudden, the B-24 went into a sharp left turn. I told Mort to hang on and climb, and then we made 180-degree turn and headed out.

It took us about ten minutes to settle down, and about this time, along came a full squadron of B-25s. Once again, we tucked in on the right wing of the rear B-25. After about only five minutes, the whole squadron of B-25's went every which way, and again we went straight up, then into a 180-degree turn, and then back out.

After we were out of the worst of it, I called Mort and told him that usually along the coast, when the weather came in from the east, the clouds would rise a bit as they approached land and leave a space we could fly in and still see what was ahead. He said, "Okay, let's give it a try." So we proceeded east to the coast and headed south. My guess was correct to some degree, as we had about forty feet between the clouds and the water, although the distance varied because the clouds kept moving up and down.

It was raining hard, and our vision through the windshield was nil, so we flew by looking out of the right side windows at the line of surf. I tried to maintain a minimum of twenty feet in altitude and hold position about fifty feet east of the surf line. Everything was working out okay, but my right engine was shaking a bit, so I feathered the right prop and shut the engine off.

About this time, Mort called and said, "Wire, I can't take any more of this. I've got plenty of gas and recently have had a lot of instrument flying. I'd like to break off and try to climb out of this." I told him, "Okay, Mort. Best of luck." He started climbing, and I found out much later that he made it fine.

In the meantime, I kept going down the coast. I was getting awfully tense and, as you can probably imagine, downright scared! I really had no idea just where I was, except it was somewhere on the east coast approaching Lae.

I kept going, and all of a sudden I saw a small landing field with some planes on it. It was just inland from the water. I immediately swung to my right to make a landing, but I was going too fast to turn to the field. I flew over the west side of the field and then headed out over the ocean. When I got out far enough so I could just see the field, I headed south down the coast. As I did, the clouds came down, forcing me lower and lower. The P-38 handles well at 220 miles per hour indicated air speed, and this was what I had been flying at this time. All of a sudden, I saw a wave that seemed to be higher than my wing. I hauled back on the stick, but it was too late. I hit the top of the wave!

Hitting the wave bounced me up a bit, and the nose started going down. I pulled back on the stick to level out, and the stick came all the way back inside my lap. I knew then that I had lost control of the airplane.

I leaned back and locked my shoulder straps, cut the mixture control off, and dumped the canopy. All this took very little time, but it felt like I was in a vertical dive. It was probably not vertical, but it was a dive nonetheless.

I don't remember hitting the water. I could not see it coming; I could not feel it or hear it. All I know was that I came to feeling as though I had needles in my ears. I unfastened my seat belt and kicked out of the plane. My clothes and parachute had enough air trapped in them to float me to the surface.

All I could think of was getting my life raft out. It took me some time and struggling to do so, and I was getting tired of trying to stay above water. Then I thought, "You fool, you have a Mae West on!" I pulled the string, the life vest inflated, and I laid back for a bit of a rest. I finally got my life raft inflated. This will show you how stupid or shocky I was: here I was in the sea with real strong winds and awful waves, trying to get into that raft over the big end! I finally figured it out, turned the raft around, and climbed in. The raft was full of water, so I spent the next fifteen or twenty minutes bailing it out. That was another mistake. With the water out, the raft rode high, like a big piece of balsa wood. The wind just threw me and my raft around like a balloon. It didn't take me long to push the small end underwater and fill the boat so it would ride better.

I think I was about half a mile off the coast when I crashed. All went well after I got water back into the raft. The wind in the meantime was pushing me toward the shore. I could see a line of huge breakers ahead of me; they were crashing over a reef and into the bay. This gave me another fright, but I must have been on the crest of the wave, for it carried me over the reef and into the bay, which had much smoother water.

Coming toward me from shore was what looked like a native dugout canoe with two men in it. Each was wearing some kind of conical hat, so I immediately thought "Japs!" I got out my .45 and tried to shoot at them, but luckily the pistol wouldn't fire. They were GIs, and they towed me to shore.

We had to wait at the landing strip for two B-24s to crash land before we could cross. The men took me to their first-aid station and made temporary repairs to my face.

I had torn off the bridge of my nose, there was a large cut in my forehead in and over my eyebrows, and my front teeth had been driven through my lip. The GIs told me that the strip was at Yami Point, north of Saidor. The next day, they sent me by LST to Saidor, and I proceeded from there by plane to an Army hospital in Sydney, Australia. They kept me there for about four months for plastic surgery and R&R, and then I rejoined my squadron on Biak in August.

First Lieutenant Calvin Wire resumed combat flying upon his return to the 433d Fighter Squadron, and was soon given command of the squadron. On November 19, 1944, he brought his final victory tally to seven Japanese fighters when he shot down a pair of Ki-43 Oscars over the central Philippines. He returned to the United States in July 1945, married the Canadian girl he had left behind during his brief RCAF stint, and left the service in 1946 with the rank of major.

THE OPPORTUNITY FIGHTER PILOTS LOOK FOR

Lieutenant DICK STAMBOOK, USN
VF-27 (USS *Princeton)*
Mariana Islands—June 19, 1944

Richard E Stambook was born on April 9, 1921, in Lancaster, California and raised in a tiny, isolated community built around the oil-pumping plant operated by his father.

After I finished high school, my dad encouraged me to go on to college, and I did, attending Palmdale Junior College for my freshman year. Fueled by conversations with my father about world unrest and by stories of my uncle's World War I experiences, I signed up for the Civilian Pilot Training program when a local barnstormer won a contract to set up a CPT course at the college. I logged forty flight hours while attending Palmdale, but since there was no CPT secondary course being offered there, I transferred to Bakersfield Junior College for my sophomore year. The course at Bakersfield was conducted in a Waco biplane, which made for good aerobatics training. I logged forty hours in the secondary course, for a total of eighty hours in the air, which entitled me to a limited commercial license as well as an invitation by the U.S. Navy to attend flight training at Pensacola, Florida. After two weeks of naval indoctrination at the Long Beach Naval Air Station (actually Long Beach Airport), three of us from the Bakersfield CPT class embarked for Pensacola via a passenger train to enroll in Class 7A-41. That was in July 1941. I left Pensacola as an ensign and a naval aviator in January 1942 with orders to report to the battleship USS *California,* which had been sunk on December 7, 1941, at Pearl Harbor.

When several of us new ensigns arrived together for our fleet assignment, we joined scout seaplane pilots from the battleships *California, Utah,* and *Arizona*—all of which had been sunk on December 7—and formed an ad hoc inshore patrol squadron. We flew our Vought OS2U Kingfisher three-place observation planes on their wheels from Pearl Harbor, doing sector searches for Japanese submarines. I saw *our* subs and many other critters, but no Japanese!

I felt trapped in that assignment, but after months of turning me away, our commanding officer relented to my constant requests for transfer to fighter training. He endorsed my orders to Lieutenant Butch O'Hare's VF-3, which was based on Maui following the Coral Sea and Midway battles. Training in the F4F Wildcat was relaxed as we ran through a syllabus of flight tactics, gunnery, and field-carrier landings. We also worked with Lieutenant Commander Jimmy Flatley's VF-10, which operated from our field for several weeks before going to the South Pacific aboard the USS *Enterprise*.

At length, I was ordered to Lieutenant Commander Lou Bauer's VF-6, which after some intensive training, headed to the South Pacific in the USS *Saratoga*. We eventually joined forces with the *Enterprise* to operate in the Coral Sea for several quiet months, until the *Enterprise* was relieved by HMS *Victorious*. That provided an interesting diversion for our squadron, which replaced the *Victorious* bombers for a time. VF-6 also flew into Guadalcanal a couple of times, but the action consisted entirely of diving into trenches at night to avoid "Washing Machine Charlie," a nocturnal visitor that buzzed the airfields and dropped bombs every now and then.

In the fall of 1943, I was given leave at home before being reassigned to VF-27, which was being reformed at Alameda Naval Air Station following a land-based tour at Guadalcanal. Initially, we flew F4Fs, but we gradually acquired a full complement of new Grumman F6F-3 Hellcats.

The Hellcat was a great airplane, without the ground-looping characteristics of the Wildcat. Grumman and Pratt & Whitney did themselves proud with that airplane and its reliable R-2800 engine, which was later observed operating for lengthy periods minus a cylinder or two shot out by enemy gunfire. Another improvement that appeared in the Hellcat was shoulder straps, which helped prevent the pilot's face from smashing into the gun sight when thrown forward in the event of a sudden stop. And we were finally issued personal parachute harnesses that actually fit. Until then, pilots of large size often temporarily relieved constant strap pressure by removing the harness, which resulted in the unavailability of the parachute when it was most needed.

Throughout our training and deployment, I served as the squadron engineering officer, but the job was made remarkably easy through the devotion of Chief Petty Officer Kenneth Colby and his rated specialists, who worked in cooperation with the excellent *Princeton* maintenance department.

Fighting 27 went to sea in the *Princeton* in early May 1944, sailing from Hawaii to the South Pacific to be part of Task Group 58.3. We made our first strike at Saipan's southernmost airfield on June 11, in preparation for Marine landings. After my strafing run, which burned and exploded several airplanes on the ground, I climbed rapidly to 10,000 feet to prepare for a riled-up Zero crowd. The only thing visible, however, was a Betty, low on the water, heading south, away from Saipan toward nearby Tinian. I made a steep dive on the Betty from 10,000 feet and almost overshot, even with the power off. A burst of about three seconds with all six rifles flamed the left engine, and the Betty crashed into the sea. Two other VF-27 pilots got kills that day; my comrade, Lieutenant Paddy McMahon, got one Zeke on his own and shared one with Ensign Hugh Lillie.

Also in early June, I was vectored from a combat air patrol (CAP) flight by the fighter direction officer (FDO) to shoot down a P1Y Frances twin-engine medium bomber. And on two other occasions, I turned the flight lead over to my second-section leader and my wingman so they could destroy similar targets. We all did the job, but I never found Navy records of these kills.

In addition to regular CAP duty, we conducted strafing missions against Japanese defenses ahead of our Marines on Saipan. The most gratifying thing that came of this was a statement on the radio from the Marine controller who assigned strafing sectors that in essence said, "Well done."

By about 1000 on June 19, 1944, my four-plane division had settled into CAP orbit at 20,000 feet over our task group. Another VF-27 Hellcat division was occupying the CAP position at 10,000 feet. I believe the second division was led by our squadron commanding officer, Lieutenant Commander Fred Bardshar. At any rate, our moment arrived when the Task Group 58.3 FDO, who was aboard the *Lexington,* came up on the otherwise silent radio net to assign us to vector 280 degrees, angels 20, and speed buster to intercept and destroy a large bogey heading about

100 degrees, angels 20 at approximately eighty nautical miles distance. Needless to say, the FDO had my full attention. No doubt the *Princeton* and the other carriers in Task Group 58.3 were scrambling more Hellcats for intercepting this bogey, and even more to follow.

I called "tally-ho" at about 1030, when I spotted the Zero high cover for the enemy bombers above the horizon. The sight of these enemy fighters prompted me to climb a few thousand more feet to gain the altitude necessary to build up performance advantage if I needed it for conversion to speed. I reported sixteen to eighteen fighters escorting twenty-one to twenty-four D4Y Judy dive-bombers.

The fighter director's instructions were excellent, and that includes his altitude assignment. Nevertheless, my extra altitude would have proved more desirable had the Zeros been more aggressive at the start of the fight.

I probably should have delayed the engagement a few seconds and made a quartering firing run on the Zeros, but their apparently unperturbed progress inclined me to first attack the leader from above at about 10 o'clock. This required a brief burst of all six rifles from a range well outside the boresight distance of about 300 yards. I was in luck. The Zero blew up!

I turned left to an easterly heading in order to parallel the flight of enemy fighters. By then, the Zeros were showing some signs of activity via some spreading of their former tight formation. I had swung a bit wide to the south during my first gunnery pass, on account of my diving speed, so I was heading back with about a 30-degree angle on the Zero formation when, almost before I could position myself, a Hellcat crossed in front of me with a Zero closing from behind.

Since all three of us were at about the same altitude and descending slightly together, it was my good fortune to get in firing position on the Zero by making only a slight left-wing dip. As I recovered with a small gunsight lead and pulling only about two Gs, I fired a short burst that blew the Zero to pieces. Although my F6F suffered no damage, the explosion of the enemy fighter was uncomfortably close.

I knew I had to kill the bombers, but some of the urgency I felt to fire my guns at them was alleviated by the many Hellcat reports cluttering the VHF channel, all pertaining to Judy shootdowns or "bomber kills."

I now believe that many of these broadcasts were in reference to the interception of follow-up attack formations by several F6F squadrons. At any rate, our critical common radio frequency was overused!

The whole melee continued to descend, probably below 12,000 feet. I was deciding on my next target (the closest Zekes), when my second-section leader came into view, leading a Zero across my flight path in a steep descent at about a 40-degree angle from my airplane. The Zeke was rapidly closing to firing range, but with the excess speed I had gained during my descent from altitude, I maneuvered rapidly to fire into it while pulling about three Gs. I saw my arcing tracers hit the target just before it exploded.

Suddenly I was alone—or so I thought. Where had everybody gone? With my adrenalin pumping, and my best fighter-pilot eyes looking for another enemy airplane to destroy, I spotted a Judy several thousand feet below my 8,000- or 9,000-foot altitude. I initially intended to dispatch this Judy with a high-side run from left to right. She was on a northwesterly heading, in a steep descent, but the Judy pilot evidently spotted me, for he turned to a westerly heading as I commenced positioning myself behind him. When still separated by about 500 or 600 feet, I discovered I was unable to fire, so I had to break off to avoid the Judy's determined rear gunner while I recharged my weapons. When I achieved a firing position again, the Judy was very low on the sea. Although the gunner was doing his job, he did not hit my Hellcat before I hit the Judy's cockpit and splashed her.

Here I was, with an operative fighter in an area where enemy aircraft were plentiful. My adrenalin was coursing!

Now my fighter-pilot eyes located another possible target. I was not close enough to recognize it as a Zero flying almost straight and level, but it did appear distinctively alien. This was the opportunity that fighter pilots look for! I made about a 20-degree heading change to close the distance for an attack, but while I was still three or four seconds from the best firing position, I was privileged to observe an expert at work in that Zero.

As I was getting into position on the Zero, two Hellcats in close formation dived over me from almost 180 degrees behind and fired at the Zeke, which at the right moment went into a violent left skid. His maneuver was a success. I personally was relieved that my own airplane had not been hit by spent cartridge casings from the overflying F6Fs. The casings might have fouled my engine.

Now it was my turn! The Zeke had only seconds more to fly. With those seconds dwindling, my concentration was again disrupted by two more fast-diving Hellcats that attempted to steal the shootdown. But once again, all they did was shower my airspace with brass. I was not hit, and neither was the Zeke, whose pilot adjusted his flight path abruptly with another pull-up and left skid, which I figured must surely have exhausted the pilot's capabilities to avoid being hit due to diminution of his airspeed.

By now, my whole outlook was fixed on dodging brass cartridge casings. I may have become shy! At any rate, I yielded the contest momentarily—long enough for a single F6F to approach the Zeke more deliberately than the others and dispatch it in a ball of flame. I found no more targets that day, and I still applaud the spirit and skill of that Zeke pilot.

The Task Group 58.3 carriers, unharmed by the enemy, were now preparing to recover aircraft. After a rendezvous of sorts and getting a reading on the *Princeton's* YE/ZB radio homing signal, we were invited aboard—and pleased to comply after safetying our guns and completing the landing checklist.

June 19, 1944 was a good fighter day for VF-27, and for other squadrons as well. The whole day's proceedings—380 confirmed kills by U.S. Navy carrier pilots—attests to the immense capability of the U.S. Navy at this stage of the conflict.

When he landed aboard the Princeton *late on the morning of June 19, Lieutenant Dick Stambook was an ace, having received official credit for shooting down three Zeros and a Judy. On September 21, Stambook raised his official score to eight when he shot down another Zero and two Imperial Army Ki-61 Tony interceptors in the vicinity of Manila. On October 13, 1944, Dick Stambook downed a Ki-44 Tojo over Formosa, and on October 18 he raised his official tally to ten when he shot down a Ki-45 Nick twin-engine fighter over Luzon. With that, Stambook's rising star had reached its zenith. The* Princeton *was sunk on October 24, and that ended Dick Stambook's combat career; he was lucky to swim away from the ship with his life and the clothes on his back.*

Following survivor's leave at home, Lieutenant Stambook reported to Los Alamitos Naval Air Station in California, where he joined VBF-101 as an instructor. He left the Navy after the war ended and went to work for TWA as a pilot, a job he held for thirty years.

ON A WING AND A WHEEL

Lieutenant BAYNARD MILTON, USN
VF-15 (USS *Essex)*
Luzon—November 13, 1944

Charles Baynard Milton was born in Waycross, Georgia, on June 29, 1921, and raised in Jasper, Florida. He entered Emory University in 1939 and had just completed his sophomore year when he signed up for the Navy flight program, because, as he put it, "I thought the program would tax my capabilities to the fullest."

Cadet Milton entered the Navy in January 1942 and earned his wings at Jacksonville Naval Air Station in September of the year. After attending the fighter school at Cecil Field, he qualified for carrier duty aboard the USS Core *in February 1943, and was shipped to the Fiji Islands in March to join VF-21, a land-based F4F Wildcat squadron. Ensign Milton survived a three-month combat tour—including two water landings—with VF-21 in the Solomon Islands; then, in August 1943, he returned with the unit to the United States. In September 1943, Lieutenant (jg) Milton reported to VF-15, a new Grumman F6F Hellcat unit based at the Atlantic City Naval Air Station, New Jersey. He deployed as a division leader with VF-15 aboard the USS* Essex *in April 1944.*

Lieutenant (jg) Baynard Milton shot down two Zeros and damaged a third on June 19, 1944, during the Battle of the Philippine Sea. On September 9, he shared in the downing of an Imperial Army Ki-57 Topsy twin-engine transport over Mindanao, and on October 10, he shot down a Tony fighter over Yontan Airdrome, Okinawa. On October 16, Milton shared in the downing of a D4Y Judy dive-bomber at sea, and on November 11, 1944, Lieutenant Baynard Milton achieved ace status when he shot down an Oscar over Ormoc Bay, Leyte.

♦

When the sixteen of us took off that day, our assignment was simple enough: sweep Luzon north of Manila and strafe and destroy targets of opportunity, especially in the Clark Field area. No big problem, no particular sweat. Air resistance by the Japanese in the Philippines had been reduced to a minimum and was no longer of any great concern. But, of course, there was the ever-present antiaircraft fire, which was always mean and nasty, and against which we had very little defense other than pure luck. And the odds of luck were now working against us, or so we were beginning to feel.

By then, Air Group 15 had been in the combat zone longer than any other carrier air group out there at the time, and it seemed reasonable to assume that we would be the next group relieved to go home. But we had no idea when that would happen. Rumors were persistent that it would happen soon, but continuing delays kept dashing our great expectations and gnawing at our morale.

As we more or less expected, there was no real air activity in our target area, although we could hear over our radios a degree of resistance to the groups attacking the Manila Bay area. After scouting around the island and along its shoreline for a while, and finding no shipping or anything else of particular value worth attacking, we prepared yet again to shoot up the Clark Field facilities. That would be a fun thing to do—recreation, almost rest and rehabilitation. Within a few minutes, we had made several strafing passes on the hangars, barracks, mess halls, fuel-storage areas, and even some of the gun installations that we could see shooting back. We also destroyed some planes on the ground, which I'm reasonably sure had been reported as "destroyed" several other times during the last few weeks. All in all, we had done considerable damage and started innumerable fires that were billowing up clouds of smoke and flame.

We then made a final farewell pass before going home. As I raced across the field at a very low altitude, firing into a hangar, my airplane was hit. My left wing dropped dangerously and the plane went into a wild, high-speed, uncontrolled left turn, barely above the ground. By kicking the right rudder full forward and slamming the stick all the way over and back, I was able to regain some control—enough to avoid crashing into the ground, at least for the moment. While struggling to maintain a straight-ahead bearing and gain enough altitude to clear the rising terrain, I took a quick look around to determine as much as possible the extent of the damage the plane had sustained. The only damage that I could see was a large, ragged hole through the port wing. There was no way for me to see or determine the condition of the underside of the fuselage or the tail section. But for the moment this really didn't matter. It was taking all I could do just to stay in the air.

After gaining some altitude to spare, and with a little experimenting, it became evident that, at best, I could only make a slight turn to starboard, and that only with great effort. And such a turn could not be maintained for long. By holding the right rudder full forward and the stick well over to starboard, a straight-ahead course could be maintained. Any relaxing on the controls, however, and the plane would go into a slightly downward spiral to port. But I couldn't start for home, not yet. First, it was necessary to gain enough altitude to clear the rough, mountainous terrain barring me from the ocean and our task force.

Then I saw my wingman, Lieutenant (jg) George Pigman, fly his plane into formation alongside me. He had not seen what had happened but had missed me and come looking. It was nice to have "Pigman"-type friends. Of course, he immediately spotted the hole in the wing and knew that I was in deep trouble. Picking up his transmitter, he called me, but I couldn't hear him. My radio receiver was dead. This information was signaled to him by pointing at an ear and then giving the thumbs down signal. In answer to my signal, he gave the thumbs-up signal. Things could have been worse, for at least my transmitter was functioning.

While continuing to gain the needed altitude, Pigman circled around and made a general inspection of my plane's condition. From his hand signals, I learned that in addition to the big hole in the wing, I had landing-gear problems. Although the port wheel was loosely and only partially extended, the starboard wheel was fully extended. Operating the controls solved nothing; the wheels stayed as they were, one up and one down. Evidently the hydraulic system was out of commission, or at least partly so. I tried the flaps, which worked. The tailhook, needed for landing on a carrier, would also extend and retract. Well, things weren't a complete washout; some luck was riding with me.

Finally, with just enough altitude to clear the island, we started for home, which was at least 150 and perhaps 200 miles away. With plenty of engine power and Pigman to watch over me, I felt we would be home in no time. But with constant pressure being applied against the rudder and stick, my right leg and arm began to tire severely, and then to cramp. I released the two controls and began stamping the leg up and down and flexing the arm to ease the cramps and restore circulation while the plane made a slow, descending spiral to the left. Watching the compass as the plane came around in full circle, I rammed the controls full right again as we came to the heading that would take us home. But the cramps kept coming back, making it necessary to periodically repeat the spiral in order to gain relief. The cramps were not severe, however—merely a nuisance. They posed no real problem, except that they were delaying our return to the carrier.

Fortunately, the plane, damaged in the manner it was, could be flown in a turn to port, which is the way one approaches an aircraft carrier for a landing. Had the starboard wing been the one damaged, with only turns in that direction possible, landing on a flight deck would have been completely out of the question. And my plans, at least for the moment, were to land aboard. No bailing out or ditching for me; I had already ditched twice in the Solomon Islands!

For the last few minutes, as we were approaching the task force, I had been observing Pigman talking on his radio. He would be reporting my condition to the carrier and receiving instructions. Directly, he pointed at me and then cupped his hands in front of his face and made a forward sweeping motion, as if diving into a pool. This was followed by his hand being held flat in front of him and then moving forward and down in a landing-type motion. He then pointed down towards the ocean.

Using my transmitter, I replied, "Porkchop, old buddy, are you asking me which I want to do, bail out or ditch in the ocean?"

He nodded.

"Well, I'm telling you and Rebel Base both that I don't want to do either one. I want to land back aboard. I presume they can hear me as well as you can?"

He nodded again. Then he used his radio again. After a slight delay, he looked back at me and again made the landing motion with his hand, but this time he pointed at the carrier. Then, with his two palms turned up at about shoulder level, he looked at me and spoke. I could almost hear him ask, "Do you think you can do it?"

I answered by transmitting to the ship, “Rebel Base, this is Rebel Six. I’m not sure at all that I can successfully escape the plane with a jump. And the idea of ditching with one wheel up and one down, plus the possibility of stalling in and cartwheeling, doesn’t really thrill me at all. Request permission to bring her aboard if possible—and I think it is. If I find it isn’t, I’ll take a voluntary waveoff and try something else.”

No longer was I simply talking to the carrier base. Permission to try to land the plane, damaged as it was and a sure washout, on the carrier’s flight deck would be a decision made only by the ship’s captain, with an admiral looking over his shoulder.

After a few moments Pigman turned to me with a grin and held “thumbs up.” I was somewhat surprised that the captain was actually granting permission for an attempted landing on the carrier. Then giving me the “I’m-turning-the-lead-over-to-you” signal, Pigman pulled away, made his approach, and landed aboard.

Knowing it would be necessary to fly in faster than usual, my plan was to hit the deck with the left wingtip and the right wheel and tailhook touching first and simultaneously, in order to minimize the possibilities of bouncing or cartwheeling. But at the last second the landing signal officer (LSO) gave a waveoff, and I had to go around again.

During the next approach, I called, “Rebel Base, this is Rebel Six. Tell the landing signal officer that that waveoff he gave me was close. I almost didn’t make it. Tell him not to worry about the excessive speed. I have to have it. Just give me an early Cut and I’ll put it on the deck.”

The LSO gave me the early Cut, and I landed aboard as planned. Slamming to a stop, the extended wheel broke off. I saw it go flying down the deck, hit something, and bounce up and over the port side of the ship and into the sea. The instant the plane stopped, a deckhand was at my side, reaching in and unlocking the safety belts and helping me out of the cockpit. Lieutenant Commander J. H. Mini, the VB-15 skipper, and the flight surgeon crowded up, both wanting to know whether I was hurt.

“To hell with that,” said the crewman, “there’s still a possibility of fire.”

The others scattered and I got out in a hurry. There was no fire, and I was unhurt. I had survived again. But I did take the time to quickly reach back into the cockpit and retrieve my navigation board from beneath the instrument panel.

A couple hours later, while I was relaxing in the ready room, a call came up from the hangar deck: "Tell the pilot of that plane that crash-landed a while ago that we have stripped it of spare parts and are ready to push it over the side. If he wants to see her make her final dive, he should come on down right away."

I went down. She was sitting there, busted and stripped, not looking like much, but I felt a kinship for her. Wounded and broken as she was, she had brought me safely home. They splashed her, and she started that last final dive to the bottom of the ocean. Though I appreciated her efforts for me, I was glad she was making the rest of the trip alone.

Shortly thereafter, Lieutenant Baynard Milton and the rest of Air Group 15 returned to the United States for a well-deserved home leave. Milton reported to Daytona Beach Naval Air Station in January 1945 and served as a fighter instructor until taking his discharge in October. After leaving the Navy, Milton never piloted an airplane again.

THE SPLIT-S THAT FAILED

1st Lieutenant BO REEVES, USAAF
431st Fighter Squadron, 475th Fighter Group
Off French Indochina—March 28, 1945

Horace Bickley Reeves was born in Stamford, Texas, on April 16, 1922. He graduated from high school in Lamesa, Texas, in 1940 and attended three semesters at the University of Texas before enlisting in the Army Air Forces Reserve on June 8, 1942. Cadet Reeves was called to active duty in November 1942 and earned his wings and commission at Williams Field, Arizona, on October 1, 1943. After he completed operational training in P-38s, Reeves shipped out for duty with the Fifth Air Force on February 2, 1944, and joined the 475th Fighter Group's 431st Fighter Squadron at Dobodura, New Guinea.

Second Lieutenant Reeves scored his first aerial victory on June 16, 1944, a Ki-43 Oscar fighter he shot down near Jefman, New Guinea. On

December 12, 1944, 1st Lieutenant Reeves downed a Zero over Leyte, and on December 26, he downed another Zero near Clark Field, Luzon. Bo Reeves's fourth aerial victory was a Zero he shot down over Luzon on January 1, 1945.

The 431st Fighter Squadron launched eight P-38s from Clark Field early on the morning of March 28, 1945. We, along with P-38s from the other squadrons of the 475th Fighter Group, were to escort a group of V Bomber Command B-25s whose mission it was to strike Japanese shipping along the French Indochina coast. Because of the great distance to the target, it was necessary to carry maximum fuel. Additionally, we had been given a secondary mission of glide-bombing the ships. For this mission, we were each loaded with a 2,000-pound General Purpose bomb on one shackle and a 300-gallon fuel tank on the other. This was the heaviest load for takeoff I had experienced in a P-38, but it turned out to be a piece of cake; I had plenty of runway left when I broke ground.

I was the element leader of the third and last flight in the 431st Squadron formation. Shortly after takeoff, a wingman up front experienced mechanical difficulty and had to abort the mission. It was necessary to move my wingman forward to fill the empty space, which left me as tail-end Charlie.

The mission went as planned. After the B-25s cleared the target, we made our bomb runs. Though no formal training had ever been conducted, I had carried two 1,000-pound bombs on numerous occasions while supporting our ground forces on Luzon. This was the only sortie on which I ever carried a 2,000-pounder.

We approached the ships in a 45-degree glide angle and released our bombs at approximately 4,000 feet. We then broke sharply to the left to rejoin the B-25s, which were heading home. I never saw my bomb explode. I feel this was simply a test run that would certainly net us greater combat range.

We then escorted the bombers toward home to about thirty miles offshore. There, because we had not seen any enemy fighters, we requested a release from the bombers, and we received an okay.

As soon as we were released from escort duties, we turned back for a fighter sweep south down the Indochina coast. Twenty to thirty minutes later, a radio call sounded: "Bandit!" And the fight was on.

My flight, which was down to three P-38s, stayed at about 10,000 feet while the rest of the squadron engaged the Japanese fighters at 15,000 to 20,000 feet. My flight swept across the area of Cam Ranh Bay without seeing an enemy airplane. Disappointed, we turned toward Clark Field and reduced power for economy cruise. We were then over Ben Goi Bay, a long way from home.

We no sooner got cruise condition set than I noted in my rearview mirror that three Hamp fighters were in shooting range—with their wing and cowl guns already blazing! I yelled, *"Bandits!"* on the radio, kicked hard-right rudder, and pushed the yoke hard forward. This action rolled me almost to an inverted position.

I managed to get full power—maximum RPMs, sixty inches of mercury, and Full Rich fuel mixture—as I completed a diving turn to the right and came up to about where I had begun my evasive maneuver. I was looking for the Japanese fighters. I saw my flight leader, 1st Lieutenant Kennth Hart, engaging a Hamp, and Hart's wingman, in trail behind and below him.

Suddenly, another Hamp came into view as it was lining up on the number-two P-38, Hart's wingman, 1st Lieutenant Thomas Martin. While this Hamp was climbing rapidly and trying to close on the P-38, I maneuvered behind it to get into a trailing position. Soon, I was rapidly closing on the Hamp. As I came into position, he was 400 to 500 feet above me and 600 to 800 feet ahead of me. I continued to close rapidly on him, but when I was nearing firing range, he executed a rapid half roll and started into a split-S. This was a typical attack maneuver used by the Japanese, and it was often effective. Usually, a Hamp or any other Zero variant would complete a split-S, then roll out and climb to a level firing position astern of his target.

Things happened quickly in the next few moments. The Hamp's diving flight path was bringing him directly in front of me. I lowered my nose to get a lead. The Hamp was by then in a vertical dive, and our two aircraft were closing rapidly. I was looking at the top side of the Hamp as I started going down. I was essentially in a right-side-up position, but I began to lower my nose to get off a short burst. Both aircraft were at about the same altitude when I fired. I observed flashes on his canopy and wing roots just before the Hamp passed from my view.

I immediately broke right to look for him. Instead of seeing the Hamp,

I saw the Japanese pilot in his parachute. My turn took me right past the parachute, and I could see that the pilot's head was hanging.

I looked again for my flight leader and his wingman, and found them engaged with three more Hamps. I kept my speed up and climbed to join them. I was nearing them when a Hamp suddenly appeared ahead of me from out of the usual afternoon cumulus. I promptly latched on to him and closed to firing range. I fired two fairly long bursts and hit him. He was burning and smoking when he hit the low-lying hills.

The fight was over. We three turned for home and reduced speed. During the fight, we had gotten farther and farther from home and had had several minutes of high fuel consumption.

We coasted out over Cam Ranh Bay and slowed to cruise speed. We kept our heads on swivels as we didn't have enough fuel left for another fight. We discussed the kills we had made, and when we were about fifteen minutes out, we fired all our remaining ammunition in order to lighten the aircraft weight and to increase our range with the fuel we had left to us.

After landing at Clark Field and filling out my action report, I noted that the sortie had lasted nine hours and twenty-five minutes. That's a long time to sit on the folded one-man dinghy.

By the time Bo Reeves returned home at the end of his combat tour, he had flown 137 P-38 combat missions totaling 496 combat hours, had participated in numerous ground-support missions, and had destroyed six Japanese aircraft—all fighters—in air-to-air combat.

"BOGEYS AT THREE O'CLOCK DOWN"

2d Lieutenant JERRY O'KEEFE, USMC
VMF-323
Off Okinawa—April 28, 1945

Jeremiah Joseph O'Keefe was born in Ocean Springs, Mississippi, on July 12, 1923, and lived there until his family moved to Biloxi in 1937. He graduated from high school in June 1941 and entered business college in September. After volunteering for the Marine Corps immediately after Pearl Harbor—his father had been a Marine in World War I—he learned that passing a two-year college equivalency test would help him qualify for flight training. O'Keefe took and passed the equivalency test and immediately signed up in the U.S. Navy Reserve, but he was advised to report to Louisiana Junior College as a civilian to take the Civilian Pilot Training primary course. As soon as he had completed the course, O'Keefe was called to active duty as an aviation cadet and ordered to Pre-Flight training at the University of Georgia. He subsequently completed Primary training at the Dallas Naval Air Station and earned his wings and Marine Corps commission at Pensacola in May 1943 at the age of nineteen. His only problem was that he had trained as a multi-engine pilot but had no desire to fly transports, which at the time were virtually the only multi-engine planes the Marine Corps owned. Through a mutual friend, 2d Lieutenant O'Keefe met Major Marion Carl, the Marine Corps' first fighter ace, who managed to get O'Keefe and several like-minded multi-engine pilots reassigned to the fighter base at El Centro, California. Once at El Centro, O'Keefe was assigned to the newly formed VMF-323, the only fighter squadron then in residence at the base.

VMF-323 shipped out of San Diego in June 1944, trained for several weeks in Hawaii, then served a rather humdrum tour at several South Pacific bases until loaded aboard an escort carrier in March 1945 to take part in the Okinawa invasion. The squadron flew off the carrier to Kadena Field, Okinawa, on Easter Sunday, and soon began a stellar combat tour in which many of its pilots achieved ace status.

On Sunday April 22, 1945, Lieutenant Jerry O'Keefe; Major George Axtell, the VMF-323 commanding officer; and Major Jefferson Dorrah, squadron executive officer, all achieved ace-in-a-day status in a single engagement against an inbound kamikaze *attack. Dorroh downed six Val dive-bombers, and Axtell and Jerry O'Keefe each downed five. In all that day, VMF-323 pilots were credited with 23.75 aerial victories.*

A lot of excitement and publicity followed our unusual April 22 fight, but I expected that aerial action would again become quiet and routine, as it had been for most of VMF-323 in the preceding weeks. During that time, and after April 22, our primary mission was to help protect the hundreds of ships that were unloading troops and supplies off Okinawa.

Most of our missions consisted of picket duty, in which case several divisions of our Corsairs would be assigned to orbit over one of the U.S. Navy radar picket destroyers stationed to the north and northwest of Okinawa. We were to be available to be directed by the destroyer's radar to intercept and destroy enemy planes flying in from Japan. We also undertook bombing, strafing, and napalm strikes for our ground troops on Okinawa.

On Saturday, April 28, 1945, I was part of a flight of twelve Corsairs led by Major Axtell. I was in my usual place as the skipper's section leader, and, as usual, 2d Lieutenant Bill Hood was flying on my right wing.

The weather was sunny and clear; it was kind of a balmy day. I did not expect to see any enemy planes. The action we had experienced the previous Sunday was so unusual that I expected I probably would never again see an enemy plane in the air.

Our twelve-plane flight was headed east at approximately 12,000 feet to the north and west of Okinawa, when I spotted five unidentified planes at 3 o'clock. They were headed south at about 8,000 to 10,000 feet.

I called the rest of the flight to say that I saw five bogeys. (We called any unidentified plane in flight a "bogey," and planes identified as *enemy* were called "bandits.") These planes were too far away for me to be certain of their identity, but I suspected they were Japanese, because the group was composed of five planes, instead of the usual four, eight, or twelve planes we usually had.

It surprised me, when I called out "Bogeys at three o'clock down and headed south," that no one else in the flight seemed to see them. After I had waited in vain for a few moments to receive a response, I asked Major Axtell to allow my section to investigate. With his approval, I began a slow turn to the south and began bearing down on the bogeys from above and behind. Unbeknownst to me, as Bill Hood and I left our flight, all ten of the remaining Corsairs led by Major Axtell started a lazy turn to the south and began descending behind us.

As I got closer, I became increasingly certain that they were bandits, not bogeys, as I had earlier reported. As soon as I was positive that this five-plane formation was indeed Japanese, I called out that our bogeys were now bandits and that we were attacking. I armed my .50-caliber machine guns and signaled by hand to Bill, who was flying on my right wing, to move farther away from me to my right. By moving Bill farther to the right of my plane, I gave him an opportunity to attack the Japanese from the right rear, at about the 5 o'clock position, while I attacked from a left-rear position, at about 7 o'clock to the bandits.

My excitement was running high. I thought we might shoot down all five of the bandits. They were old Imperial Army fixed-gear Ki-27 Nate fighters headed for a *kamikaze* run against our ships off Okinawa.

The Japanese pilots were unaware of our approach and did not make any move to evade our attack. As I was closing range on the bandits, I lost sight of Bill. But we were in tune with one other, and I was sure he would be in range to fire at almost the same instant I was.

I opened fire on the leader from 300 yards, aiming to hit his plane amidships. The Nate took hits from just in front of the cockpit to inside the cockpit, and it immediately exploded. I then attempted to fix aim on the next closest Nate, but I couldn't do so in time and missed him with a short burst as I streaked past in a shallow dive.

I pulled up and around to the left as quickly as I could, but all I found was a single plane in a dive for the ocean below. I went after him, flying straight down on his tail. I didn't miss him again. We were both flying straight down for the ocean when I fired into his plane from directly behind, and it exploded.

Bill Hood and I teamed up again, as I didn't see any other Japanese planes. I learned that Bill had exploded two Nates on his first pass, and that the fifth Nate had been shot down by Major Axtell. Bill and I rejoined the flight and saw no other Japanese that day.

With the arrival of replacement pilots in June, 2d Lieutenant Jerry O'Keefe was ordered home and reassigned to the Marine Corps Ferry Command in Columbus, Ohio. When the Japanese surrendered in September, he resigned his commission in order to resume his education at Loyola University.

ALL IN A DAY'S WORK

Lieutenant MAC McWHORTER, USN
VF-12 (USS *Randolph)*
Off Kyushu—May 13, 1945

Hamilton McWhorter, III, was born in Athens, Georgia, on February 8, 1921. He attended the University of Georgia and Georgia Tech for two years before entering the Navy's aviation cadet program in August 1941, and was commissioned at Pensacola on February 9, 1942. In November 1942, as a member of VF-9 operating from the carrier USS Ranger, *Ensign McWhorter flew Wildcats in support of the invasion of French North Africa. There, he shot up several Vichy French warships and attacked aircraft on the ground at a Vichy French airdrome, but he did not see an enemy airplane in the air. Following the surrender of Vichy French forces in the region, VF-9 returned to Norfolk, Virginia, to become the first squadron to be equipped with the new Grumman F6F Hellcat. In March 1943, VF-9 went aboard the new USS* Essex, *and then out to the Pacific later in the year.*

On October 5, 1943, Lieutenant (jg) Mac McWhorter shot down a Zero, and probably downed another, over Wake Island; on November 11, he shot down two more Zeros and claimed another probable during an attack against Japanese warships in Rabaul harbor. On November 18, 1943, Mac McWhorter downed an F1M Pete float fighter over Tarawa Atoll, and the next day he became the Navy's first pure Hellcat ace when he shot down a Betty at sea near the Tarawa Atoll. Thereafter, McWhorter became the Navy's first double Hellcat ace when he ran his score up to ten victories with credits for two Zeros over Roi Airfield in the Marshall Islands on January 29, 1944; and three Zeros over Truk Atoll on February 17, 1944.

When VF-9 returned to the United States in March 1944, Mac McWhorter was assigned to help reform VF-12 as a Hellcat squadron following its first combat tour in Corsairs. Operating from the USS

Randolph, *Lieutenant McWhorter downed a Zero while taking part in the first carrier strikes against Tokyo, on February 16, 1945.*

♦

One of the highlights of my third combat cruise occurred on May 13, 1945, when I was on the day's first combat air patrol near Task Force 58. At 0640, my division was vectored out to intercept a high bogey. I turned, headed out on vector, and began climbing. After about five minutes, as we were passing through about 20,000 feet, I spotted the bogey, a single-engine Imperial Navy C6N reconnaissance plane we called Myrt. It was about three miles ahead, at about 25,000 feet and going away from us. I quickly climbed and closed to about 500 feet behind and slightly below the Myrt. As soon as I fired a short burst, the airplane flamed. I was so close behind it that oil from its engine got all over my canopy.

Two parachutes opened alongside as the plane exploded, so I circled back to look them over. To my surprise, neither chute had anyone in it, only something boxlike, about the same size and thickness as the seat cushions and survival gear that we carried on our parachutes. One of the young ensigns in my division was too curious and went in too close to take a look, and he hit one of the boxes with his wing. Whatever it was, it must have been pretty solid, because it smashed the leading edge of the wing all the way back to the main spar. None of us saw anyone or anything fall from the plane or the chutes.

This was my highest victory, compared to my lowest one, a Betty that I shot down at Tarawa about ten feet above the water. Shooting the Betty down in 1943 had earned me the nickname of "One Slug" from my squadron commander, Lieutenant Commander Phil Torrey, because after I returned to the ship, it was found that I had expended a total of only eighty-six rounds of .50-caliber ammo—and that included a test burst of all six guns shortly after takeoff.

Also on May 13, 1945, during the task force's early morning strike against the Japanese air base near Usa, on the northeastern coast of Kyushu, one of our VB-12 SB2C dive-bombers was badly damaged by antiaircraft fire. Fortunately, the pilot was able to reach the coast and ditch about five miles offshore in the Inland Sea, about fifteen miles north of Usa Airdrome and about 180 miles from the *Randolph*. Our squadron commander, Lieutenant Commander Mike Michaelis, and his division maintained air cover over the pilot and his radioman, who were in their life raft. In fact, Mike's flight strafed one Japanese vessel and set it afire as it was heading for the downed crew. Later, two Japanese destroyers were seen heading for the area, but after heavy strafing, they changed course and departed.

My division was assigned to escort two Vought OS2U Kingfisher float planes from the cruiser *Astoria* to pick up the downed SB2C crew. We took off from the *Randolph* and rendezvoused with the Kingfishers on the way to the Inland Sea, assuming our escort position about one thousand feet above them. At first, I tried to keep our air speed up by continually weaving back and forth over the OS2Us. This was for our own safety, because at a low air speed, we would be sitting ducks for any Japanese attack, just like the OS2Us were. The Kingfisher's cruising speed was only about eighty or eighty-five knots, and with a little headwind our ground speed was even less. I estimated that it was going to take more than two and a half hours to get to the downed SB2C crew, and of course with the pickup and return time added, I could foresee a fuel-shortage problem for us at the higher power setting. So in order to be able to complete the mission, I had to take the chance that we would not see any Zeros. I reduced our power settings to the minimum and engine RPMs back to 1,200.

The F6F propeller had a two-to-one reduction gearing, so I could practically count the prop blades, which were turning at only 600 RPMs. Even at this minimum power setting, we were still ten to fifteen knots faster than the Kingfishers, so we had to make continual **S**-turns during the entire flight in order to stay over them.

After about two hours, we reached the entrance of the strait leading to the Inland Sea. Some flak started popping nearby, but none of it was too close. Somebody came up on the radio to ask if anyone saw where the fire was coming from, but someone else—I believe it was one of the OS2U pilots—immediately replied, "Who the hell cares where it's coming from. I just want to know where it's going!" I could see the flashes of the antiaircraft guns on a point of land off to our left. They was firing at a rather long range, so we pretty much ignored them.

About this time I heard Lieutenant Lane Bardeen, whose division was now providing air cover over the downed crew, call to say that he had to leave because he was running low on fuel. I advised him that we were approaching the area. Soon, we spotted the large patch of yellow dyemarker in the water. The Kingfishers landed and the first one picked up one of the downed crewmen. As the second OS2U was picking up the other crewman, I could see that its engine was idling very slowly. And then the prop stopped. I remember thinking, as we orbited overhead, that it really wasn't the wisest thing to do, cutting the engine while floating around only fifteen miles from a Japanese air base.

The OS2U had a cartridge-type starter that emitted a large puff of white smoke when it was fired. I saw the first big puff of smoke as the Kingfisher pilot tried to restart the engine, and then another, then several more. After what seemed an eternity, but in probably only a few minutes, the engine finally started and both OS2Us took off.

On the way out, we flew much farther north of the point of land at the entrance to the Inland Sea, and we received no antiaircraft fire. We had an uneventful flight back to the task force, but it was even slower going, because the Kingfishers were now carrying an extra load. Fortunately, we saw no enemy aircraft on the way up or on the return flight. The OS2Us landed back near the *Astoria* and were hoisted aboard, and the bomber crew was back aboard the *Randolph* early that afternoon.

By the time my division landed back aboard the *Randolph,* we had been in the air for 5.6 hours, my longest flight in three combat cruises. The length of the flight wasn't really excessive by the standards of this cruise, as I had already flown several five-hour combat air patrols. However, what made this and other long flights excruciating was the survival pack that we had to sit on, since it was attached to our parachute. Some sadistic, diabolical person, obviously not a pilot, had designed a system for packing the life raft, food, flares, dyemarker, poncho, medications, and cans of water in the survival pack in such a way as to place one of the water cans directly under the right cheek of the pilot's fanny. Try to imagine being tightly strapped to such a seat for more than five hours. Even though there was a seat cushion on top of the survival pack, the edges kept getting harder and harder as that water can cut deeper and deeper. I assure you that at times it was pure hell to move around. There was no room in the cockpit, so there was little you could do to alleviate the pain in your fanny.

During his third and final combat cruise of World War II, Lieutenant Mac McWhorter flew 158 combat hours on forty-three combat missions, plus another thirty-eight combat air patrols, which were not counted as combat time. On June 10, 1945, after being replaced aboard the Randolph *by another air group, VF-12 departed the combat zone for Hawaii. It reached the United States on July 19.*

Commander Mac McWhorter retired from the Navy in 1969. In 1989, he was inducted into the Georgia Aviation Hall of Fame.

1st Lieutenant Willie Y Anderson, USAAF

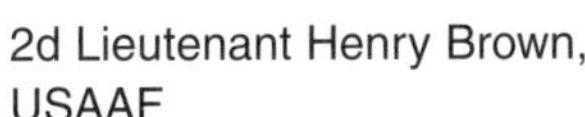

2d Lieutenant Henry Brown, USAAF

Captain George Chandler, USAAF

2d Lieutenant Roger Conant, USMC

2d Lieutenant Ben Drew, USAAF

Major Phil DeLong, USMC

1st Lieutenant Harold Fischer, USAF

1st Lieutenant Bud Fortier, USAAF

Bob Goebel (l.) and Ernst Pausinger

Lieutenant Jim Gray, USN

Lieutenant (jg) Vernon Graham, USN

1st Lieutenant Joe Griffin, USAAF

2d Lieutenant Russ Haworth, USAAF

Captain Frank Hill, USAAF

1st Lieutenant Jack Ilfrey, USAAF

1st Lieutenant Dale Karger, USAAF, (center) with his plane crew.

1st Lieutenant Jim Kasler, USAF

2d Lieutenant Lee Larson, USAAF

Flight Officer Jack Lenox, USAAF

Major George Loving, USAF

Captain Tom Maloney, USAAF

1st Lieutenant Lou Luma, USAAF (in RCAF uniform)

26th Fighter Squadron pilots display the banner presented to them by the city authorities of Nanning, China: (l. to r.) 2d Lieutenant Allan Putnam, 1st Lieutenant Lyn Marshall, 2d Lieutenant Lloyd Mace, and 1st Lieutenant Alexander Duncan.

Lieutenant Mac McWhorter, USN

2d Lieutenant Bob Milliken, USAAF

Lieutenant Baynard Milton, USN (l.)
with Lieutenant George Pigman, USN

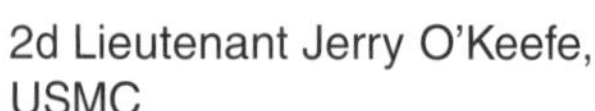

2d Lieutenant Jerry O'Keefe,
USMC

Captain Effie Pierce, USMC

Flight Office Sammy Pierce,
USAAF

1st Lieutenant Bo Reeves, USAAF

Major Robbie Risner, USAF

1st Lieutenant Duerr Schuh, USAAF

Lieutenant Dick Stambook, USN

1st Lieutenant Ernie Shipman, USAAF

Captain Don Strait, USAAF

1st Lieutenant Dick Suehr, USAAF

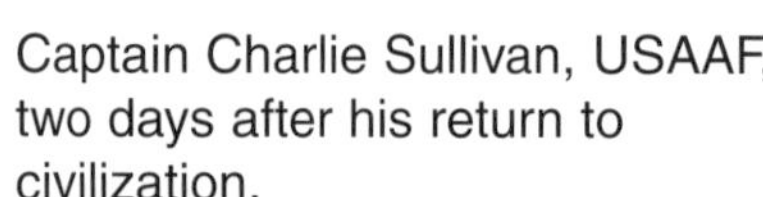

Captain Charlie Sullivan, USAAF, two days after his return to civilization.

1st Lieutenant Calvin Wire, USAAF

Part II

In Combat Over North Africa and Europe

GETTING THERE IS HALF THE FUN

1st Lieutenant JACK ILFREY, USAAF
94th Fighter Squadron, 1st Fighter Group
England to Gibraltar—November 15, 1942

Jack Milton Ilfrey was born in Houston on July 31, 1918. In 1939, while attending Texas A&M, Ilfrey joined the first Civilian Pilot Training program. He took the CPT secondary course at the University of Houston in 1940, enlisted in the Air Corps as a flying cadet in April 1941, and earned his wings at Luke Field, Arizona, on December 12, 1941.

Immediately upon graduation from Luke Field, 2d Lieutenant Ilfrey was assigned to the 1st Pursuit Group's 94th Pursuit Squadron, which soon transitioned to P-38s while guarding the California coast. In July 1942, the 1st Fighter Group, including Jack Ilfrey, took part in the inaugural stage of Operation BOLERO, the mass flight of warplanes from the United States to England. Once in England, the group began in-theater training under the tutelage of Polish pilots serving with the Royal Air Force, and soon Ilfrey and his mates began flying patrols and other missions—including the first all-American fighter sweep over France on September 1, 1942. However, no enemy aircraft were encountered, and none was shot down. In late October, the 1st Fighter Group and other USAAF units in England were ordered to stand down to prepare for a mysterious mission.

Along about this time, we learned that Major General Jimmy Doolittle had been in England for a month or so. We did not know why, but a wild rumor started floating around. The development and use of our belly tanks for extra fuel, had enabled a couple of our BOLERO P-38 flights from the United States to stay in the air eight full hours. This was more than enough time and fuel to fly to Berlin and back. Was something up for us akin to Doolittle's Tokyo Raid of April 18, 1942?

We figured that some of us might get to Berlin, but we felt sure as hell the *Luftwaffe* wouldn't let any of us return. Eventually we learned that General Doolittle was the commander of the Twelfth Air Force and that he was preparing for Operation TORCH, the invasion of North Africa.

On the morning of November 8, the news broke over the radio that North Africa had just been invaded. Then we knew where we were going and felt sure that now we would get into plenty of action. Colonel John Stone, our group commander, called us all into the briefing room on the night of the 8th and told us where we were going and what we were going to do. He said our squadrons were to fly nonstop from England to Oran, Algeria, which was about 1,500 miles away. If necessary, we could make an emergency stop at Gibraltar, which was only 1,200 miles away. Either way, it was a very long nonstop flight for a P-38. Charts and maps were brought out and we spent several hours in feverish study, with high-ranking American and British officers giving instructions on every detail. Up to this time, Algiers, Casablanca, and Oran had just been names to us. Now we could see that a new world awaited us.

This was to be a bigger adventure than flying over the Atlantic. We felt that this time we were going to get into real combat, and this soon proved to be the case. Of course, the old American custom of joking and laughing it off prevailed. Everything was so new to us—England had seemed quite different from the United States, and yet we found the British Isles very much like our own country when compared with other countries we eventually saw.

Our instructions sounded simple enough when we heard them again in the briefing room the night before takeoff. We were to fly in flights of eight, with a 319th Medium Bombardment Group B-26 bomber leading each flight. We were to fly across the Bay of Biscay, hit the Spanish coast, fly down the Spanish and Portuguese coasts, turn left, and go through the Straits of Gibraltar. We were to fly along the Spanish Moroccan coast, then along the coast of French Morocco, and then on into Oran.

Colonel Stone told us at briefing that it was uncertain as to where the enemy might be on our route, and we were cautioned to be exceptionally alert and warned again and again that Gibraltar should be our first emergency stop. It was made very clear at briefing that we were not to land at Gibraltar unless it was a real emergency, because the "Rock" was jammed tight with personnel and aircraft waiting for new fields to be opened in Algeria.

I learned much later that some of the American Spitfire groups and P-40 groups had flown off carriers at Casablanca during the invasion and in the days just after it, but our P-38s were the first to fly all the way down to Africa. It looked pretty simple on paper, but it turned out otherwise.

The ground crews squeezed every ounce of gasoline they could get into the tanks, including the external drop tanks. We were ready for our nonstop flight to Oran, and suddenly I was sorry to leave England. Somehow it felt like home. In England they knew a war was going on, and in America they had not yet awakened to that fact. The letters from family and friends told us that.

It was November 15, 1942, and I was about to embark on a journey into an uncertain future. The invasion of North Africa had begun just a week earlier, and I knew we were going to be something besides guinea pigs. Sometimes a few guinea pigs survive.

As I turned away from Chivenor Airdrome at Land's End, I had a true feeling of "This is it." We knew things were rugged in North Africa, and we knew the chance of survival was going to be low. But I didn't think about death; I thought of living and a lot of other things, too. I wondered what my mother was doing in Houston. By then it was difficult to picture in my mind's eye what my mother looked like. Everything that wasn't about the war had become abstract; I no longer had a vivid mental picture of things back home.

Some thirty minutes into the journey, at 0700 hours, I began to feel a little tired. We had left England at around 0630 hours, just as daylight was breaking, but I had been up since 0200. That morning, England was cool and damp and misty.

Strict radio silence was maintained across the Bay of Biscay, and we flew low—just above the wave tops—so we would not be detected by the enemy's radar. We saw no German planes on November 15, but several days later some long-range German fighters came out and shot down a few of our planes that were going to North Africa.

There was a low overcast that morning. Good weather had been forecast all the way to Oran, but I felt an uneasiness I was unable to analyze. It's good we didn't know the higher-ups had prophesied that only 50 percent of us would complete the flight to Oran. Nevertheless, as the minutes passed, the flight proved to be quite a bit less difficult than we had thought.

Suddenly I felt a slight jolt, and by the time I realized what had happened my right engine went out. One of my long-range belly tanks containing 150 gallons of gasoline had fallen off. I reflexivey switched to another tank and the right engine caught on again. But one fact was crystal clear: I had lost 150 gallons of gasoline.

I was still flying low when I saw Lieutenant Tony Syroi coming close to me. In his hand he was waving a map for me to see. He had printed in large letters, ONE BELLY TANK. I nodded that I understood. Maintaining radio silence meant that he couldn't tell me over the radio that I had lost a belly tank.

I didn't want to go back to England; I wanted to stay with my outfit. I got out my maps and charts, and after a few quick mental calculations, I decided I had enough gasoline to get as far as Gibraltar. With that, I dismissed all thoughts of turning back. I was not going to miss out on operations in Africa and I was not going to be separated from the gang. To be honest, I have to say that I wasn't about to miss the big adventure ahead—Africa. Maybe I was thinking of lions and tigers.

We kept on flying. When the B-26 that was leading us dodged a thunderhead by turning west, I had the feeling we were getting off course. We flew for another hour, and then I began to get a little worried. After another hour passed, I began to get alarmed. My gas was running low. We had used a great deal of fuel in dodging thunderheads. There was still no coast in sight; we were pretty far out to sea. I knew that much, and I knew we were flying in a southwesterly direction. I decided to leave the flight because my gas wouldn't last much longer.

I turned southeastward and hoped to hell I would run into the Spanish or Portuguese coast. The clouds were dispersing by then. I hoped I would be able to see the coast when the sun came out. And in a few minutes, I did see land. At the moment, I was flying at an altitude of about 9,000 feet. I got out my maps again and figured that I was close to a point on the coast that marked the Spanish-Portuguese border. I then turned parallel to the coast, but after only a short time, I realized I would never make it to Gibraltar. My gasoline was almost gone; I did not have enough left to reach Gibraltar.

There are no words to describe the feeling you have when you are 8,000 to 10,000 feet up in the air and know your gasoline is going to be exhausted soon. The best description I can give is that you have a kind of paralysis, with parts of your mind focusing between what to do next and hoping for something you know isn't going to come true. One minute I decided to bail out, and the next minute I thought I'd try to crash-land on the coast. While I was still wavering, I arrived over the mouth of the Tagus River. According to my map, the river ran twenty or thirty miles into Lisbon. We had been poorly briefed about what to do if we were forced down in Portugal or Spain, but I vaguely remembered someone saying the Portuguese were friendlier than the Spaniards and might even be bribed to help get downed pilots out of the country. I also knew that it was the duty of every pilot forced down in enemy or neutral territory to destroy his plane and equipment. Still without a firm decision as to what I would or should do, I turned inland and headed toward Lisbon.

Presently I saw a beautiful airdrome just outside the city of Lisbon; it had long beautiful runways and big administration buildings. Everything looked inviting and seemed eager to beckon me. Without another thought about duty, I put my wheels down, circled the airdrome, and landed.

When I had completed my landing roll, I saw six men mounted on horseback galloping out to meet me. The horsemen looked like something out of a picture book. They wore big, plumed hats, sabers, pistols, and multi-colored trousers. For a split second, I thought of the changing of the guard at Buckingham Palace. The horsemen gestured wildly for me to taxi my plane toward a building, which turned out to be the administration building. As I did, I hurriedly tore up maps and papers, and threw them to the wind. With more frantic gestures, the horsemen signaled me to stop on the apron just in front of the building.

As soon as I had I killed my engines, I looked up and saw people rushing toward my plane from every direction. Some of the people in the crowd gave me the V-for-victory sign, but most of them just stared. By this time, the six horsemen had surrounded my plane.

I stepped out of the cockpit onto the wing and looked down at the crowd. I felt like a stranger to myself. It was almost impossible to believe that I was in Portugal, about to become an internee. When I inquired whether anyone spoke English, a young fellow who looked like some sort of official came up and said he did.

"You are an American, yes?" the fellow asked.

"I certainly am an American."

The Portuguese smiled and said, "Yes, I thought so. I see the star on your airplane. It is the first American warship that I have seen." (A distinction of sorts here; I was the first P-38 pilot to be forced down in Portugal.) Then he added, still smiling, "In trouble?"

My reply was serious enough. "Yes, I am in trouble. I need some gasoline. Is it possible for me to get any?"

The fellow gave a short laugh. "Come with me and I will take you inside." As I walked away from my airplane, I glanced back. Everyone was staring at me and my plane in utter amazement. I felt a sudden alarm about my airplane, so I asked the Portuguese official if anyone would bother it. He spoke to one of the guards, who commanded the people to stay away from the P-38.

As I started into the administration building, I was jolted to see several Douglas DC-3 airliners, each with a big German swastika on it. Then, when I got inside the building, I saw the German pilots of these airliners. It made me furious to see that they had our planes, but of course the planes had probably been bought before the war.

I was taken into the restaurant at once and given cake and coffee. The coffee was terrible and the cake was even worse. By this time, more Portuguese officials had arrived and I was being asked my name, home address, and questions about everything under the sun. One of the officials, who spoke excellent English, told me the American Legation had been notified of my arrival. I wondered whether this could mean anything but decided it didn't—at least for the time being.

As the questioning continued, I heard a commotion outside and looked out just in time to see a big car skidding to an abrupt stop and some excited Portuguese pouring out. They made it into the restaurant in no time flat. There were more questions. Where was I going? I said I could not tell them. Where did I come from? I refused to answer that one, too.

I could see the Portuguese officials did not like my attitude. They had expected a little information but had received none. No doubt, any information acquired from me that day would have been in the possession of the Germans by night.

Then a new tack was tried. They had seen some American planes passing over earlier in the day. Had I done any fighting against the Germans? I neither denied or affirmed this. One of the officials made the comment that since I was flying a warship and was a fighter pilot, I must have fought the Germans. All this time, the German airline pilots were gathered around me, listening intently. Their faces were grim. It was hard to believe I was in a neutral country, the atmosphere was so tense. It seemed definitely pro-German here, anything but neutral. I didn't have to be psychic to feel hatred coming from the Portuguese officials. Their politeness was only surface dressing. The people outside had not seemed at all antagonistic, and the contrast with the officials was a curious one.

The questioning went on for an hour or more. The Germans stood rooted; they did not move once. At first I thought I had been the one who had stood still. I felt like I was in a trance at times. I could hardly believe where I was. But one thought crowded out all others: I must not say anything; I must not say one word that would give aid to the enemy.

One of the Portuguese officials who had been in the background stepped up and told me in cool, crisp English that it was the policy of Portugal, a neutral country—I had the greatest urge to laugh at this—to intern all foreign pilots and their planes. That was a shock. If I ever felt alone, it was at that moment. My friends had gone on, and I would not see them for a long time. I was out of the war. The great adventure had come to an end. My airplane would be taken away. That hurt! A plane is as close to a pilot's heart as a ship is to a sailor's. When your plane goes, a part of you goes, too. I had had no desire to fight a war, but my country needed help, and that was all I knew. Now I was in Portugal, about to be interned, cut off completely. I'd never get any mail and I'd never know what was going on.

I was next introduced to a Portuguese Air Force pilot who spoke good English and asked me whether I would show him something about the P-38. He said he had never seen a P-38 before and that he was amazed by its looks. He also told me the Portuguese Air Force was made up mainly of interned German, British, and French planes, and he repeated that my airplane was the first American warship he had seen. He said he was going to take the plane and fly it over to a military airfield.

When we walked outside, it seemed there were thousands of people looking at me. I forgot to be self-conscious. I knew people were looking at me. I saw people, and that was all. Something had happened to my consciousness. I was floating along, coming out of a dream that was both real and not real.

The Portuguese Air Force pilot asked me what type of fuel the P-38 used. When I told him 100-octane gasoline, he said they had no 100-octane fuel, and would 85-octane gasoline do? I thought for a moment before answering, and finally told him "Yes."

The Portuguese pilot asked me to show him the various mechanisms of the P-38. I saw nothing wrong with that because the plane had to be taken off the commercial field and flown to a military base. The mechanics finished gassing up the plane just as I climbed into the cockpit. Almost everything of mine had been removed. My Mae West and parachute were gone. I had stuffed my billfold and overnight bag behind the seat, but these also had also been discovered and removed. However, a few maps had been overlooked.

The Portuguese aviator sat on the wing while I explained the use of the various switches that controlled the operation of a P-38. All the time I was talking with the foreign pilot, my conscience kept bothering me. I kept thinking I should have destroyed my plane; I felt disloyal because we had been told to destroy our planes in the event we were forced to land. I glanced at the hundreds of people who were still standing around the P-38 and at the guards who still surrounded the airplane. My emotions were really mixed up. Some of the officials were still in evidence, jabbering among themselves, but as yet no one from the American Legation had put in an appearance. I was one forlorn fighter pilot.

Suddenly, I heard a familiar, faint sound, and then a louder noise. I looked up and saw a lone P-38. It was in trouble and preparing to land. The six guards on horseback dashed off, and all the people started running toward the end of the ramp to watch the landing. The P-38, which was just putting its wheels down, was landing on only one engine.

I held my breath, and all of a sudden it struck me. "Ilfrey," I said to myself, "what the hell are you waiting on?" With that, I threw on all the switches. But while I was doing this, the Portuguese pilot realized what was about to take place, and he tried to reach inside the cockpit to turn off some of the switches. But lightning had struck. I had already turned over my left propeller and the engine had started right up. The Portuguese pilot, who was sitting on the left wing, lost his hat when the propeller created a terrific wind that also sent what was left of the crowd scurrying away. When the pilot tried to get a better grip on the plane, I started my right engine and threw on lots of power, which created a bigger wind than ever. I managed to keep the airplane still. My idea was to blow the pilot off the wing, which I did in the next second or two. I looked back and saw that the Portuguese pilot had cleared the plane. I also saw some officials holding on to their hats while many others were chasing their headgear. Believe me, there were plenty of Portuguese hats flying in the air just then.

As soon as I knew that people were clear of the plane, I threw the canopy shut, came to full power, and without looking back, went straight across the field, disregarding runways and everything else in my path. As I was leaving the field, I saw the identification mark on the P-38 that had just landed. It belonged to Captain Jim Harman, a member of my squadron. Beyond this, I didn't think or see. I was too busy rolling up the windows and doing other things I needed to do.

As soon as I was in the air, the full realization of the harrowing takeoff fairly shook me. I had no parachute and no helmet, and most of my other belongings were gone. But I gave no further thought to these things as I set an estimated course for Gibraltar that would take me across Portugal and Spain. I just hoped they had put in enough gasoline for the 400-mile trip.

I was flying in bright sunlight, which was certainly a contrast to the muggy overcast of England. The Portuguese villages passing beneath me looked pretty and picturesque. My conscience still bothered me, however. Although I knew I had violated international law in wartime and was heading for Gibraltar by the quickest and safest route, I did not realize the extent or degree to which I had broken the law.

The Rock was like a beacon. As I approached Gibraltar, I had no trouble finding the airdrome or receiving landing signals. I landed safely and, on my way to the operations office, I met several other boys from my squadron who had been forced to stop on their way to Oran. Of course, I had to explain where I had been and how I had gotten out of Portugal, a story that my mates listened to with expressions of amazement and near-disbelief. When I repeated the story to the base operations officer, he also looked at me in disbelief and hinted of complications.

It wasn't long before I was taken in to see Colonel Willis, who was in charge of American operations at Gibraltar and who had been a member of the Lafayette Escadrille in the last war. After I told my story once more, to say that he was mad is saying nothing at all. He was blind, furious, *raging* mad. He gave it to me up one side and down the other. Half the time he was incoherent. And so was I. All I remember was that he kept storming on about international complications, and why didn't I use my brain, why didn't I think, why didn't I destroy my plane, and why and why and why?

After about forty-five minutes of this tongue-lashing, the colonel suddenly broke out into a big, healthy laugh and said it was a good trick after all. In fact, he almost congratulated me on getting out of Portugal. Finally, he dismissed me.

I joined my squadronmates in the officers club at the other end of the Rock, but later on in the evening—after I had celebrated a little too much—Colonel Willis sent for me again. The captain who came for me decided I was in no condition to see the colonel, and I certainly was in no condition to discuss such a grave problem as "international complications." When the captain left, he warned me to be at the colonel's office at 0900 hours, sharp.

My good friends who had celebrated with me didn't wake me up until 1000 hours. When I finally got into the colonel's office, he was madder than ever. He not only repeated the previous day's performance but really gave me the works. I stood there shaking, both from the dressing down and also from the hangover. My brain wouldn't function. I couldn't have thought of anything to say even if the colonel had stopped for a moment. He commented acidly on my unshaven appearance, said my airplane had been locked up, and that he had a good mind to lock me up, too. At last, I mustered enough courage and energy to tell him I hoped he didn't really expect me to go back to Portugal, that surely Colonel Stone, the CO of my group, would be able to figure out something. With that, Colonel Willis gave me a frosty smile and dismissed me. Despite his noncommittal air, the slight smile gave me hope. I couldn't believe Colonel Willis would send me back to Portugal, no matter what Washington told him to do. I knew it wouldn't be long before Washington would be in the picture, but I had a great faith in the Army's ability to circumvent civilian officialdom.

I felt so optimistic that I relaxed and proceeded to look Gibraltar over thoroughly. The weather was warm, even at that time of year, so I went swimming, toured the Rock in a jeep, and walked through its many tunnels. It was amazing to see the compactness and the efficiency of the offices in the Rock.

The city of Gibraltar is built just like a fortress, and only grim business went on there. There were many warships in the harbor, and the airstrip was a one-way affair on a flat spot behind the Rock. Thirty feet on the other side of the airstrip was the Spanish border, and I was told the Spaniards would shoot you down if you flew over Spanish territory. It gave me a curious feeling to see German observers with telescopes watching everything that went on in the harbor and on the airstrip.

Late that afternoon, I was summoned again to Colonel Willis's office. He was brief, telling me that the Portuguese government had notified Washington and that he was under instructions from the War Department to send me and my plane back to Portugal to be interned. I just stood there, stunned, refusing to believe what I had just heard.

I must have looked pretty pathetic, because the colonel got up and came around to me, gave me a friendly pat on the shoulder, and said not to worry. And I was again dismissed.

Hope was soaring so high that I rejoined my buddies. We met a Spanish boy who had offered to take us on a little sightseeing expedition into Spain. We were all dressed in khaki clothes and looked exactly like civilians. The Spaniard took us in his little boat across the harbor to Algeciras, and much to my surprise, we found a nightclub doing a thriving business. The liquor was plentiful but not very good. We watched the dancers and thought them fair. The Spanish women seemed to put everything they had into their dancing, but there it stopped as far as I was concerned. They didn't have much to appeal to the American male. Their unwashed anatomies did not attract.

The next morning, rumor reached me that Colonel Willis had cabled Washington that the "dumb John" pilot who had landed at Lisbon and later at Gibraltar had been sent to join his outfit in North Africa; he was sorry that Washington's instructions had been received too late. I never saw Colonel Willis again, but I've thought of him a thousand times with a gratitude that will not diminish with time.

I left that day for Oran, once again with high hopes and in high spirits. But soon I was to wish I had never heard of North Africa.

News of my adventure in Lisbon reached very high circles at the time. Captain Harry Butcher, General Eisenhower's naval aide, wrote in his memoir, *My Three Years With Eisenhower: The Personal Diary of Captain Harry C. Butcher, USNR, Naval Aide to General Eisenhower, 1942-1945* (New York: Simon and Schuster, 1946): "As if Ike didn't have enough worries—one of our American pilots flying a P-38 from UK to Gib landed at Lisbon for gas, having lost one spare belly tank, was told he was thereby interned. Told the Airdrome official he wanted to clear his superchargers or something, got back in plane, started motors, and dashed away, leaving his jacket with identification papers. Fearful of a diplomatic upset for thus flouting Portugal, and of indicating a 'mightier than thou' attitude, Ike had Gruenther radio our Ambassador at Lisbon the story and to be prepared to answer questions frankly. Consideration would be given to return the lad and plane for internment."

Tafaroui Airdrome, fifteen miles outside Oran, was not a place where you'd plan a honeymoon. Everything was fouled up and everybody was confused, but it gave me a good feeling to be back with my squadron as I was brought up to date. Lieutenant Bob Neale, one of my buddies, had missed Oran on his way down, had run out of gasoline between Oran and Algiers, crash-landed, and spent several days with the French. One of the boys in another squadron had been shot down by the Spaniards when he had flown too close to Spanish Morocco. Our ground troops had come by ship from Southampton and had taken part in the invasion of North Africa, but they were not yet at Tafaroui when I arrived.

Everyone was anxious to know what had happened to me, and I got pretty tired of telling people about my escape from Portugal. In fact, I preferred not to think about it; there was always the chance that the State Department might outwit the Army and send me back to Portugal to be properly interned. It was too bleak a thought to consider.

The sequel to the Portugal story is that Jim Harman, who had landed behind me in Lisbon, joined our outfit in North Africa about four months later. By then, he was quite angry with me. One of Jim's engines had started acting up, and he got the same idea about landing in Portugal that I had. He had seen a P-38 take off as he was landing and thought to himself, "It looks simple. I'll just get some work done on my engine and be on my way." But it turned out differently. The minute he stopped his plane and chopped his engine, the Portuguese grabbed him by the back of the neck, and Jim never saw his P-38 again. He was thrown into the local jail for a few days and later sent to an internment camp on the Spanish-Portuguese border. He said I was to blame for the rough treatment he received. I felt a little guilty at first, but then I consoled myself; I had acted according to the first law of nature. Jim was nearing the end of the third month of his confinement when the American Legation supplied him with civilian clothes and spirited him out of the country on a Dutch liner. He told me that, a few days after he landed in Lisbon, six P-39s were forced down there and also interned. But thanks to the good old American Legation, all six pilots eventually got back to their organizations.

First Lieutenant Jack Ilfrey more than made up for all the trouble he had caused. He shared in the downing of an Me-110 twin-engine fighter over

Tunisia on November 29, 1942; shot down a pair of Bf-109s over Gabès Airdrome, Tunisia, on the morning of December 2; and downed two FW-190s near Bizerte on December 26. On March 3, 1943, Jack Ilfrey achieved ace status when he shot down a Bf-109 near El Aounia Airdrome, outside Tunis.

After flying 208 combat hours on seventy-two missions with the 94th Fighter Squadron, Ilfrey returned to the United States in April 1943. He served as a P-38 and P-47 instructor until he was again shipped to England, and there he assumed command of the 20th Fighter Group's 79th Fighter Squadron, an VIII Fighter Command P-38 unit. Ilfrey downed two Bf-109s over Berlin on May 24, 1944, but he was himself downed by flak while strafing a train in France on June 11. He successfully evaded capture and, dressed as a French civilian, walked into British Army lines on June 20.

Captain Ilfrey resumed command of the 79th Fighter Squadron upon his return to England. Shortly thereafter, the 20th Fighter Group transitioned to P-51s. On November 20, 1944, Major Ilfrey landed his P-51 in a field near Maastricht to pick up his wingman, who had just been shot down. The rescue was a success.

During his two action-packed combat tours, Jack Ilfrey flew 528 combat hours in 142 missions. He served the last few months of the war at a Stateside base, then left the service to begin a successful career in banking.

DEADLY MISTAKE NUMBER 109

Captain FRANK HILL, USAAF
309th Fighter Squadron, 31st Fighter Group
Near Pont-du-Fahs, Tunisia—April 22, 1943

Frank Ackerman Hill was born March 20, 1919, in Nyack, New York, and raised in Hillsdale, New Jersey. From an early age he dreamed of flying airplanes, and with members of his high school flying club, took part in purchasing, restoring, and flying an old Cessna glider. After graduating from high school in 1937, Hill took an aircraft mechanic course at night while working days as a plumber's assistant.

Hill attempted to enlist in the Army Air Corps at the beginning of 1939, but he had to wait nine months for an opening. In September 1939, he paid his own way to Chanute Field, Illinois, and enlisted in the aerial photography school. Later, he passed a two-year college equivalency exam and thus qualified for flight school. He joined Class 40-G as a flying cadet and earned his commission and wings at Kelly Field, Texas, on November 15, 1940.

Immediately after graduating from flight school, 2d Lieutenant Hill joined the 31st Pursuit Group, a P-39 unit based at Selfridge Field, Michigan. After transitioning to P-39s, the group took part in maneuvers in Georgia and Mississippi. Hill crashed in a P-39 during the latter exercise and was in a full body cast from September 1941 to February 1942. He thus missed being shipped out when the 31st Group's three fighter squadrons (but not the group headquarters) were dispatched to Australia. When Lieutenant Hill returned to duty with the 31st, he was one of only a few experienced pilots, and was he assigned as the commander of a flight of eight airplanes and pilots in the new 308th Fighter Squadron.

Frank Hill was still a flight commander when the 31st Fighter Group was shipped to England in June 1942—without its airplanes. In England, the group was equipped with Spitfires and taught up-to-date combat tactics by experienced Royal Air Force pilots. Its combat baptism came on August 19, 1942, when the group provided support for Canadian troops taking part in the ill-fated Dieppe raid. On the first of two missions over Dieppe, Captain Hill left an FW-190 trailing dense black smoke and heading toward the ground, but he could not follow it because of the intense air battle, and no one saw it crash. The encounter was played in the U.S. press for a time as the first USAAF fighter victory over Occupied Europe, but in the end it was officially scored a probable.

Captain Frank Hill's first official victory was a Junkers Ju-87 Stuka dive-bomber that he downed over Tunisia on February 22, 1943. He next downed an FW-190 over Tunisia on March 25, after which he was reassigned to the 31st Fighter Group's 309th Fighter Squadron, as commanding officer.

On April 22, 1943, the 309th Fighter Squadron was flying out of La Sers, which was about eighty miles southwest of Tunis. We went out on two missions that day. On the first, we escorted a squadron of 33d Fighter Group P-40 fighter-bombers as they dive-bombed and strafed targets of opportunity from the bomb line near Pont-du-Fahs to the coast. At the time, German ground forces were heading north toward Tunis. I was leading a three-plane flight of Spitfire IXs at 18,000 feet, providing top cover for the other planes of our squadron (which were Spitfire Vs) and the P-40s they were escorting. My two wingmen were 1st Lieutenant Bob Rahn and 1st Lieutenant Claude McRaven.

Except for some heavy flak encountered along the way, the mission went off okay. At the coast, the P-40s regrouped and flew off to their base, and the Spit Vs from my squadron headed back to La Sers, which was about sixty miles to the east.

As we were weaving over the Spit Vs at 18,000 feet, either Rahn or McRaven spotted a group of airplanes milling around to the east. It looked like they were fighting. We flew toward the milling airplanes, and as we got closer, I could see that six or more Bf-109s were mixing it up at about 13,000 feet with some Spitfires.The Spits might have been from the U.S. 52d Fighter Group, but they were probably British.

I dove and increased power to attack the 109s. As I did, I also rolled to the right and cut left across the arc to the left rear of a 109 that was following another 109. I opened fire with all my cannon and machine guns at about 200 yards and I continued to fire bursts all the way down to about twenty-five yards. Smoke and debris were coming from the 109; pieces of it were fluttering away in the air. I had to pull up to avoid hitting it as it went into a dive from which it didn't recover. The 109 went down to the northeast, streaming glycol and thick black smoke until it crashed. Stormy Rahn had also fired at it, so we shared the victory.

I then started to climb for altitude and called for my flight to reassemble over the dry lake at Pont-du-Fahs. As I passed through 10,000 feet over the assembly area, I came up under a lone fighter. I automatically assumed it was one of my flight, so I waggled my wings to signal it to "follow me." Then I went into a turn to the left. No sooner had I turned my head to see if he had joined me than I saw gunfire coming from his propeller spinner. I had made the unforgivable mistake of not recognizing a Bf-109 from low in the rear, and now I was about to be blasted out of the sky at my own invitation.

With a quick jerk on the control column, I yanked the plane into a steep vertical turn. The turn was so fast and abrupt that the canopy came out of the rails from the twisting strain on the fuselage. I must have been pulling five or six Gs, but the 109 followed me around for two turns. He fired at me, but he couldn't quite bend it around enough to get a good bead on me. Looking directly across the small circle described by our two planes, I could see that I was gaining on him. I could see the enemy pilot in his cockpit straining under the G forces, trying again to get on my tail.

All of a sudden, I saw his plane shake and stall. He rolled over and went straight down. I immediately followed and caught up to him, firing all the way down to the deck, where I was still on his tail. He was going all out, and I had everything full forward. We were skimming across the desert sands, and my machine guns were blasting away. I could see hits on his right wing and some of the bullets kicking up the dirt. I didn't realize it at the time, but the torque of the prop going full out put the plane in a skid that threw my bullets to the right.

I was so intent on nailing him that, without my realizing it, I was following him directly to his airfield, El Aiouna, which was at the east end of the city of Tunis. Here we were, on the deck, going right down the main street of Tunis! When I noticed the tops of buildings going by, I realized where we were and gave up the chase. I pulled up over the buildings and got the hell out of there. A few more seconds of chasing him would have placed me directly over the airfield, where I knew they had plenty of accurate flak.

By that time I had no idea where the other two members of my flight were. I was alone and almost out of ammo, so I headed back to La Sers. There I found out that my number-three, Lieutenant McRaven, had also picked off a Bf-109 during our initial attack.

On my second mission that day, I was leading Yellow Flight—four Spit IXs. Once again, we were escorting a squadron of about twelve 33d Fighter Group P-40 fighter-bombers. There were also two other flights from our 31st Fighter Group in Spit Vs. As before, the Spit Vs were escorting the P-40s and the Spit IXs were providing top cover.

At about 1645 hours, we were at about 9,000 feet near Medjez el-Bab, about fifty miles southeast of Tunis and about the same distance from La Sers. Yellow Flight was weaving back and forth, trying to keep the other two formations in sight. Suddenly, someone yelled that 109s were diving on us. I just had time to see that about nine Bf-109s were coming down on us from about 12,000 or 13,000 feet.

I rammed the throttle forward and called, "Break right!" This placed us pretty much head-on to them, but not in time to get good aim or fire. They flashed by and we didn't get in any shots because they quickly pulled up and over us, out of range. This was their usual tactic, using speed gained during their dive on us to pull up rapidly and get up to run another pass. As far as I knew, they hadn't scored any hits on us or on the lower formations.

This was at a time when we were fighting highly experienced German fighter pilots, some of them aces many times over. I knew they would probably make another attack, and they had our full attention as they formed up out of range. We were at once anxious and super alert as we positioned ourselves to meet the second attack. We were in a standard finger-four formation, with my element to the left and the second element to my right.

To gain speed, we increased power and nosed down as the 109s came down from high up toward my left rear. I called, "Break left!" and the flight snapped left and up as we all went to full power.

The break placed most of us head-on to three 109s, which were all firing their machine guns and cannon. The first 109 flashed overhead, probably firing at our second element. But the other two 109s were in trail formation to the right, a few hundred feet behind the first, and slightly high. They were in position for me to get a good lead and bead on one of them. I fired everything at the second 109 and hit the engine, cooling system, and belly. As it passed to the right and slightly higher than my airplane, glycol streamed out; it looked like a contrail and marked a long, billowing white path from 10,000 feet to the deck, where the airplane crashed. The pilot must have been hit, because he made no attempt to pull out of the dive.

The rest of the mission went off uneventfully. After I landed, I was surprised to learn that my second-element leader, 1st Lieutenant Carl Payne, had also fired at the same plane, and thought he had hit it. He had fired after I hit it, but we couldn't decide who should get the credit, so we each took a half credit.

♦

Major Frank Hill achieved ace status on May 6, 1943, when he shot down a pair of Bf-109s over Tunisia. He was the 31st Fighter Group's first ace of the war. On June 10, he downed an Italian Air Force Macchi Mc.202 over Pantelleria Island; and on July 11 he scored his seventh and last official victory when he shot down a Junkers Ju-88 medium bomber over Sicily.

Only twenty-four years old at the time, Lieutenant Colonel Frank Hill assumed command of the 31st Fighter Group in mid-July 1943. He was ordered home in September and, following a leave, spent the remainder of the war in command of a P-47 operational training unit. He remained on active duty after the war and earned a degree in industrial engineering. After commanding the 33d Air Division, he retired from the Air Force with the rank of colonel in August 1969. In 1992, Colonel Frank Hill was inducted into the New Jersey Aviation Hall of Fame.

ACTION OVER ATHENS

Flight Officer JACK LENOX, USAAF
49th Fighter Squadron, 14th Fighter Group
Athens, Greece—December 20, 1943

Jack Lenox, Jr., was born February 20, 1922, in Enid, Oklahoma. During his school years, he enjoyed building model aircraft and reading flying magazines; on weekends, he often hitchhiked five miles to the local airport, where he would spend the day walking around and looking at the airplanes.

I graduated from high school in the spring of 1941 knowing that, with six children, my parents would not be able to send me to college. I went to both the Navy and Army recruiting offices to get information about their flying cadet programs. The Navy indicated that it would not be possible for me to be enrolled without a college degree, but the Army recruiter attempted to get me information about taking the two-year college equivalency exam. He told me that he would be on leave for two weeks, but if I would come back after that time he would try to have more information for me. After the two weeks, I returned to the Army recruiting office and was informed by the recruiting sergeant that a new act had been passed in Congress and, as of June 3, 1941, the Army Air Corps was authorized to train enlisted men as aviation students. The Army regulation covering this act was published on August 1, 1941, so after that date I again returned to the recruiting office for more information. To be eligible for pilot training, I had to be enlisted in the Army, unmarried, between the ages of eighteen and twenty-two, have a high school diploma with at least one and a half years of math, pass the flight physical exam, and appear before an aviation cadet examining board. Also, after graduation from flying school, I would have to re-enlist in the Army for an additional three years. So, with that information and knowing I had to be in the Army before I could apply, I enlisted on August 15.

During my Army entrance physical in Oklahoma City, I was being examined along with three college graduates who were applying for aviation cadet training. When my height was recorded at five feet, three-and-a-half inches, the examining doctor stated that I was a half-inch too short for the cadet program. The recruiting sergeant intervened and said that I was enlisting in the Army, not the cadet program.

After I went through basic training and had attended the aviation mechanics' school at Chanute Field, Illinois, I got all my paperwork together and applied for aviation student training. When I went to take the flying school physical, and remembering what had happened at my enlistment physical, I conveniently forgot to remove my shoes. No one noticed I had my shoes on when my height was measured, and so I passed the physical with flying colors.

I received orders to report to Kelly Field, Texas, for Pre-Flight training in January 1942. My class, 42-I, was the first class to attend Pre-Flight. Prior to this, the cadets reported directly to Primary flight school. All of my flight training took place in west Texas. I completed Advanced flight school at Lubbock Army Air Force Base on October 9, 1942, and was sent through another physical before receiving my wings. At this physical, I had to remove my shoes. When my height was measured, I was a half-inch too short. The examining doctor, who could not understand how I could have lost one inch of height during flight training, drew a line on the office wall and told me to back up against the wall and stretch. I did this and was able to meet the minimum requirements. I received my wings and staff sergeant rating the next day.

After graduation, I was assigned to duty with Air Training Command to fly student bombardiers. After a few months, all sergeant pilots were discharged and given the new warrant flight officer rank. I volunteered for combat duty and ended up in P-40 and P-51 training in Florida. Upon completion of fighter training, our entire class was sent to North Africa in September 1943 as P-51 replacement pilots. There were no P-51 groups in North Africa at this time, and the P-40s and P-39s were not effective against the German Bf-109 fighters, so we were divided between the three P-38 groups then in the Twelfth Air Force. We spent about thirty days in Constantine, Algeria, checking out in the P-38. After that, I was assigned to the 14th Fighter Group's 49th Fighter Squadron, which was then located about forty miles southeast of Tunis. Our group became part of the new Fifteenth Air Force, and we moved to Foggia, Italy, about December 1, 1943.

On December 20, 1943, I was on my third combat mission, a raid on Athens, Greece. I was flying as wingman to the group commander, Lieutenant Colonel Oliver Taylor. Our group was providing top cover to the B-17s that were attacking the Eleusis Airdrome at Athens.

As we approached the target, the 49th Fighter Squadron was at about 28,000 feet, well above the bomber stream, which was at about 22,000 feet. From our position, we were able to observe fifteen to twenty Bf-109s as they moved into position behind the bombers. Colonel Taylor half-rolled his P-38 and dove to attack the enemy aircraft, and I followed him down in a vertical dive.

As I looked out the right side of my cockpit, I spotted a formation of four 109s below me. My airspeed was fast approaching the red line on my airspeed indicator. I was at 90 degree to the enemy formation, so I pulled off the power and rolled the aircraft to the right, ending up above and behind the flight of four enemy aircraft. By then, I had lost sight of the group commander.

Because our P-38s were not equipped with dive flaps, it was not a smart thing to stay in a vertical dive—the P-38s had compressibility problems that made the control surfaces freeze up, and pilots did not understand this phenomenon. I shallowed out my dive and applied power to both engines, turned on my gunsight, and ended up in a position dead astern of the last 109 in the flight of four.

I started firing from about 400 yards and continued to fire until I was less than 100 yards from him. At this point, a thin stream of black smoke was trailing back along each side of the 109's fuselage. My overtake speed was a lot greater than the 109's, so I pulled my nose up and fired a short burst at the lead aircraft. I saw three or four puffs of white smoke just forward and above that aircraft's wing root.

I was then passing through the enemy formation. I realized that the enemy aircraft were now in a position to attack me, so I pulled the P-38 into a steep climb in an attempt to outrun the 109s behind me. While climbing, I must have pulled somewhere between four and five Gs on my body, which caused my vision to gray out. After I had climbed a thousand feet or so, my vision returned to normal and I started looking around desperately for a P-38 to tag on to. As I circled to the left, I observed another P-38 above and to my right. I quickly slid into formation beside the other P-38 and, lo and behold, it was the group commander.

The squadron reformed on the two of us, and we set course for our base at Foggia. As we passed over Bari, where the Fifteenth Air Force maintained its headquarters, I dropped out of formation and landed, because I wasn't sure I had the fuel needed to get to Foggia. I refueled at Bari and flew on to Foggia.

That evening, we attended the mission critique. Colonel Taylor reviewed the mission, stating how successful it was and how we had flown good formation. I'm not sure, but I don't think he realized I was not on his wing for a few minutes.

All in all, the 49th Fighter Squadron was credited with nine 109s shot down on that mission. Colonel Taylor was credited with one confirmed kill, a probable, and a damaged. The other member of our flight, 2d Lieutenant Bob Seidman, shot down three 109s that day. Bob made the statement, "I bet the Huns would be real mad if they knew a little Hebrew boy had shot down three of them." I was credited with one aircraft destroyed and one damaged. The next day, however, I went by the intelligence tent and had them change my one destroyed to one probable, because I felt there was not enough information to support a claim of one destroyed. Years later, while talking to the Colonel Taylor at a reunion, I found out that he had also reached compressibility during his dive and had had a difficult time recovering.

This mission to Athens was my third combat mission and my first encounter with the German Air Force.

On April 1, 1944, Flight Officer Jack Lenox was ordered to report to Fifteenth Air Force headquarters. There, Lieutenant General Nathan Twining awarded him a battlefield commission, the only means by which an Army Air Forces flight officer could attain commissioned rank. On April 3, 2d Lieutenant Lenox damaged a Bf-109 over Budapest, Hungary. On May 23, he was awarded his first victory credit for a Bf-109 he shot down over Ferrara Airdrome in Italy; the next day he shot down an Me-210 twin-engine fighter over Wiener Neustadt, Austria. Lenox became an ace on June 14, 1944, when he shot down three Bf-109s over Petfurdo, Hungary.

Second Lieutenant Jack Lenox flew his last combat mission on July20, 1944, returned to the United States, and flew P-38s and P-61s until the war ended. He was released from active duty shortly after the end of World War II but remained in the Reserves. After being called to active duty for the Korean War, Lenox remained on active duty until his retirement from the Air Force in 1967 with the rank of lieutenant colonel.

NIGHT STALKER

1st Lieutenant LOU LUMA, USAAF
418 RCAF Squadron
Hildesheim, Germany—January 21, 1944

James Forrest Luma was born in Helena, Montana, on August 27, 1922. He was interested in aviation and flying from early childhood, and made model airplanes and saved pictures of military aircraft. During the 1930s, when there were many pulp magazines filled with fictional stories about World War I air combat, he bought stacks of old, unsold magazines from the local distributor and read them from cover to cover. As a teenager, he rode his bicycle to the local airport to watch the mechanics work on the wire and fabric airplanes.

In his junior and senior years in high school, Luma took an aeronautics class that provided, as part of the syllabus, his first airplane ride, a thirty-minute flight in the school's Fleet. After Luma graduated from high school, his parents moved to Seattle, Washington, but he remained in Montana and enrolled as a student at Carroll College in Helena. During a spring break, he hitchhiked to Seattle to see his parents. On his return to Montana, he hitched a ride with an American who was a sergeant pilot in the Royal Canadian Air Force (RCAF). The sergeant pilot told Luma that the RCAF was accepting Americans who were at least eighteen years old. Luma saw this as a golden opportunity to learn how to fly—and be paid for it to boot. When he got out of the sergeant pilot's car, he changed his mind about returning to Montana, turned around, and hitchhiked back to Seattle. From there, he went to Vancouver, British Columbia, to join the RCAF. He was told by the Canadians that he was too young and thus needed the written consent of his parents. Back in Seattle, he smooth-talked his parents into giving their permission. The first trip to Vancouver had exhausted Luma's finances, so he hocked his watch to get bus fare for the second trip.

After enlisting in the RCAF, Luma was sent to Brandon, Manitoba, where he was issued gear and taught the basics of military life. From Brandon, he went to Edmonton, Alberta, where for several months the new recruits attended classes designed to separate them into pilots, observers, and gunners. In addition to classes in mathematics and air navigation, the recruits were given several sessions in a Link Trainer to determine their coordination and suitability for flight training. Upon completion of the schooling at Edmonton, some recruits were sent off to pilot training, some to observer training, and some to gunnery school. Lou Luma, as he was known to his fellow recruits, was selected for pilot training. He received his elementary flight training in Tiger Moths at Boundary Bay, British Columbia, and got his wings at Claresholm, Alberta, after flying Cessna Cranes. He was commissioned with the rank of pilot officer and, following a short stint as a staff pilot at a bombing and gunnery school in Dafoe, Saskatchewan, he was posted overseas to England.

♦

I arrived in England in January 1943 on a troop ship out of Halifax, Nova Scotia. After debarking in Scotland, I was posted to Bournemouth, on the south coast of England. There, a sorting-out process took place. I am sure that the needs of the various operational squadrons largely determined where one was posted. At any rate, some pilots and observers were sent to Bomber Command and some to Fighter Command. Through some sort of error or mixup, I received an exceptionally high grade in a night-vision test. As a result, I was assigned to night intruders, though at the time I had no idea what a night intruder was.

Because the British night fighters had radar superior to that of the Germans, they were not permitted to operate over occupied territory for fear they might be shot down with the result that their advanced technology would fall into enemy hands. Instead, the British night fighters were restricted to hunting over England and the English Channel. Night intruders, on the other hand, operated over the Continent, but without radar.

After a short stint with an advanced flying unit at Grantham, Lincolnshire, I was sent to No. 60 Operational Training Unit (OTU) at High Ercall, Salop. It was there that I was introduced to the Mosquito, a twin-engine airplane made of plywood that had a crew of two. The pilot sat on the left and the observer (navigator) on the right. The throttle was on the left, as in a single-engine aircraft, but the Mossie was powered by two Rolls-Royce-Merlin engines. Its armament was four .303-caliber machine guns and four 20mm cannon, all concentrated in the nose. Extra fuel could be carried in drop tanks, one under each wing, located outboard of the engines. The drop tanks could be replaced with 500-pound bombs.

At OTU, we learned to fly the Mosquito and practiced air-to-air gunnery and air-to-ground gunnery. After several weeks at OTU, we intruder trainees were instructed to informally pair ourselves off into crews. Colin Finlayson, a Canadian from British Columbia, and I agreed to crew up together. It would be a permanent arrangement, sort of like the marriage vow—"'til death do us part."

It was while at OTU that I decided to transfer to the U.S. Army Air Forces. The official policy at the time, agreed to by the Americans and

British, was that a crew would not be broken up, so after I was sworn in as a first lieutenant, I was permitted to return to the RCAF to finish my tour of operations before returning to the USAAF. I was a U.S. Army Air Forces pilot on detached duty with the RCAF. After finishing OTU, Fin and I were assigned to No. 418 RCAF Squadron, which was based at Ford, Sussex.

Ford was located on the beautiful south coast of England. Like many RAF aerodromes, it consisted of two paved runways at right angles to each other. Circling the perimeter of the aerodrome was a paved taxiway. The aircraft were parked in blast bays located outside this perimeter. Blast bays were **U**-shaped revetments that protected the aircraft from all but a direct hit by a bomb. The blast bays were in clusters with a taxiway leading from each cluster to the perimeter taxiway. The taxiways and runways were lighted at night, but only when aircraft were using them.

Life at Ford was good. We had a comfortable officers mess and were billeted in private homes that had been taken over by the government. We had our own rooms and were awakened and brought tea in the morning by a batman, who was a Royal Air Force enlisted man.

418 Squadron consisted of "A" Flight and "B" Flight, which alternated duty. Fin and I were posted to "A" Flight. The squadron's Mosquitoes had the paintings of Al Capp's "Li'l Abner" characters on them; each aircraft had a different character from Dogpatch. The aircraft that was assigned to Fin and me,"D for Dog," had a painting of Moonbeam McSwine on it.

Sometimes when we were on standby, we would conduct a night-flying test. Fin and I would fly the airplane for thirty minutes or so to determine its mechanical fitness. Sometimes we would also practice air-to-air gunnery, using a camera gun. At other times we would do an in-flight compass swing. After landing we would leave our parachutes and helmets in the seats in order to save time in case of a scramble. The "erks" (ground crew) would correct any mechanical problems we might have experienced and would top off the fuel tanks. The erks were a hard-working, dedicated, loyal part of the team, and they did not receive the recognition they deserved. At least not from me. I was too young and egotistical to think that anyone other than myself was contributing to any success that I might achieve.

After we had finished our night-flying test, we would have supper at the officers mess before reporting in at the ops room for the night's duty. The ops room was a medium-size room with reasonably comfortable chairs to lounge in while we were on standby. It had planning tables for the navigators, and the walls were plastered with silhouettes of German aircraft for boning up on aircraft recognition. We killed time by reading, talking, and listening to the radio. Sometimes we would listen to the English-speaking "Lord Haw Haw," who broadcast Nazi propaganda from Germany. The music on his station was usually better than what the BBC offered.

Usually we were given our targets as soon as we arrived at the ops room, and would plan our flight accordingly. At other times, we reported to the ready room and remained there on standby, waiting for a scramble. We were dressed and ready to go. Pilots had flying gloves made of thin chamois that fit tightly to the hands. The preferred style of flying boots had a dress shoe on the foot with fleece lined uppers. In the event you bailed out over occupied territory, you would cut off the uppers after you were on the ground by using a small knife carried in a pocket in the boots. This left you with black, low-cut dress shoes that could pass as part of your civilian attire when being helped by the Underground to get out of the country. Each crewmember carried a packet containing the currency of the country they would be flying over (usually French francs) and a map printed on cloth.

British intelligence was excellent. Each time the Germans sent bombers to raid England, the British knew where the bombers were taking off from, how many aircraft there were in each flight, and where they were returning to. In many cases, they knew the names of the officers leading the flights. The RAF control center would dispatch night intruders to each of the aerodromes that the bombers were expected to return to and to those from which German night fighters were operating. This type of operation was known as a "Flower." The Mosquitoes would time their takeoffs to arrive at the German aerodromes when the Hun aircraft were preparing to land. Since the intruder had no radar, he had to hope that the Germans would turn on their navigation lights prior to landing. Normally they didn't, but if they did, consequences were usually fatal. I can recall being at a German airport on a black night, seeing nothing but every once in awhile getting a jolt when the Mosquito flew through the slipstream of a Hun aircraft. If the Germans were returning to a field deep within Germany, they would feel safer and be more likely to put their navigation lights on. One of our crews was at Munich one night, deep inside Germany. The Germans apparently felt they were too far from England to be in any danger and they put on their navigation lights prior to landing. The Mossie pilot immediately shot down two of them. The crew said the sky was full of aircraft with their nav lights on, but they had to leave after shooting down the two, because they lacked fuel to remain any longer.

The Germans did not like the night intruders, and it made them uneasy knowing they were being stalked. One night, a squadron of German bombers was diverted to an alternate airport, because a Mosquito was lurking at the destination airport. The alternate fogged in before they got there, and all of the aircraft ran out of fuel and crashed.

There was a green phone on a raised dais at one end of the ops room. The phone was a direct link to some mysterious place (mysterious to me, at any rate) from which we received the word to scramble. The target would be given to us, and we were to take off as soon as possible. The navigator would quickly draw some courses on our charts, and we would be driven to our airplane by an enlisted WAAF (Womens Auxiliary Air Force). We were expected to have our engines started within five minutes from the time we were given our target. Included in that five minutes was a nervous pee behind the airplane before climbing in.

After starting our engines and calling the tower, we were given the runway in use for takeoff. We did not use our navigation lights. There was the possibility that some Hun could be waiting to do unto us as we would do unto him. After takeoff, we would set course across the English Channel, flying several hundred feet off the water. Even on a clear night, we were completely on instruments. Crossing the Channel could be nervewracking. You were inside of a pitch-black nothingness. You knew the water was a few hundred feet below you, because you had a radio altimeter that told you so. In training, we had been warned that we would eventually experience vertigo, where your senses tell you that you are in a turn, yet your instruments tell you that you are wings level. The compulsion to believe your senses is overpowering. You swear that the instruments are lying, that they are malfunctioning. You really believe that you are in a turn. Fortunately, in training we were emphatically told, "Believe your instruments!" In the beginning, there were times that I had to force myself so hard to believe the instruments that it made me sweat. Later in my combat career, I learned little techniques to more rapidly dispel the vertigo, like forcing myself to make a gentle bank one way followed by another gentle bank the other way. Another means of diminishing the vertigo was to take my eyes off the instruments and slowly look around the cockpit. This would reset the inner ear to neutral (wings level). Then, when you returned to the instruments, everything was normal (hopefully).

One night on a Channel crossing we saw RAF bombers being shot down, most probably by some *Luftwaffe* night fighters. We would see a light glow appear at the bottom of the overcast, followed by the burning bomber spinning out from underneath. It was an unforgettable sight, to say the least.

For navigating across the Channel and making an accurate crossing of the enemy coast, we were aided by Gee, the forerunner of Loran. It generated a single "line of position" that could be followed to intersect the enemy coast. This gave us a very accurate means of crossing the coast exactly where we wanted to. After crossing the coast, we would climb to a thousand feet above the ground if there were no mountains below us, or 2,000 feet above the ground in mountainous areas. Usually we were flying on instruments, because black sky blended into black ground. Yet it was possible to navigate by planning a course that went between pinpoints that were unique. On the blackest of nights, a point on the ground where land meets water is visible when looking straight down at it. The navigator planned his course utilizing unique pinpoints—oddly shaped bends in a river, for instance.

We were given permission to shoot at trains, an option later withdrawn. Shooting at a train on a black night was deceptively dangerous. A train could be spotted when the engine's firebox door was open to shovel in more coal. You could not see the rest of the train or the surrounding terrain, just the firebox. We would dive on the firebox, and I would fire when I got it in my gunsight. My navigator would read out the altitude, and tell me when to break off the attack and pull up. It was always tempting to fire for just a second or two more, but that could be fatal because of to your close proximity to the ground. German trains were known to deliberately stop in a cut and open their firebox. When the intruder dived on it, the crew would see the firebox but not the high ground. The high risk involved in shooting trains was probably why the option was later withdrawn. A locomotive wasn't worth the loss of a Mosquito and its crew.

Sometimes the Germans flew decoy aircraft at night. The decoy would fly with its navigation lights on. The gunner in the tail would be just waiting for you to suck in. Fortunately for the intruders, the navigation lights of the decoys were inordinately bright, because they wanted us to be sure to see them. We were told to stay away from bogeys with extremely bright lights.

The Germans used different combinations of colored flares as a means of identifying friend and foe. These color combinations were changed daily. British intelligence was so good that we usually knew what the German colors for the day on every mission that we flew. If we mistakenly flew over an area heavily defended by antiaircraft guns, we could fire the correct colors of the day, and the enemy, thinking we were a friendly aircraft, would cease shooting at us. The Mosquito flew close to the ground so the amount of time that the aircraft was within range of the guns was not very long. Because we didn't want the Hun to know that we knew his colors for the day, we used our speed to our advantage. The navigator would fire any flare other than the correct colors of the day. In the brief time it took the gunners on the ground to associate the correct colors of the day with the colors that we shot, we would be out of range.

When returning to England from an ops, we would turn on our IFF after crossing the enemy coast. IFF (Identification, Friend or Foe) was an electronic device that would identify us on British radar screens, both ground and airborne, as friendly aircraft.

When we were well on our way back to England, we would use our VHF radio to contact our radar control center, which would give us vectors or steering to base. As we neared the base, we would pick up the outer circle, a ring of lights over a mile in diameter that surrounded the aerodrome. We would follow this outer circle as we prepared for landing. From the outer circle another set of lights funneled the aircraft into the runway in use. These lights guided the pilot as he descended to the runway. It was thus possible to make an approach and landing under extremely poor weather conditions.

After landing, we would have a debriefing session with the intelligence officer. That would be followed by breakfast, where we were rewarded with fresh eggs. Fresh eggs were a precious commodity in wartime England, and only young children and aircrew got them.

On one of our early ops, we inadvertently flew over a defended area, where we encountered our first enemy flak. When the flak was behind us, the compass needle was swinging wildly because of the violent maneuvering that we had done to evade the exploding shells. The British aircraft compass was like a marine compass, with the glass on top. Under normal circumstances, it was customary to gently tap the glass to get the compass needle to settle down. My first experience with enemy ground fire resulted in an adrenalin high, causing me to "tap" the glass so hard that I broke it, rendering the compass unusable. Fortunately, we still had heading information available from the directional gyro. It was a clear night, so we had the North Star to crosscheck the accuracy of the precessing gyro. Unfortunately, we were unable to spot any good pinpoints on the ground to accurately determine our position as we pressed on in a westerly direction. As a result, we crossed the coast at Abbeville, which was one of the Germans' most heavily fortified coastal areas. Fortunately, Fin and I were the beneficiaries of techniques developed by preceding night intruder crews, who had learned through experience to develop ways to cope with a situation where the night turns to day because of the seemingly infinite number of searchlights and obscene amount of flak.

Our best defense was our low altitude and high speed. The procedure in this situation was to turn into the searchlights and away from the flak, which was visible because of the tracers. By turning into a searchlight, you made it more difficult for the searchlight operator to lock on to you. The reason for turning away from flak is self-evident—the farther from it the better. I would duck my head down so as to be just a few inches from the instrument panel. Fin would hold his map over the top of my head to shield me from the glare of the searchlights. He would tell me when to turn, and which way. Our turns were steep and violent. In addition, I would abruptly change altitude several hundred feet up and down. At one point during that night over Abbeville, we were so low that, during one of the steep turns to the left, I saw nothing but water out of the corner of my eye. I hopefully asked Fin whether we were over the Channel. He replied that we were still over Abbeville, that it was a river I saw.

I do not remember any night-intruder crew that liked a clear, moonlit night. Although it was easier to see and thus to navigate under such conditions, it was also easier for the Hun to see us. We didn't have the security of a moonless night's total blackness. Whenever we did have an ops on a moonlit night, we always entertained the hope that we might spot and destroy enemy aircraft that didn't have any of their lights on. Spotting such aircraft was called a "cat's eye." One night, we finally realized our dream—at least the cat's eye part—when we spotted a bogey over France. We immediately took out after him, since all bogeys over the Continent were fair game. Because the bogey was flying in a direction that put him up-moon, I had to position the Mosquito behind so that we were down-moon from him. As I eased into position to shoot at him, Fin shouted, "Don't shoot, Lou! It's a B-24!" I immediately broke off the attack. (After I returned to the United States, I was based for awhile at Victorville, California. One night in the bar at the officers club, I was talking to a B-24 pilot. We had become barroom buddies, because he, too, had flown at night out of England. He had flown clandestine trips over France to make drops to the French Underground. He related a story of one night when his tail gunner spotted a bogey on their tail and was about to open fire when he recognized it as a Mosquito. The barroom buddy and I rushed to our quarters and compared dates in our logbooks. We had indeed crossed paths over France!)

My most memorable flight was the one that entitled us to have our first swastika painted on the side of our Mossie. It began on the night of January 21, 1944, and it was my seventeenth mission. My navigator, Fin, was sick, so another navigator, Flight Lieutenant Al Eckert, was assigned to my plane. We took off from Ford at 2215 hours on a Flower to Hildesheim, Germany, near Hannover. By now, ops were pretty much routine for me. On each of my early flights, I fully expected that I would see an enemy aircraft, but it didn't happen. Now, I was pretty much resigned to the fact that I might put in a whole tour without ever seeing an enemy aircraft. It was possible; some of our crews did come up scoreless.

When Al and I took off, there was no reason to believe that this wouldn't be just another uneventful op. The weather was sour with a lot of low cloud and haze, which made navigation difficult. We reached an airfield that was lighted with perimeter lights. After orbiting the airfield, we found a pinpoint that fixed the airfield as Wunstorf. Shortly after that we saw two bright lights on the other side of the airfield. We came in to meet them very nearly head-on. They proved to be on an aircraft that had just taken off from the base. We were at 1,500 feet and the enemy aircraft passed over us at 2,000 feet. As he passed over us, we identified him as a twin-engine aircraft with one white light just under the nose and one under the tail.

We did a quick orbit to port, coming in behind him, and chased him for fifteen to twenty miles. As we closed, he was climbing through about 4,000 feet. In my excitement at seeing my first enemy aircraft, I very possibly came close to losing the opportunity to chalk up my first kill. I had overestimated our closing speed and overshot him. As I threw down the landing gear to slow us down, the thought that my buck fever was going to cost me the chance of destroying my first enemy aircraft left me with a sick feeling in the pit of my stomach.

With the gear down, the Mossie rapidly slowed, but we were still not in a position to shoot at him. We were directly below him. By now the nervous excitement had disappeared. I did a quick turn to port, followed by one to starboard. This brought us under his tail—about 500 feet below and 250 to 100 yards behind. I was calm, and I knew we had him in the bag. We were in position.

I pulled back on the stick, placed the center of the gunsight slightly forward of and midway between the points where the exhaust flames emerged from the engines. Then I fired all my cannon and machine guns. Strikes on the fuselage were followed by a big ball of fire, which enabled us to identify the aircraft as an Me-210. A large piece broke off to the left, and he went down. Al Eckert saw him go in, explode, and burn on the ground. After our return to base the erks found two pieces of plywood from the enemy aircraft embedded in the leading edge of the Mosquito's starboard wing.

Not long after destroying the Me-210, there was an article in the Air Ministry Weekly Intelligence Summary about a *Luftwaffe* ace by the name of Major Prinz Heinrich zu Sayn-Wittgenstein, a highly decorated *Luftwaffe* night-fighter pilot who was killed in air combat on the night of January 21–22, 1944. The Intelligence Summary went on to say that he had shot down eighty-three aircraft. It also said he had shot down five RAF aircraft within a few hours of meeting his death. I found it interesting that I was the only RAF/RCAF pilot who had shot down an enemy over the Continent that night.

Lou Luma's second aerial victory was an He-177 he shot down over Bordeaux, France, on February 13, 1944. On March 6, he downed an FW-190 fighter over Pau, France; and he achieved ace status on the night of March 21, 1944, when he downed a Junkers W-34 light transport over Luxeuil, France, and a Ju-52 trimotor transport near Luxeuil.

First Lieutenant Lou Luma flew his final RCAF mission with 418 Squadron on the night of April 30, 1944. He then transferred into the U.S. Army Air Forces and flew a Mosquito weather plane for the Eighth Air Force until, in November 1944, he rotated to the United States for duty at Victorville, California. He left the service in September 1945.

OUT OF AMMUNITION

2d Lieutenant HENRY BROWN, USAAF
354th Fighter Squadron, 355th Fighter Group
Berlin Area—April 11, 1944

Born in Dallas on January 25, 1923, Henry William Brown enlisted in the Army Air Corps in December 1941 and was accepted into the flying sergeants program in June 1942. He earned his wings and the rate of warrant flight officer when he graduated in Class 43-C from Spence Field, Georgia, on March 25, 1943. He was assigned directly to the 355th Fighter Group, and was soon commissioned a second lieutenant.

When it began flying combat operations from Steeple Morden Airdrome in September 1943, the 355th was equipped with P-47s. During Brown's first thirty-five missions in Thunderbolts, he destroyed 4.5 German aircraft on the ground but none in the air. Things changed after the group transitioned to Mustangs in March 1944. On March 18, Brown downed a Bf-109 and damaged an Me-110. Then he downed an FW-190 on March 29; shared in the downing of an Me-108 staff plane and took a one-fifth share in a Do-217 on April 5; and shared in the downing of a Bf-109 on April 8, 1944.

On April 11, 1944, the 355th Fighter Group, based at Steeple Morden, England, was ordered to escort bombers to Sorau, east of Berlin, to attack aircraft engine plants. According to our field order, fighters were permitted to dive to the deck and attack airfields and other military targets after being relieved of escort duties with the bombers upon the arrival of replacement escort fighters.

The mission was expected to take approximately six and a half hours and cover 800 miles—400 out and 400 back. Counting the extra miles we would put on weaving over the slower bomber formation, this was about the maximum range for our P-51B aircraft with two 75-gallon external fuel tanks attached. I later flew the P-51D with two 110-gallon external fuel tanks and logged nearly eight hours on a shuttle flight from England to Russia. This is an indication of the performance the P-51, which left the *Luftwaffe* no place to hide and, in a short period of time, contributed greatly to its destruction.

Another thing that led to the destruction of the *Luftwaffe* was an Eighth Air Force field order issued in February 1944 that stated, "Seek out and destroy the German Air Force in the air and on the ground." This authorized the fighter groups to leave the bombers when the relieving fighter group arrived to take up the escort: the fighters released from escort duty would dive to the deck on the way home, looking for airfields, truck convoys, and railroad trains to strafe.

The order to strafe on the way home kept the *Luftwaffe* from saving their aircraft and aircrews for attacks on Allied air forces that were preparing the way for the impending invasion of France. The Germans knew the invasion was coming soon, but they did not know exactly when or where. This strategy was working; we were destroying hundreds of German aircraft parked at airfields throughout Germany. Unfortunately, it also increased the number of deaths among American fighter pilots and resulted in more of our pilots being captured.

The April 11 mission began for me at 0400 hours, when the squadron intelligence officer banged on my door to tell me to report to the group briefing room. I put on my clothes, jumped on my bicycle, and headed for the briefing room. Lieutenant Colonel Everett Stewart, the group commander, briefed us on the operational part of the mission, and the intelligence officer briefed us on the latest German threats and how they would affect us. The weatherman gave us the local, target-area, and return weather from the target area back to England. He could brief only in general terms on the winds aloft because his information was limited. The British had weather flights off the northern coast of Europe, but reports on the winds aloft for the interior were very inaccurate.

After the group briefing, we pedaled on down to the squadron operations hut for our detailed briefing on how we were to accomplish the mission. The pilots were told who was to fly in each flight position. For example, I was to fly as Blue-4, the number-four position in Blue Flight.

Blue Flight had its own aircraft to maintain, and I was given a P-51B with the squadron letters WR-Z. This was the airplane identification I had been assigned when I joined the 354th Fighter Squadron and the airplane I flew whenever it was ready to fly. This airplane had the "Hun Hunter from Texas" painted on the nose and the number of German aircraft destroyed painted on the side of the fuselage. I had 3.2 German aircraft credited at the time of the April 11 mission.

The Blue Flight commander was Captain Curtis Johnston, with whom I had flown on many occasions in both the P-47 and the P-51.

Because they bore a passing resemblance to the Germans' Bf-109, P-51s had been fired on (and some shot down) by our ground troops when they were first used in combat. To help alleviate the problem, yellow stripes had been painted on the tops and bottoms of the wings and around the vertical stabilizer. This yellow paint job was changed to white-and-black on some camouflaged aircraft.

After all the briefings, the pilots went to the mess hall and had breakfast. It started with orange juice hopped up with vitamins, then powdered eggs, toast, marmalade, and coffee. On occasion, we had creamed hamburger, referred to as S.O.S., or pancakes and syrup. Getting food, and lots of it, was no problem for the aircrews in England. From the mess hall, we went back to the ready room in squadron headquarters, which was a Nissen hut, to check our personal equipment.

All this time, the B-17 and B-24 bombers were getting airborne, forming up, and climbing up to cruising altitude. We got into jeeps and drove out to our aircraft. I talked to the crew chief about the status of my P-51. He informed me that the plane had been run up, the two external fuel tanks checked for proper fuel transfer, that no leaks had been found, and that all fuel tanks had been topped off. I climbed into the cockpit and hooked up the shoulder harness, lap belt, radio, and oxygen hose. At the proper time, I started my engine, the crew chief again checked for leaks, and I taxied out to join the other members of my flight. We took off in elements of two, joined up in a flight of four, then joined up with other flights in the squadron.

The fuel sequence check on the P-51 was very important for safety reasons and as a means of achieving maximum range. After becoming airborne, the fuselage tank is used, then the external wing tanks are used in case they have to be dropped if your plane is bounced by a German fighter. The reason for using forty gallons of fuel from the fuselage tank was to establish the optimal center of gravity, one that would enable us to maintain the stability of the aircraft. If this procedure is not performed immediately, the aircraft could be uncontrollable if subjected to hard and heavy stick forces: it might pitch up, stall, and spin out of control.

The weight of all the fuel on board (approximately 500 gallons), and the 2,000 rounds of .50-caliber armor-piercing and incendiary ammunition, plus the weight of the aircraft itself, could make the P-51B difficult to handle on the take-off roll. Nevertheless, I got off without a problem.

The climb-out and join-up with the bombers was routine, and the weather during the join-up was very good, with only high clouds. The group pilots took up their positions on the bomber force. The 354th Fighter Squadron, led by the 355th Fighter Group commander, took the lead, in front of the bombers. The 357th Fighter Squadron took the left side of the bomber track and at a higher altitude than the 358th Fighter Squadron, which was on the right side of the bomber track. In this configuration, the bombers were surrounded by our fighters, which meant that the Germans had to come through the escort squadrons to get to the bombers.

On the way to Berlin, a group of single-engine and twin-engine aircraft was observed forming up to attack the bombers. My squadron, the

354th, and the 357th dropped fuel tanks and attacked the German force while the 358th stayed with the bombers. Seven twin-engine fighters and two single-engine German fighters were shot down; the rest scattered and dived away to fight another day.

As we approached Berlin, flak began to explode in the bomber formation, but the bombers continued on as planned. After passing over Berlin, the target, Sorau, came into sight and the bombers dropped their bombs right into the middle of the target. Black smoke in the target area indicated that the bombers had caused great damage.

The fighter group assigned to relieve us in escorting the bombers showed up on time, and we left the bombers and headed home.

One of the pilots reported an airfield below—it was Strausberg Airdrome—and Lieutenant Colonel Stewart radioed to the other two squadrons to separate from us and attack other targets. The group leader started his attack on the airfield, and Blue Flight Leader, Captain Johnston, called out that he had the target in sight and for Blue Flight to get into a string formation. That left me on the end of the attacking Blue Flight aircraft.

Johnston increased the dive angle, and our airspeed jumped to more than 300 miles per hour. It had increased to 400 by the time we reached the outer edge of the airfield. The trees were zipping by and looked like a picket fence. Blue Flight paralleled the runway on the attack and eased over toward the aircraft hangars, where many aircraft were parked. Blue Flight Leader headed for the parked aircraft and flamed three in three passes. Blue-2 and Blue-3 were also firing, and I shot up a Ju-52 troop carrier that burst into flames.

The flak was heavy. Johnston called in that he had been hit by ground fire. Then another pilot called in that he was also hit. In all, approximately fourteen German aircraft were left burning. I lost sight of the other Blue Flight aircraft, but I heard Blue Flight Leader say he was going to bail out.

As I circled to make another pass on the airfield, I saw a Ju-88 medium bomber and started firing at it. I got hits all over the aircraft, but it would not burn. A ground target had to burn for a pilot to get credit for a kill. If it didn't burn, I would be credited for a damaged plane.

As I was pulling up from my pass at the Ju-88, I saw an FW-190 taking off on the runway at the far edge of the field. I cut back on the throttle and turned a bit to the left to get in trail with the German fighter. He had retracted his landing gear and flaps, and was picking up speed. I opened my throttle full and closed in on him. I was closing into firing range when he must have seen me or received a radio warning from the ground that I was coming up behind him. At 100 feet off the ground, he started making sharp turns to the left and right, but even so I was reducing the distance between us.

At a range of approximately 250 yards, I put the gunsight aiming point on him and squeezed the trigger. I saw hits on the wing root and around the fuselage, below the canopy. The German slid sideways, and I almost ran into him. I backed off and fired again. Parts flew off the side of his aircraft as bullets firing at a rate of more than eighty rounds per second hit it.

The FW-190 jerked to one side and headed for an open field. It was smoking and flames had begun to come from its left side. It hit the ground at about 200 miles per hour and bounced several times before sliding sideways and coming to a stop. The pilot jumped out and ran for cover to a ditch with a small tree. I banked around and fired at him, and he ran back toward the FW. I made another pass to strafe the crashed aircraft and pilot, who was running all around the aircraft. I finally used up all of my ammo, so I pulled up. I wobbled my wings at the pilot and picked up my navigational heading home.

I checked the fuel gauges and found I had plenty of gas but no ammo. I also determined that I was about 400 miles from home. I knew that Blue Flight Leader had bailed out, so I called Blue-3 and asked for his position. He answered that he was heading home and climbing through 10,000 feet approximately fifty miles west of Berlin. I rogered that. It would be thirty minutes or more before I caught up with the remainder of the flight.

I kept climbing and turned my head around continuously to make sure no Hun was going to attack me, and to see if I could find some other P-51s to join up with. About this time, black puffs of smoke began to pop up around me and I realized the antiaircraft guns around Berlin were firing at me. I dived for the deck to get out of range of the antiaircraft guns, but red balls from small-arms fire were flying all around me. The fire was heavy, so I pulled up again in sharp turns and varied my rate of climb from time to time. I wasn't hit, so I began to climb slowly back to 15,000 feet on a heading home, and again began looking left and right to make sure I was not going to be attacked by the Hun.

Up ahead, I spotted four fighters climbing in formation, so I flew toward them, still looking around to make sure I was not being attacked. I closed on the four fighters and, since they were heading west, I just assumed they were P-51s. It had been a long day. I had fought hard to destroy the Hun's aircraft, but right now I was heading home and had P-51s in sight to join up with.

As I got closer to the four-ship formation, I got a feeling that something was not right. I began thinking: is the vertical stabilizer too small, is the canopy too small, is there a bulge under the wing—a radiator—and should it not be underneath the fuselage? Am I failing to recognize that the four aircraft could be Bf-109s instead of Mustangs? I got closer and I realized that I *had* made a mistake. These *were* 109s! This was not the first time I had made such an error. Months earlier, when the group was still in P-47s, I had been flying on Captain Johnston's wing when we jumped a 109. Johnston fired on the 109 and, when it took evasive action, I saw it was really a P-51! I yelled on the radio that it was a P-51, but Johnston had stopped firing by then. That P-51 was able to fly back to England and the pilot was not injured.

I immediately pulled the throttle back to slow my closure rate and figure out the best escape route. Then I saw two Mustangs crossing in front of the four 109s, which were preparing to attack. I immediately got on the radio and yelled, "Two Mustangs climbing on a western heading, angels twelve or thirteen—there are four one-owe-nines jumping you." But there was no reply. The two were maintaining radio silence. I again yelled, "One-owe-nines are jumping you. Break left, break left!"

The Mustangs suddenly turned sharply to the left. They were still at a disadvantage, but at least they seemed to have heard me. The 109s also turned left and were in a good attack position. I believed if I jammed the throttle full open I could close the gap and blast through the 109 formation to break up the attack.

The two Mustangs, out in front below, were in a sharp left turn, and the 109s were right behind them. I yelled on the radio, "Two Mustangs turning left—keep turning. I'll break into the one-owe-nines at six o'clock." At last there came a reply: "Okay. We've got 'em in sight and we see you."

Of course, all the action taken by the two Mustangs got the 109 pilots alerted that something was going on. The number-three 109 pilot looked to his rear and saw me boring down on his flight. He immediately rolled over and dived for the deck—just as the three other 109s opened fire on the two Mustangs. I yelled for the Mustangs to break right. One of the Mustangs did break right and either spun out or split-essed in a dive for the deck. A moment later, the other Mustang half-rolled and drove for the ground. The three remaining 109 pilots, who were caught flatfooted by the sudden maneuver and knew I was still at their 6 o'clock position, held to their steep turn with me on their tails.

We ended up in a tight Lufberry. They were poor shots. They must have been new pilots, because they put no lead on me when firing. I could see the tracers and white puffs from their 20mm cannon, all in back of me.

When I began to move in extremely close to the tail of the last 109, it flipped over in a split-S and dived for the deck. I could not move any closer to the other 109s without stalling, so I put down ten degrees of flaps, which were called "combat flaps," and rolled the elevator trim to full back. I decided to hold what I had until I ran out of gas and then try to bail out. It seemed that I was closing on the last of the two 109s, and the pilot must have noticed my movement closer to him, for he also split-essed and dived away. That left the German flight commander, who circled a couple of turns before diving for the deck and leaving me all alone.

I reduced power, lifted the flaps, pulled the prop RPM lever back to cruise speed, and started to turn west for home. But I heard a rattling noise, and the aircraft began to shake and shudder. I realized that I was taking hits. I jerked back on the stick and climbed into the 109 that was firing at me. It flashed over me and climbed straight up. I then realized that one of the 109s that had left the Lufberry must have climbed back up to get back into the fight, or that one had stayed outside the circle until I reduced throttle. He fired on me, overshot, and left the fight. I immediately rolled over and dived for the deck in the hope of getting out of sight before he came after me again.

When I got to the deck, I noticed that I could not get a compass reading on my instruments. I looked out at my wing, where the compass was located, and saw holes that the 109 had put in the compass area. I knew I had to have some help to guide me on a westerly heading, so I got on the radio and said, "This is Haywood Blue Four. I just got shot up by a one-owe-nine. Compass knocked out. Will someone who is flying home tell me what position the sun is on the canopy?" In a few seconds, there came a strange voice, unknown to this day, "Put the sun on the second screw from the front on the top left railing." I thanked the guy and started home, checking left and right to see that I was not being attacked. I put the sun on the canopy, as directed.

I got to the coast and could see water through breaks in the clouds. There were no contrails from the bombers and no other aircraft visible. I thought I was in range of the British Air-Sea Rescue Service, so I punched the number-two button on the radio and called for a heading back to England. I was told to continue on the same heading by someone who also said, "I think I have you." Then the voice said, "Make a ninety-degree turn to the left." I made the turn, and the voice said, "We have you. Turn right." I started right, and in a minute or so the voice said, "Stop your turn; you are heading for England. Give me a call in five minutes." The heading I was on before I called Air-Sea Rescue was too far north and I would have gone out into the North Sea had I not been able to reach the rescue unit.

After five minutes, I called Air-Sea Rescue again and was told, "Your heading is good; you will make landfall near Dunwick. To what base are you going?" I said I was going to Steeple Morden, and he put me on a heading to the group airfield. I began my let-down and saw a couple of fighters going my way, so I knew I was getting close to an airfield.

A familiar voice came on the radio and asked how badly I was shot up. I stated that the area of the wing where the remote compass was located was the only place I could see damage, and that everything else seemed to be working.

When I landed, I was told to park the aircraft in front of squadron headquarters for easy access by the mechanics. It was now 1515 hours, and I was very tired, physically and mentally. I needed help getting out of the aircraft, and a crowd was on hand to greet me.

My main thought after several hours was, who were the pilots who had been jumped by the Hun? They were identified as belonging to another squadron. When asked why they had left the fight, they stated, "We were out of ammunition."

Lieutenant Henry Brown was awarded a Distinguished Service Cross because he attacked the four Bf-109s even though he knew his own Mustang's ammunition bays were empty.

Brown was credited with a Bf-109 downed on April 11, and he achieved ace status on April 24, 1944, when he downed two Bf-109s near Munich. He also scored on April 29, when he shot down another Bf-109, and again on May 13, when he downed an Me-210. This made him the 355th Fighter Group's leading ace.

Following a leave at home—he missed the invasion of France—1st Lieutenant Henry Brown added to his score. He shot down three Bf-109s near Kassel on September 11, 1944, a feat for which he was promoted to the rank of captain. Brown next downed a Bf-109 on September 18; and he brought his score to 14.2 aerial victories on September 27 when he downed a pair of FW-190s near Eschwege. At this moment, Brown was the leading Army Air Forces ace in the European Theater.

On October 3, 1944, Captain Henry Brown's P-51 was riddled by ground fire as he was strafing an airfield near Nordlingen, Germany. Brown crash-landed in a field while members of his squadron looked on, and then the squadron commander, Major Chuck Lenfest, a 5.5-victory ace, set down in the same field in the hope of picking up the downed pilot. But Lenfest's P-51 became mired in deep mud, and the two aces headed for the woods and thus failed to see the landing of yet another Mustang, this one flown by Captain Al White, who was able to take off after failing to attract the attention of the two downed pilots. (Superior officers later subjected White to harsh criticism for his heroic action.) Chuck Lenfest and Henry Brown were both captured, and they spent the remainder of the war in captivity. At the time he was downed, Henry Brown had 14.2 official air-to-air victories and 14.5 official ground kills.

Henry Brown remained in the service after World War II and served in numerous assignments until he retired as a colonel in 1974.

♦

NO JOY

1st Lieutenant BUD FORTIER, USAAF
354th Fighter Squadron, 355th Fighter Group
Bremen Area, Germany—May 24, 1944

Norman John Fortier was born in Pelham, New Hampshire, on May 30, 1922, and raised in Nashua. While attending St. Anselm College in Manchester, New Hampshire, he completed both phases of the Civilian Pilot Training program, then dropped out of school in January 1942 to enlist as a U.S. Army Air Corps Flying Cadet.

Fortier attended flight school as a member of Class 43-A. He was commissioned at Spence Field, Georgia, on January 14, 1943, and assigned to the newly formed 355th Fighter Group's 354th Fighter Squadron in Orlando, Florida. The group initially trained in P-40s, but was re-equipped with new P-47 Thunderbolt high-altitude fighters before being shipped to England and assigned to the VIII Fighter Command in July 1943.

On March 6, 1944, 1st Lieutenant Bud Fortier joined two other pilots in the downing of a Bf-109 near Dummer Lake. Then, shortly after the group transitioned to P-51Bs, he shot down a Bf-109 and shared in the downing of another near Munich on April 24. On May 13, Lieutenant Fortier downed a twin-engine bomber (probably a Ju-88) near Landsberg, Germany, and an FW-190 near Bremen.

This mission is etched deep in my memory.

I had been flying combat missions for about ten months, with only the occasional two-day pass to London to ease the strain—and there is considerable doubt in my mind about the therapeutic value of a two-day pass to London. It was a lively town, and we usually came back to base sorely in need of rest and recuperation. But it *was* different, and it *did* serve as a pressure-relief valve.

Occasionally we went elsewhere on pass: Brighton, on the south coast, and the picturesque city of Torquay, near Portsmouth, were favorite alternates to hectic London. Except for these occasional diversions, our lives were limited to the humdrum routine of the base, and the not-so-humdrum routine of combat missions.

On May 24, 1944, the bombers were headed for Berlin. We were to escort them from our rendezvous point, about 100 miles west of the city, to Berlin and back as far as our fuel allowed. The 358th Squadron was leading the group that day, followed by the 357th. We brought up the rear with three flights, and I was leading the third flight.

Shortly after switching over to my external fuel tanks, I knew I had a problem. The ever-increasing aileron trim changes made it obvious that the right external tank wasn't pumping fuel. I checked circuit breakers and tried flicking the switches on and off, but nothing worked; there was no fuel flowing from the right tank. A quick mental calculation convinced me that I could get by without that fuel; I'd simply use all the fuel in the left tank, then drop them both off. I'd have to keep adding aileron trim, but that should pose no great control problem.

The weather was lousy. There were scattered layers of clouds all the way up to at least 30,000 feet. Most of the time we flew between layers, sometimes slipping in and out of cloud patches.

The bombers were about twenty minutes late, so we just milled around at about 29,000 feet, waiting. Finally, three combat wings of B-17s appeared, and we took up our escort positions. Our squadron was with the rear-most box of bombers.

About five minutes from Berlin, we received reports of seventy-five-plus Bf-109s and FW-190s just west of Berlin, at an altitude of about 23,000 feet, climbing toward the bombers. Our group leader told us to stay with the bombers, and he took the other two squadrons ahead to intercept the fighters. By this time, my left wing tank was empty and I had almost full left aileron trim cranked in to keep the wings level.

Our squadron leader called for us to "drop babies" as the radio transmissions from ahead brought back the sounds of a dogfight. I flipped the tank release switch. The empty left tank dropped, but the full right tank stayed on.

"Falcon Blue Leader. Bogeys at four o'clock high," my wingman called. I looked back over my right shoulder and saw two 109s coming toward us in a slanting dive.

"Wait till I call the break," I replied. "We'll break into them at my call."

I didn't want to call the break too soon, because the 109s would simply have broken off the attack and kept going. I wanted them to commit themselves. They'd be coming at us at high speed and, if we could get them turning with us, we'd have them for sure. I know this sounds as if we were cool, ice-in-our-veins pros, but I can assure you that the blood pressure and pulse rate were considerably elevated.

Just as they got into shooting range, I called, "Break right . . . *now!*"

I rammed the stick hard right and pulled back sharply. I had forgotten about that right drop tank. The Mustang shuddered, snap-rolled viciously to the right, and started spinning toward a layer of clouds.

It was a thin layer, and by the time I got through it, I had the airplane under control again. I looked around quickly and saw a fighter right on my tail, about 200 yards behind me, in perfect position for a kill. I yanked the stick to the right and hard back, with the same result that I had gotten the first time—the tank was still attached. I spun through another thin layer of clouds and felt a thump as the wing tank fell off.

I recovered from the spin and immediately went into a sharp left turn, because of the extra aileron trim I had cranked in to compensate for the full tank. I looked back, and there was that fighter still sitting directly behind me! I tightened the turn as much as I could.

"Relax, Bud. It's only me." It was 2d Lieutenant Herbert Fritts, my wingman. How he had managed to stay with me during those wild gyrations, I'll never know.

By this time, we had no chance of rejoining the group or finding the bombers. After all my spin exercises, we were below 10,000 feet; I could see the ground through breaks in the clouds. "Might as well go home on the deck," I thought.

We headed down in a gradual high-speed dive and turned to a westerly heading for England. As we passed through 2,000 feet, I spotted a freight train a few miles to our left. At that stage of the war, it was open season on all German trains and trucks, so I told Fritts to get in a trail position and follow me in. We made a low pass over the locomotive to give the engineers a chance to bail out—and to check for flak—and then we came around on our firing run.

I lined up the gunsight on the front end of the locomotive and squeezed the trigger on the stick. I watched as flashes from the API (armor-piercing incendiary) shells seemed to crawl up the side of boiler. A huge column of steam shot straight up from the locomotive. I flew through the steam, and since there was no sign of flak or small-arms fire, I pulled into a climbing turn to the left to see how Fritts was doing.

I saw his plane streaking toward the train, firing as he came. As he passed over the steaming boiler, I saw his aircraft lurch as it struck the top of it, then smash to the ground beyond it in a ball of bright yellow-orange flame. I knew there was no way he could have survived that crash.

Through my shock, I felt a great weariness descend on me. I was tired. Tired of flying. Tired of the war. And tired of seeing young lives snuffed out in a ball of fire.

Alone now, and shaken, I started a climb through the layers of clouds. I leveled off at about 20,000 feet, still in the overcast, headed for England. I figured it would be safer to stay in the clouds as much as I could. The thick stratus layer of clouds provided smooth flying. The silent gloom of the clouds and the purring of the engine were a soothing balm for my frayed nerves.

Sudden flashes of red-orange light shattered my reverie as the jarring thumps of antiaircraft shells bursting too close jolted me back to reality. I jammed the throttle full and started a climbing turn to the right, straightened out for about thirty seconds, then executed another turn while still climbing. It was all I could do: change headings and altitude. That, and pray.

After about two minutes, which seemed more like an hour, the flak decreased, then stopped. I throttled back and resumed my original heading. I learned later that I had blundered over Bremen, a large, well-defended German city.

England was socked in, as usual. After an instrument approach, I landed in a drizzling rain. The sopping English countryside looked dreary and dark, matching my mood.

At the debriefing, our flight surgeon took one look at me and said, "I'm sending you to the Flak Home!"

The "Flak Home" was a peaceful, rural estate in southern England, where aircrew could spend one week completely isolated from the war. No uniforms, no rank, no schedules, no pressure—just quiet days of reading, chess, golf, horseback riding, a few beers at the local pubs. A time to get it all back together.

I guess I needed that.

On June 6, 1st Lieutenant Bud Fortier shot down a Ju-87 near Chartres, France, and on July 20, 1944, Fortier, now a captain, achieved ace status when he downed a Bf-109 near Oschatz, Germany.

Bud Fortier returned to the 354th Fighter Squadron following home leave in August 1944, and he was commanding the squadron with the rank of major when the war in Europe ended. In his 112 combat missions and 457 combat hours, his aircraft sustained damage only once.

Fortier returned to school after the war, then flew war-surplus aircraft for several civilian non-scheduled airlines. Within three months of joining Northwest Orient Airlines, he was recalled to active duty in 1947 to take part in the Berlin Airlift. Bud Fortier remained in the service until retiring with the rank of lieutenant colonel in 1964, and thereafter served his community as a school teacher and principal.

THE INVASION

1st Lieutenant WILLIE Y ANDERSON, USAAF
353d Fighter Squadron, 354th Fighter Group
Normandy—June 6, 1944

Born in a log cabin in Kramfors, Sweden, on June 28, 1922, William "Y" Anderson was less than a month old when he arrived in the United States and settled with his parents in Chicago. On graduating from high school in June 1939, Anderson worked as an auto mechanic until he enlisted in the U.S. Army Air Corps on September 11, 1941. He passed his aviation cadet examination and trained as an aircraft mechanic while awaiting a posting to flight school.

Second Lieutenant Anderson graduated from Luke Field on September 28, 1942, and was assigned to the 20th Fighter Group. When that unit was split, Anderson was transferred to Tonopah, Nevada, on January 20, 1943, as an original member of the 354th Fighter Group's 353d Fighter Squadron.

Although Lieutenant Anderson claimed an Me-210 on April 1, 1944, his first official victory award was for an FW-190 he downed near

Darmstadt, Germany, on April 14. He next downed a Bf-109 over Neuhaldensleben.

June 6, 1944. D Day."Come on, Lootenant, you gotta get up. The colonel says we got a mission" I sat up and promptly hit my head on something hard and solid. God, I can't see; my damn eyes are glued shut. I pulled off my gauntlets and spit on my finger to rub the gook that the ole Sandman had put in my eyelashes. Finally got to where I could see enough to let remembrance flow back into my soggy brain. I was under the sink on the concrete floor of the mess hall of the emergency field we had been diverted to after last evening's mission, on account of bad weather over the Channel and our own field. We had landed around 2300 hours last night, and by the time we debriefed, ate a Spam sandwich, and drank a cup of coffee, it was almost 0130 hours. The warmest place that I could find was under that sink, where the hot water had been running.

After briefing, we went out to pre-flight our airplanes. There were no ground crews to do it for you here; they were back at our home base. We had to drain water from fuel tanks, check oil and Prestone, and top off our fuel tanks. It was a dirty job, especially if you were tired and cold. After I had finished my chores and warmed up my engine, I had twenty-two minutes left before takeoff. I sat in my cockpit, smoking a last cigarette, listening to my warm engine cooling down. I'd shut it down to save fuel. It was just before daybreak, with hazy cold rain squalls passing by. I couldn't help but shiver. It was a grim morning.

After we had taken off and kept our rendezvous with the gliders, we began flying our lazy-eight pattern over them. That placed fighters on either side of them, to the front, and to the rear—in good position to fend off an attack by German fighters.

About fifteen minutes out from the beachhead, the sun broke through a big hole in the clouds and it looked beautiful down there along the coast. There were green grass and houses, and very little destruction, except where ack-ack batteries and long-range coastal guns had been knocked out.

The weather closed in again, so we dropped down from 700 feet to be with the gliders at about 500 feet. I was pretty nervous about flying that low and that slow along the French coast, but it turned out to be the first time in more than forty missions that I didn't run into any flak. Amazing!

I could see a sunken ship just off a beach. There didn't appear to be anyone aboard, but an oil slick indicated that it had been sunk only recently. The water was so shallow that the superstructure stuck out, but we were unable to tell if it was one of ours or one of theirs. Just the other side of the beach was a barrier built from coils of barbed wire stretching as far as the eye could see. And a little ways inland was a road on which we spotted a motor convoy. I wondered for a split second if it was ours or theirs.

By this time, the C-47s had begun to spread out and release their hitchhikers. Most of the gliders, when cut free, headed straight for what looked like a postage stamp and plopped it in. A few did some fancy turns to line themselves up for a cushy landing. Some overshot their targeted field and crashed into fences, brick walls, and trees. A few even ran into each other, and this of course was quite catastrophic. Wings were torn off, fuselages broke right in half, wings buckled, tails flew off.

One glider overshot its field and hit a clump of trees. It immediately burst into flame and burned like a thermite bomb for about thirty seconds. Then it smoldered and gave off a long black plume of smoke that rose into the clouds. I'm pretty sure that no one got out of that glider alive.

Some of the gliders used parachutes as brakes. The chutes would blossom out and, just as the gliders touched the ground, I could see the ungainly ships break speed to settle in almost on the spot.

In most cases, soldiers ran out of the gliders, including the many crashed gliders, within moments of landing, and they all literally melted into the countryside. In about ten seconds, there was no one in sight from any given glider. We were unable to see if there was any immediate contact between our glider infantry and friendly troops who were already there, but it was apparent that there was no contact with the enemy in this area.

Once released from towing their gliders, the C-47s circled back across the drop zone, tossing out supplies in blue, red, purple, orange, and yellow parachutes. These chutes were scattered for miles, hanging in trees and off telephone wires, lying in fields, and even dangling off roofs.

I spotted a farmer plowing a field that was littered with colored parachutes. He just kept going along, seemingly oblivious to the war going on around him.

I could see lots of people in the streets of small towns and in wagons on the roads. There were cows in the fields and livestock in the yards. Smoke was rising from chimneys. It did not seem possible that the great Allied invasion was taking place not too far away. There were no signs of destruction down there. It was just too peaceful.

After dropping their supplies, the C-47s headed back toward the English coast. As we were heading home, we could see that the stream of C-47s and gliders was still coming in from England; it seemed to stretch all the way back across the Channel.

Upon crossing out over the beaches, the peaceful scene disappeared. There were what seemed to be thousands of ships and boats, many flying large aerial balloons from their decks. There were destroyers, battleships, cruisers, and supply ships of all kinds along the coast.

The C-47s in our care flew right on the deck all the way home. That low, when something goes wrong, the best and safest thing to do is ditch. And that's what some of them did. The Channel was dotted with quite a few C-47s and gliders. A C-47 struck the water with a huge splash and skipped a couple of times like a flat rock. Then one wing went down, slewing the airplane around. Then the nose dug in for an instant and quickly popped out again. The crew was out within thirty seconds, paddling away in dinghies. The Air-Sea Rescue boats certainly had their hands full this day, but they were quick. In a few cases, they arrived to pick up C-47 crewmen before the crewmen really had a chance to get their feet wet.

Down below, also, we could see thousands of ships and boats shuttling between England and France. And there were destroyers and cruisers escorting them all along the way. We were really piling stuff into the invasion beaches. Tremendous numbers of aircraft were in the air—fighters, transports, gliders, and bombers of every type and description, each and every one of them sporting its special invasion recognition stripes. We could see whole squadrons fly right through other squadrons proceeding in the opposite direction, and guys doing snap rolls to the right or left to get out of the way. It was very chaotic, very exciting.

We were all pretty belligerent out there; we were aching for Jerry to show his nose. But none of them dared to show up.

After three hours and fifteen minutes of this escort duty, we returned to our own base, Boxted, in Colchester, and got debriefed, had a bite to eat, and took a snooze.

Lieutenant Willie Y Anderson downed two Me-410s on June 21, 1944, and achieved ace status when he downed a Bf-109 near Tours on August 1. On August 7, he brought his final tally to seven when he shot down a pair of Bf-109s over Mayene.

Anderson was rotated back to the United States in October 1944 and served as a combat-tactics instructor for West Point cadets at Stewart Field, New York, until he took his discharge from the service in May 1945. He was immediately hired by United Airlines, and he flew airliners for United until he retired in 1981.

MASSACRE AT MIELEC

1st Lieutenant ERNIE SHIPMAN, USAAF
307th Fighter Squadron, 31st Fighter Group
Mielec, Poland—July 25, 1944

Ernest Shipman was born in Jackson Heights, New York, on April 6 1923. He graduated from flight school as a second lieutenant in April 1943 and was assigned to fly P-40s in the Panama Canal Zone with the Sixth Air Force's 24th Fighter Squadron. Later he flew P-39s with the 51st Fighter Squadron in the Galapagos Islands.

In the Spring of 1944, following his tour in the quiet backwaters of the war, 2d Lieutenant Ernie Shipman was assigned to the veteran 31st Fighter Group, which was then transitioning from Spitfires to P-51s in preparation for serving combat escort duty with the new Fifteenth Air Force. His first aerial victory, an Italian Air Force Fiat G.50 fighter, was scored over Ploesti, Romania, on May 5, 1944. On June 13, 1944, Lieutenant Shipman shared in the downing of an Me-210 twin-engine fighter over Landshut, Austria; and he shared in the downing of a Bf-109 on June 26. Thereafter, Ernie Shipman was credited with downing an Bf-109 over Budapest on July 2, and an FW-190 on July 7. He achieved ace status when he downed a Bf-109 on July 21, 1944.

I scored my last two victories on the same mission. This mission was unusual and needs some explanation. The Eighth and Fifteenth air forces had begun, with the cooperation of the Russians, a series of task force missions that came to be known as "shuttle missions." Initially, B-17s of the Eighth Air Force in England had flown to Russia, then to Italy, and finally back to England in a triangular circuit. After this first mission, a task force was sent from Italy, but after spending several days in Russia, it came directly back to Italy. Our group, the 31st Fighter Group, was part of the third task-force mission to Russia. This mission was unique in that it was an all-fighter force that went out. Our group, equipped with Mustangs, flew as top cover for two groups of P-38s. All three groups went on to Russia and stayed there for about a week. It was on a mission from Russia, on July 25 1944, that I shot down two enemy aircraft.

On this particular day, the 31st Fighter Group's assignment was to fly top cover for one of the two P-38 groups while it strafed a German airfield at Mielec, Poland. The early part of the mission went off as planned. We stayed around until the 38s left the target after starting a number of fires, and then we left for our temporary Russian base at Piryatin. We were quite close to the front on the German side, and the *Wehrmacht* was in full retreat. There wasn't a cow path that wasn't clogged with men and vehicles. Our guns were full of ammunition, and the enemy was literally crawling over the ground below us, but we did not attack. This was because of orders that had come down from the top. I believe our mission to Russia was as much to impress the Russians with the power and the glory of the United States Army Air Forces as it was to inflict losses on the Germans. I had the impression that we were to go to Russia in one piece, fly pretty formations, and come home in one piece. For this reason, Captain Sam Brown, whose element I was leading, simply kept acknowledging the frequent references to the troops below that he was receiving from the rest of us. Finally, however, we went down after them. After three firing passes, we pulled up and headed for home.

We were on course for only a short time when someone sighted enemy aircraft and called them out. Lieutenant Colonel Yancey Tarrant, the group commanding officer, immediately got nasty on the radio and said we were over Russian lines and the planes were probably Russian—and for us to stop clowning around. I have no idea how he knew this; the squadron he was leading was not in sight at the time. As soon as Colonel Tarrant got off the air, an unidentified voice came on saying,"Russian, hell, these planes are Stukas."

It was just then that I saw them, black angular ships, swooping low over what appeared to be a mill by the side of a stream. One look convinced me that our squadron, which numbered twelve ships that day, was heavily outnumbered. On the other hand, the enemy ships were Stukas, and they were heavily out-gunned by the P-51s; they were a flock of sitting ducks. The enemy planes were dive-bombing in threes, a stunt I had never seen before. The building they were attacking shuddered with the impact of their bombs as each wave pulled up from its bomb run.

We were at 2,000 feet and approaching at what was about 10 o'clock to them. Sam Brown peeled off in a diving turn to the left, and the rest of us followed. What happened in the next five minutes will always be a little confused in my mind.

We hit them at the third or fourth wave back from the lead ships. I noticed that the Stukas had stopped making bomb runs and were salvoeing their bombs.

My curve of pursuit brought me out on the tail of a Stuka, and I opened fire. My first burst went wild, but a little correction put my guns right on the target. In spite of the hits I was getting on the fuselage, the enemy aircraft showed no ill effects. I fired again. Before I had a chance to see what happened, I saw tracers going by my canopy, so I broke around to the left. The ship whose tracer I had seen was a P-51. He was shooting at the same Stuka I was and I had been clumsy enough to get between him and his target. I never found out who that eager beaver was.

There were plenty of other enemy ships in the neighborhood, so I chose the nearest one and again opened fire. He began to smoke almost immediately. It looked as though I almost had one in the bag when tracers began to come over my canopy again. After what had just happened, I decided to ignore the tracers. I was on the point of getting this Stuka, and whoever was behind me could look for his own; the sky was full of them. I took another squirt at the plane ahead of me and then noticed something about the tracer arching over my head. Instead of the usual two lines of tracer that we fired for aiming purposes, there were four or more coming from behind me. I looked over my shoulder into the gaping air scoop of a Stuka. The model we were attacking carried two 20mm cannons, one under each wing. These were blazing away, accompanied by machine guns in the wing roots. (Besides being a dive-bomber, these Stukas were used for strafing, which requires heavy armament.) I got the hell out of there fast. The only reason I didn't "get it" there on the spot was, I suppose, that the pilot had little experience at air-to-air gunnery, because he was trained to fly a type of plane that was used exclusively for attacking ground targets.

Almost immediately, I found myself in a pass to the right on three more of them. I opened fire at 90 degrees on the lead ship and got some strikes in the engine and the front cockpit. Flames belched from his belly, and he flew out of my line of sight. I tried to shift over to the second ship of the group of three. We were all turning as tight as possible. The Stuka can make a mighty tight turn, and I was really wasting ammo, because I couldn't pull enough lead. I closed as much as I could and began to break away.

The third Stuka was in a vertical bank to the right. As I pulled up, I looked over at him. Looking down into the cockpit, I could see the pilot and the rear gunner, both of whom were looking up at me. Then the German wrenched his ship into a bank that could only crash his ship straight into mine. I pulled back on my own stick harder than I ever had before. The Stuka rolled up at me and disappeared under me. The last thing I saw of it was its left wing, black with a white cross on it, as it arched toward my plane. I stared, fascinated, at my right wing, expecting to see it dissolve as that Stuka went through it. In a second the danger was past, for my wing remained as big and beautiful as it ever had been.

This episode rattled me, but not to the point where a passing Stuka had no appeal. I started after him and noticed that he was smoking and wobbling badly. I assumed that he was on his way to auguring in, which he was. Another was not far from this one; it was taking off for the tall timber. I screamed down on him from above, not realizing that in so doing I was giving his rear gunner a beautiful shot. I was getting fine hits up and down his fuselage when I felt something hit my ship with a severe jolt that was more of a shock wave than a sound. I stopped firing and thought to myself, "I'm hit." Nevertheless, my controls responded and my engine sounded okay, so I decided that the damage couldn't be too serious. The Stuka was still in front of me, so I went back to work on it. But then smoke began seeping into the cockpit. I was on fire.

I forgot about the Stuka and everything else. The only thing I thought of was getting out of that machine before the tanks went. I pulled up, since at all times during this engagement, I had not been above 2,000 feet, and the hills in the area were up to 800 feet high. I wanted to bail out, but I paused in my stampede, because I did not know whether I should roll over, drop out of my seat, and then open the canopy, or whether I should jettison the canopy and then roll over and drop out.

It may sound silly, but that minor conflict kept me in the plane long enough for the fire to burn itself out. I realized suddenly that I would not have to bail out after all, for the smoke was subsiding. When I realized this, I banked over to take a look at the Stuka I had been after. As I watched, it crashed in flames against a hill. Simultaneously, the smoking Stuka I had passed up crashed and exploded not fifty yards away.

I checked my tail and, seeing that it was clear, took a look around. The Stukas had disappeared, and so had the squadron. On the ground, in the vicinity of the two crashed planes I had shot down were eight or ten other burning planes. I had never seen anything like it. With my ship in the condition it was in, I decided to head for home.

As I turned to get on the course for home, I began scanning the sky ahead for the squadron. I soon spotted several P-51s and began to gain on them. As I approached, a flight of Russian P-39s came over the 51s ahead of me and started into a dive after them. They were making a pass from the rear, and that brought them close to me. When I was sure that they could see me, I waggled my wings like hell. The lead 39 waggled acknowledgment, and the Russians swung off to our right and were soon gone.

I was closing the gap between my ship and the ships ahead when another 51 came up from the left. By an odd coincidence, it was my wingman. I was surprised and relieved to see him. We closed up with the other ships and continued on course for home. Then I began checking on my battle damage. My hydraulic pressure was at zero, there were several holes in my wings, and the joints around the cover of the ammunition box on my right wing were smoke-stained. There was a hole in this cover, and from these signs, I concluded, wrongly, that a stray slug had set off some rounds in the ammunition boxes, causing the smoke that had given me such a scare.

Between the strafing, the Stukas, and the length of the mission, none of us had an overabundance of fuel when we reached Piryatin. Though no one was making emergency landings because of dwindling gas reserves, there were some emergencies from people who had been shot up. With my hydraulic pressure at zero, I knew that my gear would not lower in the usual way and that I would have to rock it down. This involved putting the gear handle in the down position and allowing gravity to pull the gear into place. When I felt the gear hit bottom, I rocked the ship wildly to throw the weight of the oleo struts into a fully down position. This causes the spring-loaded locking pins to snap into place, which locks the gear in the down position. I did not call in for an emergency landing, because I wanted to give others with immediate problems a chance to land first. There really wasn't any need for me to get on the ground quickly.

I told my wingman to keep an eye on my wheels when I put them down. We went into our landing peel-off, I went through the procedure to lower the gear. My wingman, who was flying behind and below me, where he could see my wheels, called back that they looked down and locked. But as I glided down toward the landing strip, a red flare arched up in front of me. I poured on the coal and went around. I wondered if my wheels *were* down as I rocked the ship all over the sky. On my next try, I got another red flare. My gas was getting dangerously low now, so when I got a flare on my third pass, I called the tower to ask whether my wheels looked down and locked. The tower operator called back assuring me that they were. I then asked, "Why all the red flares?"

The tower came back blandly with the answer that my flaps weren't down. The flaps, like the wheels, are hydraulically operated, and zero hydraulic pressure means no flaps. I got on the radio and told the tower that my hydraulic system was shot out. If I recall correctly, my exact words were a bit more expressive and left no doubt about my displeasure with such nonsense. I then landed without any greater mishap than several good bounces. This business about the flaps is a good example of how far the asinine regulations of the swivel-chair Air Force back in the States could reach.

As I sat filling out my Form 1, the crew chief, who had been inspecting my plane, climbed up on the wing root next to the cockpit with an excited expression on his face. He wanted me to take a look at the battle damage to my ship. I undid my lap belt and shoulder straps, and stepped down and very quickly discovered what had got him so excited.

The smoke I had mistaken for a hit in the ammunition box had actually come from a burning gas line in the right wing. An incendiary bullet had neatly severed the gas lead from my right drop-tank installation. The gas in the line had been set on fire and would certainly have fired the whole ship if the drop tank had been attached. As it was, a fire must have burned gaily for thirty seconds or so in the wheel well, not more than a few inches from the rubber tire.

The slug that had clipped the gas line was about the size of a .30-caliber round. I assumed at the time that it was from the rear gun of the Stuka I was attacking, but it may have been a Russian bullet. I say this because there was quite a bit of tracer coming from the ground, which was Russian-held territory. During our squadron's attack on the enemy planes, the Germans, after salvoeing their bombs, were bailing out one after the other. As soon as they got clear of their ships they would open their chutes. Immediately, streams of tracer from the ground would cross and recross the forms of the Germans as they hung under the canopies of their open chutes. It may have been a slug from a gun of the Russian ground forces that hit my gas line. It may also have been a Russian slug that went into my other wing, splitting open the hydraulic actuating piston of my left landing gear, causing the thump I had felt earlier. I still think that the Stuka shot me up, but I will never be completely sure, because those Russians were shooting at everything. There were several other holes in my plane, in the nose and around the wing roots. Their angles of entry indicated more than one source. I know positively of only one Stuka shooting at me, but the evidence of the bullet holes indicated two or more directions from which the firing had come.

My gun-camera films were fairly clear. They recorded the strafing of the enemy vehicles and, along with the films of others in the squadron, dozens of enemy planes. One of my films came close to giving me heart failure a week or so after we were safely back at our base in Italy. My camera showed a Stuka at fairly close range with one or two others farther ahead of it and off to the sides. Toward the end of that particular sequence, the scene shifted downwards revealing another Stuka, which appeared huge on the screen. That one had been out of sight under my nose, and with his rear gunner working away furiously, as all the while I was firing at the Stuka ahead of him. Until we ran off the films, I had no idea he was there, or how close he was. In my combat report, I claimed two destroyed and several damaged.

The total count of enemy planes downed by our squadron was twenty-one Stukas. We did not lose a plane. The final count of enemy planes present during the engagement came to eighty-five or so. This force was broken down into two large groups of fifty and thirty Stukas, and some top cover consisting of FW-190 fighters. The 190s took off as soon as we started our attack on the main body of the Stukas. It was the group of fifty that took all the losses, as the smaller group was spotted only when we were leaving for home. We might have gone after them if we hadn't been ordered to proceed to base. As it was, we put half of the fifty Stukas out of the war, for certainly some of those that did not go down were badly damaged. I have gone into much detail concerning the particulars of this fight because, to my knowledge, it constituted one of the biggest mass shoot-downs of enemy aircraft in World War II.

On July 30, 1944, 1st Lieutenant Ernie Shipman was shot down near Budapest—by a Fifteenth Air Force P-38. He spent the rest of the war as a prisoner. After the war, Shipman completed his bachelor's degree at Columbia College in 1948 and a master's degree at Columbia in 1950. He served with the New York Air National Guard until leaving the service in 1957 with the rank of major.

Ernie Shipman passed away in 1987.

DESCENT INTO HELL

Captain TOM MALONEY, USAAF
27th Fighter Squadron, 1st Fighter Group
Near Aix-en-Provence, France—August 19–September 1, 1944

Thomas Edward Maloney was born in Cushing, Oklahoma, on March 21, 1923. He enlisted in the Army Air Corps shortly after graduating from high school and was inducted on June 13, 1941. He qualified for flight instruction in early 1942 and began training in September of that year. Cadet Maloney completed Primary flight training at Thunderbird Field, Arizona, in March 1943; Basic at Pecos, Texas, in May 1943; and Advanced at Williams Field, Arizona. He was commissioned as a second lieutenant and pinned on his wings as a member of Class 43-G at Williams Field on July 2, 1943.

Second Lieutenant Maloney was selected for fighters, and was trained in P-38s at Muroc Army Air Base and Lomita Air Force Station, California, then departed the United States in September 1943, bound for North Africa. He was assigned as a replacement pilot to the veteran 1st Fighter Group's 27th Fighter Squadron, then a part of the Twelfth Air Force. Based at Mateur, Tunisia, the 1st Fighter Group had served chiefly as escort for medium bombers flying against tactical targets in Italy. However, on December 9, the 1st Fighter Group was transferred to the new Fifteenth Air Force and assigned to long-range escort duties for B-24s and B-17s attacking strategic targets throughout southern Europe.

Tom Maloney drew first blood on March 28, 1944, when he shot down a Bf-109 (and probably shot down a second) over Italy. On April 23, he shot down two Me-110s (and damaged a Bf-109) while escorting heavy bombers over Hungary and Austria. Next, on May 28, 1944, he shot down a Do-217 medium bomber over Buzim, Yugoslavia, and on May 31, 1944, he achieved ace status when he shot down a Bf-109 while escorting the heavy bombers over Ploesti, Romania. First Lieutenant Maloney's sixth victory credit was for an FW-190 he downed over Oberstdorf, Germany, on July 18; and he rounded out his score with a pair of Bf-109s he shot down near St. Tropez, France, on August 15, 1944. By doing so, he became the 27th Fighter Squadron's highest-

scoring ace of the war, a distinction that one of his squadronmates would subsequently match but none would exceed.

During the Allied invasion of southern France, which commenced on August 15, 1944, two P-38 groups—the 1st and the 14th—were sent on detached service from Foggia, Italy, to Corsica in order to support the landings. The main reason for the P-38 being there was to fly cover over the beachhead. It was felt they were easily recognizabe to Allied troops as friendly planes, which meant that trigger-happy American, British, and French gunners on the ground wouldn't be shooting at us, as they had done in earlier landing operations.

I would like to comment briefly on the plane we flew, the Lockheed P-38 Lightning fighter. Many aviation writers tend to downplay the effectiveness of the P-38 because of the various troubles and lack of success endured by the three Eighth Air Force fighter groups flying the P-38 out of England. I was fortunate to be given some insight into their problem when I was sent to England along with five squadronmates to bring back three-month-old P-38s from a group that was getting the latest model. As it was, this group's old P-38s were newer models than what we had! I was reunited there with many of my Class 43-G classmates who had been assigned to this group before it was shipped overseas. These pilots were scared to death. They had many engine failures, suffered from a lack of leadership, and suffered especially from a lack of combat experience. The entire group had started combat with no experience, and the pilots gained it only as they went. By contrast, I was fortunate to be sent to one of the very first units to fly the P-38 in combat, so when we went on missions, the 27th Fighter Squadron was composed of experienced pilots with fifty or more missions, as well as new pilots with few to no missions.

I have never encountered a pilot who flew the P-38 in combat who didn't love the plane, and that included many who also flew the P-51. In fairness, I must say that the P-38's engines were very touchy and needed to be handled with kid gloves. Most writers overlook the fact that the P-51 was originally the A-36 ground-support fighter, and that the A-36 used the same Allison engine the P-38 used. The A-36 was certainly no great shakes as a fighter. I've always wondered what the P-38 could have been with two Merlin engines, the same engines the P-51 finally received.

The flying characteristics of the P-38 were superb. It was gentle as a lamb, gave plenty of notice of a stall, and could turn with any fighter except the Spitfire and the Zero. Plus, its counter-rotating props eliminated the problem of torque so common to single-engine fighters. Very early in its operational history, the P-38 developed a reputation for being very difficult to fly. This wasn't the case, but being the first really high-performance fighter to enter service in the Army Air Forces caused it to be feared by many people who felt it was too complicated for one man to fly.

On the morning of August 19, 1944, I flew a beachhead cover mission, and that afternoon our new squadron commander, Major Frank Pope, wanted to lead a four-ship flight from the 27th on a dive-bombing mission that was led by a four-ship 94th Fighter Squadron flight commanded by Captain Ed LaClare. The target was a railroad bridge in the city of Avignon, just below the confluence of the Durance and Rhone rivers. There was the possibility we might be intercepted by German fighters that far north of the invasion area. Major Pope had flown a tour in Alaska prior to joining the 27th as its CO, and he didn't have much combat experience with the Germans at this time. I was the 27th Squadron's operations officer, and the most experienced pilot in the group, so I thought it was advisable for me to fly the mission as Major Pope's element leader, in case we were jumped. This was my sixty-fourth combat mission.

The mission proceeded as planned, but with only fair results. Since we carried only one bomb apiece and had used belly tanks most of the way to the target, we still had practically full internal fuel tanks. One of the 94th Squadron P-38s developed a problem during the dive-bombing and returned to base, but the rest of us went looking for targets of opportunity by following the rail line leading to the west-southwest looking for a train or military trucks to shoot up.

We skirted Nimes and proceeded down the railroad line, and in short order we came upon a train in a small station later identified as Le Cres. The locomotive appeared to be taking on water. First the locomotive was disabled by our guns. The cars it was pulling appeared to be flatcars loaded with German Army trucks, a tank or two, and other military gear. This small station was in relatively open country and there were no soldiers visible in the area. There was no evidence that anyone was firing at us.

Because the train seemed to be carrying valuable military cargo, our mission leader, Ed LaClare, made a decision to violate our strafing code of one pass only. I agreed with him. We formed a circle and took out each rail car in order. Quite a number of the rail cars exploded, which caused us to fly through the resulting fire storm. The debris this created was like flak.

As I came off my third target, a 94th Squadron plane which was third in the circle flew straight ahead with its right engine on fire. Since he was the last 94th plane, no one in his own flight saw him go, so I flew up just behind him on the right and urged him to bail out. After about five miles, the pilot made a left 170-degree turn and belly-landed on a fairly level area. He went running off the wing before the airplane came to a complete stop. I didn't know until many years later that the pilot was 1st Lieutenant Dick Arrowsmith, and that he successfully evaded capture, was later led back to our lines by French Resistance fighters, and returned to his squadron to finish his combat tour.

As I was returning to the train, my right engine began knocking. A check of the oil pressure and temperature revealed that I'd lost the oil from that engine, so I feathered the propeller and called Major Pope to inform him that I was heading out to the Mediterranean and returning to Corsica. The major and the other two 27th Squadron planes broke off their strafing passes to escort me.

After about ten minutes, I noticed that my left engine nacelle had oil dripping from it. A check of the oil pressure revealed I'd soon lose that engine, too. I was five or six miles off the French coast, and there was a solid overcast at about 800 feet. I decided to land in the water, even though there were waves crossing my line of flight. I had no trouble landing on the crest of a wave after I jettisoned my canopy, but I immediately discovered that the P-38 floats like a crowbar.

My dinghy was attached to my Mae West by means of a woven half-inch strand, and as I jerked on the strand it appeared the dinghy wouldn't separate from the parachute pack and was going to take me under with it.

After a frantic last pull, it came up, and I inflated it. What a surprise! The dinghy was just large enough so that one side fit under my knees and the other side was below my shoulders. Only my head and knees were out of the water.

The three P-38s from my flight stayed over me as long as their fuel permitted. Shortly after the last one left, two ships came up over the horizon, moving slowly toward me from the direction of our beachhead. Though it was near dusk when they arrived, it appeared at first that the nearer ship was going to run right over me, but as it came closer I could see that it was 150 to 200 yards seaward of me. I could see sailors on deck looking for me, but the swells kept me from their sight. They slowly sailed past me about a mile, turned around to seaward, and came back. But they never came as close as on the first pass. It was dark by then, but they stayed in the area at least another hour, shooting flares and lighting up the sea. Eventually they left, and I was alone on a pitch black night.

Much later, near midnight, I began hearing breakers, faintly at first and then louder. It dawned on me that the tide and waves coming from the south had washed me to shore. I knew that I went down roughly twenty-five miles west of Marseille, and since this was four days after the invasion, I thought the shoreline here would probably be heavily patrolled by German soldiers. Nevertheless, I made it ashore without incident. I was quite tired and sleepy because I had been up since 0600 hours and had flown two missions, but I needed to find someplace to hide my dinghy and Mae West. If these were found by a sentry at daybreak, the Germans would surely know that someone had made a mini-invasion during the night.

I crept cautiously inland, looking for some shrubs in which I could hide the dinghy and Mae West and conceal myself so that I wouldn't waken to someone prodding me with a gun. The night was so dark, I could not see my hand in front of my face.

I had moved inland between fifty to seventy-five feet when I froze at the sound of a *click,* like someone working the bolt of a rifle.

On the ship that had carried me from the United States to North Africa, I had had plenty of time to think about going to war. I often thought how very lucky I was to be a pilot. I was glad I wasn't going to be in a submarine, where I could be drowned or marooned forever; and

I was glad I wasn't an infantryman, who would have to contend with land mines he couldn't see. Immediately after hearing the *click,* I realized one of my two worst fears was about to be realized.

The mine that went off under me shattered both of my feet, and inflicted compound fractures in both legs just above the ankles. In addition, several large pieces of metal had been driven into my left knee, gaping holes had been torn in both legs from the calves to the hips, a piece of metal had cut through my left bicep and numbed my arm, my face was torn by shrapnel and powder-burned, and my pantslegs had been blown off six inches below the waist.

I was aware of a king-size hotfoot on my left foot. My right shoe was blown off, but my left shoe had remained on. When I tried to remove the left shoe, I found the foot had been impaled by a shard of the mine that had penetrated the bottom of the shoe, gone through the foot, and on through the top of the shoe. The pain was unbearable, but I had to pull the shard back through the bottom of the left shoe in order to remove the shoe.

My escape kit was still attached to my belt, so I opened it and found a little tube of sulfathiazole ointment. I spread the pitifully small contents of the tube on the wounds I could feel on my feet; then I passed out.

When I awoke on the morning of August 20, I saw that I had come ashore on a quite level, somewhat sandy area covered with very low scrubby vegetation. There was no one around. Very close to me were several trip wires for more mines. Knowing I was seventy-five or more miles behind enemy lines, it seemed to me that there was no hope of my being rescued. Having been raised a good Catholic boy, I said as good an Act of Contrition as I could and resigned myself to dying there.

The truth is, few of those who made it through the war are luckier than I am to be alive. By all odds, I should be dead.

On the morning of the second day, I tried to get a drink from the canteen in my escape kit, but it was empty. For the rest of the day, I alternately passed out and woke up. I was conscious for short periods only.

During the third and fourth days—August 21 and 22—it became apparent that I was going to die of thirst, if not from my wounds, so I started moving toward a two- or three-foot rise that had a row of bushes on top. The bushes were about fifty feet away. I would pick up one leg, set it down, then move the other, all the while being careful not to hit another mine or tripwire as I dragged myself along. Because I was conscious for only short periods of time, it took me several periods of consciousness to move the fifty feet. On the other side of the rise was a six-inch-deep pool of standing water, and I gratefully drank from it even though it was dirty. I spent that night and the next day, August 23, by the edge of that pool. As before, I was unconscious most of the time.

During one of the periods when I as awake, I became conscious of a feeling of movement in some of my wounds. A check revealed that all my open wounds were full of maggots, which caused me to think I was being eaten alive. Each time I was conscious thereafter, I killed as many maggots as I could. (It wasn't until much later that doctors told me the maggots were only eating the dead flesh, thereby delaying the onset of gangrene.)

On the fifth day, August 24, I raised my head as far as possible to see whether there was anything nearby that I could try to reach for help. To the east, about a half-mile away, I could see the top of a tall wooden observation tower. Surely, I thought it would be manned, and by this time I would have welcomed a German coming to take me prisoner. By the end of the day, however, I had made no progress toward the tower, and I slept where I had awakened.

On the sixth day, August 25, I moved toward the tower and had gotten to within a hundred yards of it by nightfall. There was a swamp between me and the tower, and by sunset I could see that there was a log cabin—it appeared to be a hunting cabin—at the base of the tower. Both the tower and the cabin were obviously abandoned.

On the seventh day, August 26, I entered the swamp, which turned out to be about two to four feet deep. It so happened that I had come ashore in a vast swampy area known as the Camargue, at the mouth of the Rhone River.

I was able to move along quite well in the water because my legs were buoyant. I pulled myself to the cabin as cautiously as I could, because there were signs in German —*Achtung! Minen*—and I knew what that meant.

The swamp next to the cabin was about 100 feet wide and 150 yards long, and at the far end it turned a corner. There was a footbridge that crossed from the cabin to the shorter side of the swamp. It was made of rough timbers about ten feet long and three feet wide, and held together with a kind of baling wire.

During the next two days, August 27 and 28, I labored to take the bridge apart and construct a raft with four of the timbers held together with the wire. Late the second day, I completed the raft and, with two long sticks, poled my way down the swamp, hoping it would lead to the open ocean.

Upon rounding the corner, however, I found that the swamp dead-ended about twenty-five feet further on. It was quite late, so I poled ashore, secured the raft as best I could, and pulled myself about six feet out of the swamp. I spent the night there on the bank. I later learned that the Camargue was one of the top five mosquito-infested areas in the world. The mosquitoes were so big and so thick, they created a continual hum. I simply covered my face with my hands and let them have at me.

The next morning, August 29, I got back on the raft to return to the cabin. As I rounded the corner, I could see people at the cabin, and I called out to them as I got near. They were six Frenchmen who had come out to start cleaning up the mess made by the Germans.

They placed me in the bed of their old truck and started to drive up a trail. The jolting of the ride was more than I could physically bear, so they took the long front seat from the cab and placed me on it. Four of the men picked up the seat, one at each corner, and carried me up the trail. The truck driver drove ahead to arrange for an ambulance. The last man spelled one of the men who was carrying me, and they continued to spell one another until we reached the road, where an ambulance was waiting.

On the way to the hospital, the ambulance stopped at a house where a French lady fed me some soup, my first meal in ten days. Needless to say, I thought the soup was the best I had ever eaten. Next, the ambulance took me to a hospital in Aix-en-Provence, which was close to the by-then liberated city of Marseille.

My stay in the French hospital was almost as bad as my ten days on the beach and in the swamp. Until then, shock had spared me the excruciating pain that now came over me. No one at the hospital spoke any

English, and I spoke no French, so there was little communication with the hospital staff. On my second day there, August 31, they put me on an operating table, and ten or twelve people stood around me. The doctor had antiseptics but no anesthetics, and the additional people were there to hold me down while the doctor dug shrapnel out of my legs and left knee. After this ordeal, I found an orderly who understood a little English and I convinced him to go find any Allied soldier and bring him back to the hospital. Shortly, the orderly returned with a British soldier whose Cockney accent made him almost as hard to understand as the French. I gave the soldier one of my dogtags and begged him to find an American officer and explain to him where I was. I asked the soldier to hurry, because I was not sure I would be able to endure the medical treatment I was receiving.

When no one showed up that day or the next, September 1, I became very discouraged. Late that night, however, I was awakened by a U.S. Army captain with medical insignia on his shirt collar. He gave me a shot for the pain, and I passed out.

I was taken by ambulance to a field hospital, which had been located near our base in Mateur, Tunisia, when I first joined the 27th Fighter Squadron. Back then, the nurses had been very popular with my squadron mates, and we had socialized with them. When I woke up, I was being tended by a nurse I recognized. My spirits improved rapidly. During my stay at the field hospital, necessary surgery was performed on my numerous wounds in order to prepare me for evacuation.

In short order, I was flown to the 118th Station Hospital in Naples, Italy, where I received a lot of medical attention. When word was sent to the 1st Fighter Group commander, Colonel Robert Richard, that I was alive and in a hospital in Italy, he issued an order that every day the weather permitted, a 27th Fighter Squadron P-38 pilot was to land at the nearby Capodichino Airdrome and visit with me.

In Naples the doctors decided it was best to amputate my legs. I implored Colonel Richard to get the doctors to reconsider. With his help, and the help of our wing commander, the doctors decided to try to save the legs.

They flew me back home in October. The date of the flight was known at 1st Fighter Group headquarters, so after the C-54 I was aboard lifted away from Capodichino and leveled out at altitude, a dozen red-tailed P-38s from the 27th Fighter Squadron appeared and settled down on both sides of the transport. They looked like silver ghosts. They escorted me for a hundred miles out over the blue Mediterranean, then silently peeled off, one by one, and went back to the war.

Years later, I learned that Colonel Richard had issued an order that from then on, in the 27th Fighter Squadron, any plane with the number 23—my old plane number—would forever be known as *Maloney's Pony.* This order was not followed for thirty years after World War II, but ever since 1975, when the 27th, 71st, and 94th squadrons were rejoined as the 1st Fighter Wing, plane Number 23 of the 27th Fighter Squadron is named *Maloney's Pony.*

I arrived in the United States in November 1944, and was stationed as close to my home as possible, at McCloskey General Hospital in Temple, Texas. I was operated on many times and was bedridden until September 1945, at which time I was able to take a few steps with the aid of crutches. I went home on leave, married my childhood sweetheart, Miss Patricia Jean Driggs, and returned to the hospital for another operation.

In February 1946, with McCloskey Hospital scheduled to be closed, I was transferred to William Beaumont General Hospital in El Paso. While there, I received only rehabilitative care. Next, I was transferred to the neurological center at O'Reilly General Hospital in Springfield, Missouri, in order to repair damage to the peronneal nerve in my left leg. When the doctors at O'Reilly decided the nerve injury was inoperable, I was transferred in September 1946 to Pratt General Hospital in Coral Gables, Florida, for further treatment. I received only rehabilitative treatment there, and the hospital closed in April 1947. I was finally sent to Letterman General Hospital in San Francisco, and there I received treatment to both legs and feet. I was sent before the retirement board in October 1947 and was retired for physical disability with the rank of major, to which I had been promoted in April 1946.

After leaving Letterman General Hospital, Tom Maloney enrolled at Oklahoma State University and began the spring semester there in January 1948. In January 1951, he received a degree in accounting and went to work for an oil-and-gas drilling company. In 1954, he helped form his own drilling company, but in December 1976, problems related to his injuries forced him to sell his share. He later returned to work at the firm, finally retiring in 1985.

In 1992, Tom Maloney was inducted into the Oklahoma Aviation and Space Hall of Fame.

In late 1995, Tom Maloney was contacted by Jean Robin, an amateur historian who lived in the vicinity of the Le Cres railroad station, which had been the target of the August 19, 1944, strafing attack. The letter revealed that, in a matter of minutes, the flight of seven 1st Fighter Group P-38s had done extensive harm to the German war effort in recently invaded southern France.

There were two trains in the station when the attack commenced at 1920 hours. One was on a siding without a locomotive. It consisted of thirteen closed rail cars containing "fire bombs"—possibly incendiary ammunition of some sort. Explosive and incendiary bullets fired by the P-38s' .50-caliber machine guns and 20mm cannon started fires in these cars, and the rail cars and their contents were "entirely destroyed and blown to pieces."

Moments before the strafing attack commenced, the second train had been brought to a halt in the station by a red-light signal. This was no doubt the train Captain Tom Maloney saw when the attack got underway. It was composed of fifty-two flatbed cars and closed goods wagons. A number of Royal Tiger heavy tanks were on the flatcars, and ammunition was stored in many of the closed cars. Waffen SS *tank crews and* Panzergrenadiers *were also in the closed rail cars.*

As the strafing attack began, the locomotive was perforated by bullets and stopped for good. Of the fifty-two cars it was pulling, nineteen were blown off the rails and destroyed. Twenty-six others remained on the rails but were "entirely blown, torn to bits." When the P-38s left the scene, only seven flatcars and goods wagons were left intact.

Beyond the outright destruction of the engine and fifty-eight rail cars and their contents, the attack blocked the main rail line with all the neighboring rail sidings with debris that, in some cases, continued to cook off through the night and burn out of control for several days. Live ammunition was scattered all over the station area and several nearby vine-

yards. The switching station was demolished and phone lines running through the station were severed. Apparently, many Waffen SS *troops were killed in the attack or trapped in the wreckage, where they perished in the subsequent explosions and fires.*

Jean Robin, who passed through the area after the war, described it to Tom Maloney as "a tangled heap of ruins, an absolute hell!" He also reported that only one French railwayman was injured by an ammunition explosion. "Your action," the Frenchman wrote in 1995, "completely disrupted the German retreat by railway. All convoys [up the line] from Montpellier were then destroyed by Allied planes or by the Germans themselves."

HORRIDO!

2d Lieutenant BEN DREW, USAAF
375th Fighter Squadron, 361st Fighter Group
Near Rostock, Germany—August 25, 1944

Urban Leonard Drew was born in Detroit, Michigan, on March 21, 1924. He entered the Army Air Forces in October 1942, several months after graduating from high school. Upon receiving his commission and wings at Bartow Field, Florida, as a member of Class 43-I, 2d Lieutenant Drew was assigned as a P-51 instructor. After a year on the job, he was reassigned as an overseas replacement in May 1944 and sailed for England, where he was sent to the 361st Fighter Group's 375th Fighter Squadron.

On June 25, 1944, 2d Lieutenant Ben Drew scored his first victory, a Bf-109 he downed near Lisieux. On August 7, he damaged a Bf-109 over Chartres Airdrome.

It was a gray day in England on August 25, 1944, when the 375th Fighter Squadron took off to escort B-17s of the 91st Heavy Bombardment Group, 1st Bombardment Division, VIII Bomber Command, to targets in the vicinity of Rostock, Germany. I was leading White Flight, the lead flight in the squadron.

Unfortunately, when the squadron crossed the near side of the English Channel, my P-51's supercharger failed to kick in. This limited high-altitude performance and was a "mandatory abort." I returned to base, where I knew there was always a reserve airplane, armed and fueled, for each squadron. Flight leaders and squadron leaders had the option to take the reserve aircraft without authorization if they felt they could still catch up with the group.

I jumped into the reserve aircraft and hurriedly taxied out for take-off. A pilot from another squadron had also aborted, and he had jumped into his squadron's reserve aircraft. He called me to ask if he could fly my wing. I said, "Fine. Let's go!" We took off to catch up with group and the bombers.

We climbed at maximum power, and I soon could see that we were catching up with the formation. The bombers appeared as faint specks on the horizon, far, far away. My head was, as usual, on a swivel, and so I caught a glint of reflection up-sun, about 15,000 feet above me as I climbed through 18,000 feet. The glint turned out to be about sixty Bf-109s and FW-190s.

I called the identity of the bandits to my wingman and cautioned him to continue to slowly climb with me. Then, dead ahead at 12 o'clock level, four P-38s appeared. They were flying almost a show formation.

In England at that time, when fighter and bomber units were briefed for their missions, they were told about all friendly aircraft that would be in their sky space. I had not heard any mention at our briefing that morning about any P-38s in our area. But before I could do anything about them, twelve Bf-109s peeled off from the gaggle above and descended to attack the P-38s, which were not on a common radio channel with the 361st Group. There was nothing I could do to alert the P-38 pilots as the 109s pulled up behind them and shot all four down in less than thirty seconds. It was a devastating sight, but there was nothing I could have done.

I called my wingman and said, "Let's just keep climbing slowly and hope they don't see us. Sixty against two are not good odds, and maybe we can sneak through." Unfortunately, that was not to be the case.

As my wingman and I climbed through 26,000 feet, another twelve bandits peeled off and dived to the attack.

I called to my wingman and explained, "When they get in range, I'll break sharply upwards into them, and you do the same. Seesaw your rudder pedals and hold your trigger down. We'll try and discourage the attack as much as we can. After that, buddy, you're on your own. Do your best. I'll try and take the leader on as he dives through." And that is what happened.

Most fighter pilots start firing a little out of range, and that is what the German leader did. When I saw the flames from his gunports, I pulled sharply up into him, in about a 60-degree climb. I seesawed my pedals and held my trigger down. As he flashed by me, I pulled the Mustang into a hard hammerhead stall, flipped over on my back, and went after him. He immediately turned into a Lufbery Circle, and I entered the circle with him. [The Lufbery Circle, named after Major Raoul Lufbery, America's third-raking ace in World War I, is circling defensive maneuver.]

As soon as I entered the Lufbery, I went for him. He was exactly 180 degrees across from me, and I went for him with full power on, full power off, full flaps down, full flaps up—whatever it might take to get inside him. But I couldn't get inside him, and he couldn't get inside me. We stayed on opposite sides of the Lufbery starting at 28,000 feet and, of course, descending all the time, as is the nature of a Lufbery. Neither one of us could lay a gun on the other.

This was unbelievable. In all my combat encounters with Bf-109s and FW-190s, I had never had any trouble. I could outfly and outfight every one of them. But this guy was different. I had never fought an adversary with the skill this pilot exhibited in handling his 109. At that time of the war, the pilots left in the *Luftwaffe* were either very experienced aces or fledgling pilots with not even 100 hours in the air. I have always believed that this pilot was an ace and probably the *Geschwader* (wing) commander. I am well aware that, unlike ourselves, the Germans did not always have the commander in front, so that he would not be targeted as the leader. But with a gaggle of some sixty-plus fighters against only two of us, I strongly suspect that the *Geschwader* commander had led the attack and was the one I was tangling with.

As I flew through 16,000 feet, my flying suit was sopping wet, and I could feel water sloshing in my flying boots. I was rapidly dehydrating, and for the first time in my combat career, for just one fleeting instant, I thought, "Is this guy better than I am?" And as fast as that thought crossed my mind, I had to put it out, because if I continued to think that way, I can assure you that the wrong mother's son was going home that night.

I concentrated on pulling inside of him, but with no joy. There is one end to a Lufbery Circle, and only one. As you turn, you are always losing altitude, so the one pilot who has to "break" first, before crashing into the ground, is the loser. I managed to hold about 100 feet of altitude on the German ace, and when we hit the treetops, he had to break first.

Immediately, like a cat on a mouse, I was on him, less than fifty feet behind him. I squeezed my trigger, but found, much to my dismay, that my three left-side guns as well as my two right inboard guns were also jammed. I only had my right outboard gun firing.

I realized immediately what had happened: the thin aluminum .50-caliber feed chutes in the wings had collapsed due to the high G forces I had been pulling in the Lufbery. Fortunately, since my right outboard gun was at the top of the G forces, it was still able to fire. It was no problem to saw my rudder pedals and shoot the 109 down. He crashed and burned in the trees. I took gun-camera film of his crash site.

When I flew home that early afternoon, I was truly sad. I knew I had shot down and killed one of the world's great fighter pilots. I do not know his name or his unit, but in the legions of honor we fought in, and in the skies that we aces dominated, he was among the best that ever flew. Rest in peace; and, as the Germans fighter pilots say, *"Horrido!"*

On September 11, 1944, 1st Lieutenant Ben Drew shot down a third Bf-109 near Gottingen, Germany; on September 18, he downed an He-111 medium bomber over the Baltic Sea near Fehmarn Island; and on October 7, 1944, he achieved ace status when he shot down two Me-262 jet fighters over Achmer Airdrome.

Ben Drew left active duty after the war but served with the Michigan Air National Guard until he retired with the rank of major. He operated an aviation service for many years in England and South Africa.

LONER

2d Lieutenant RUSS HAWORTH, USAAF
338th Fighter Squadron, 55th Fighter Group
Meiningen, Germany—September 11, 1944

Russell Carroll Haworth was born on October 13, 1922, in Wichita Falls, Texas. During the Great Depression, Haworth's father, a sign painter, was continually on the move with the family in tow, seeking jobs wherever he could find them; as a result, Russ Haworth spent each year of high school in a different city or town. He thus became, in his own eyes, a loner.

Haworth attended business school and got a job with a Dallas-area oil company, but when a promised pay raise failed to materialize, he enlisted in the Army Air Forces in May 1942. Although accepted for flight training, he was not called up until February 1943.

Haworth received his commission and wings as a member of Class 43-K at Luke Field, Arizona, on December 5, 1943, and thereafter trained in Piper Cubs, P-39s, and P-38s. He sailed from Boston on June 6, 1944, listening to the D-Day invasion news as his ship left the harbor. In England, after advanced theater training, he was assigned as a replacement pilot to the 55th Fighter Group's 338th Fighter Squadron at Wormingford Airdrome.

I flew a few local P-38 flights until July 13, when the base closed operations to convert to P-51 Mustangs. I credit that event to saving my life. The P-38 as a fighter plane was a bad joke.

After fifteen hours in the P-51, I flew my first mission on July 28; we were escorting bombers. Then, during August, we flew bombing and strafing missions against transport facilities around Paris while the Germans were evacuating the city. On August 10, as I was raking a long train, my right wing was hit by two 20mm cannon shells fired from a flatcar in the middle of the train. Because I was banked left, I was able to recover as my right wing dropped. Otherwise, it would have been all over. The cannon shells barely missed the right-wing spars and just tore up the aluminum skin.

On August 28, I was flying the number-four position in a four-plane flight when we caught a bomber towing a troop glider leaving Paris. The flight leader and his wingman destroyed the bomber, and the element leader and I destroyed the glider. I received a one-half credit but no combat victory.

On September 11, 1944, at 1145 hours, I was flying a bright aluminum P-51 Mustang at the extreme right of a sixteen-plane squadron formation. We were south of Meiningen, Germany, at 20,000 feet, on our way to our assigned box of bombers.

I always flew the number-four position in my flight, because I always broke formation when any action developed. I did not expect to survive the war and did not worry about dying. Because I had no religious superstitions, I considered death to be an extremely long and peaceful sleep. Nevertheless, I intended to avoid the inevitable as long as possible and have fun doing it. The other pilots did not appreciate my joke about our being expendable.

Someone called, "Bogeys at twelve o'clock high." Dead ahead was a bunch of German fighter planes, so numerous they reminded me of a swarm of bees. Then another radio call reported, "One is diving through the formation." I glanced to the left, and there was a Bf-109 in a vertical dive right in the middle of our formation.

I simultaneously slammed the control stick and the rudder full left, hit the external fuel tank release, pressed the mike button, and yelled, "This is Haworth. I'll get him." When I took off after the German, no one was surprised.

I did a split-S into a vertical dive and came down right behind the 109. I quickly overtook the German and gave him a long burst from my six .50-caliber machine guns. I was directly behind him, in a vertical dive, about 500 yards back. I saw hits over his entire airplane, which began to trail heavy black smoke and small pieces of metal as it disappeared into a low cloud bank.

I had only just begun my first dogfight with the enemy. I looked around and saw that the sky was full of fighter planes at my level and higher. I headed for the closest plane and met it head-on as we approached each other at a combined speed in excess of 500 miles per hour. I did this several times. I had just a fraction of a second to identify friend or foe and, if foe, to aim and fire. With some planes, I had to climb to meet them head-on. I saw hits on one enemy plane, but I did not seem to be doing very well.

The adrenalin was flowing and I was gasping to get enough air through the oxygen mask. I could not afford to concentrate on the wildly gyrating altimeter in order to see whether had lost enough altitude to remove the mask.

Suddenly one of the Germans made a fatal mistake: he turned away from me. I pulled up directly behind him and pressed the trigger at a range of about 200 feet. I saw a few hits in the wing roots and fuselage, but not nearly as many as I wanted. The 109s were tough airplanes. Then my guns stopped firing. I was out of ammunition!

I pulled into close formation with the German plane, on its right, almost in the slipstream of its wing. I was planning to shoot the pilot with my .45-caliber pistol if he tried to escape. He had already jettisoned his canopy and had his legs and one arm hanging over the side. Apparently he pushed the stick down with the other arm, and that caused him to tumble out backwards. I don't think he saw me on his wing. His parachute opened. I watched the plane hit the ground and explode, then I did a quick 180-degree turn and photographed the pilot in his parachute with my gun camera. The pilot may have thought I was going to shoot him—I am sure he needed a change of pants when he hit the ground—but I wanted him to survive to have the opportunity to bring up another plane for me to destroy.

Since I was out of ammunition, I immediately returned to base. I was credited with two Bf-109s destroyed and one Bf-109 damaged.

The next day, 1st Lieutenant Russ Haworth downed two Bf-109s while escorting bombers to Frankfurt, but because of a bookkeeping error arising from a belated claim for an assist by another squadron pilot, he was given official credit for only a half victory. Later, the missing credit for the missing full victory was added as a fictitious victory dated December 24, 1944—after Haworth had been transferred from his group. His final actual victory was another Bf-109 that he downed on November 2, 1944, over Merseburg, Germany. Counting the half-credit for the glider, which was officially awarded in July 1945, this edged Haworth into ace status, but he was not notified at the time and did not learn of the honor until 1984.

After leaving the 55th Fighter Group, Haworth served as a theater ferry pilot until he returned to the United States in May 1945. He flew RP-63s (armored Bell King Cobra fighters) as a targets for bomber gunners until he left active duty in October 1945. He remained in the Air Force Reserve until 1955.

"BREAK RIGHT!"

2d Lieutenant BOB MILLIKEN, USAAF
429th Fighter Squadron, 474th Fighter Group
Near Aachen, Germany—September 12, 1944

Robert Carl Milliken was born in Hanna, Wyoming, on June 6, 1922. He graduated from high school in Hanna in June 1940, then attended the University of Wyoming. After completing the Civilian Pilot Training course at the university in June 1942, Milliken enlisted in the Army Air Forces. He underwent Pre-Flight training at Santa Ana, California; Primary at King City, California; Basic at Merced, California; and he graduated as a member of Class 43-J at Williams Field, Arizona.

Upon completing an operational training course in fighters, 2d Lieutenant Milliken was shipped to England, where he was assigned to the Ninth Air Force and then to the 474th Fighter Group's 429th Fighter Squadron at Warmwell, which he joined on April 23, 1944, as the group was completing its theater training. The 474th Fighter Group flew its first combat mission on April 25, and 2d Lieutenant Bob Milliken flew his first combat mission on April 30.

Milliken's first encounter with enemy aircraft came on May 7, during his third combat sortie—an escort mission over France. He flew numerous missions during the D-Day build-up and invasion, and he scored his first aerial victory, an FW-190 he downed near Nogent, France, on July 6, 1944.

On August 6, following on the heels of the Allied breakout from Normandy, the 474th Fighter Group moved to Advance Landing Ground A-11 in Normandy—the better to conduct missions in support of the advancing U.S. First and Third armies.

♦

On September 6, 1944, an advance flight echelon of the 474th Fighter Group—including me—moved into a new advance field, A-72, at Perrone, near St. Quentin. Much of this installation, which had been a *Luftwaffe* base, had been destroyed when the Germans pulled out of the area. In fact, as I was taxiing out for the first time, the P-38 in front of me set off a land mine. It went off behind him and in front of me!

One of our 429th Fighter Squadron's September 12 missions was aimed at suppressing German flak batteries near Aachen, Germany. Two of our P-38s were assigned to bomb the flak batteries from low level, and six of us were escorts. If we had the opportunity, we would also strafe the flak positions. It was an afternoon mission, and the weather was clear.

After the two P-38s with bombs attacked the flak battery at about 1500 hours, they and the rest of us split up and began strafing targets of opportunity in the area. I went down alone and strafed a truck that was parked in the shade of some very tall trees. I also strafed the outer area of the antiaircraft emplacements. We were not fired on during these passes. These were large-caliber guns—too large to fire on us at such low altitude. After I strafed the truck and several searchlights, I began searching for other targets.

I noticed a very suspicious-looking installation. As I dived down for a closer look, I saw that it was covered by netting. I flew along, just skimming the ground, so I could look under the camouflage netting and see what was there. It was a long, low building with a veranda on the side. As I flew by, I saw that a woman dressed in white clothing was running down the veranda from one end of the building to the other. I assumed that it was a hospital, because this woman was dressed like a nurse. I don't remember seeing any red crosses, but I decided not to strafe that particular target.

As I completed my pass at the camouflaged building, we received a call from the mission leader, Captain Paul Munger, to form up and get ready to go home. We were all low on ammo, although some much less than others. I hadn't found many targets, so I might have had more ammo than most of the other P-38 pilots.

We were given a rendezvous point and a heading to form up with the flight led by Captain Munger. My flight of four, which I was leading, formed up, and I led it in a high-speed climb, though we weren't really bustering at full throttle.

As we climbed toward Munger's flight, I looked up and saw a whole gaggle of FW-190s as it crossed over us diagonally, from left to right. We called, "Bandits, nine o'clock high." They were right up above me. From my position, it seemed like we were all suspended in midair; it seemed they were flying very slowly. As I watched, I thought, "Why don't they hit us?"

As we continued to climb and weave, going all out, I lost sight of the 190s. Seconds later, they attacked Munger's flight.

We continued to climb and weave on our original heading. As we were getting ready to join the fight, one of my pilots called, "Break right!"—just as some of the 190s bounced us from the right rear and above.

During our right turn into them, my number-three and -four men split off. That left me with 2d Lieutenant Richard Stein on my wing.

After I made the right turn, I went into a slight dive to gain more airspeed. Then I pulled into a slight right-hand turn and a shallow climb to retain my speed and to get into the fight.

I looked up. About 1,000 feet above me was a 190 on a course that crossed my flight path to the left. I was still pulling up a little bit, gaining speed and coming around to a path that would put me slightly behind him. He sighted me and made the first of several tactical errors. He had the altitude advantage, but instead of trying to position himself to where he could get on my tail, he made a slight banking turn and entered a dive toward me. When he did this, we were committed.

I pulled up to meet him. I felt I had no option, really. To turn left or right would have exposed me to a deflection shot. And if I pulled up—same thing; he would have had a deflection shot at my belly. Or if I kept up the turn I was in, he could have made a weaving turn, set up a pursuit, and come in on my tail. One option for me was to depress my stick, but things were happening fast, and I didn't feel that was a viable option, at least not initially.

He came in slightly off from head-on. I would say he was heading toward me from about a 355-degree angle, just slightly crossing from my left to my right. We both began firing. As his tracers converged over my canopy, I was really awestruck by the fire power that was coming out of his wings. It looked like cannon fire. It all happened in a millisecond. I just executed a very slight left roll to put my fire into him. His tracers were going over my canopy, and my tracers were going under his right wing root. He failed to press his attack; he had a momentary advantage, but he blinked first. If he had pressed his attack, he might have hit me first, because his tracers were going right over my canopy; it was just a matter of a few feet. He failed to depress, but I pulled back on my stick, just slightly, and my fire—all four .50s and the 20mm cannon—went into his right wing root and fuselage. He blew up.

The 190 was approximately 150 yards away, and my airspeed at the time was about 250 miles per hour. We would have been closing at 500 feet per second. I closed my eyes, fully expecting to get his engine in my lap. But I pulled through the smoke and flames without any large fragments hitting me. I estimate that from the time we sighted each other to the time I flew through his debris, about four seconds had elapsed. He flipped over and went straight in. My wingman, Lieutenant Stein, saw this and reported that no chute had opened.

As I led Stein into a turn to the right, I saw another 190 below me, attacking a P-38. I made a 20-degree dive on him, closed to about 250 yards, and made a 20-degree deflection shot, a three-second burst. My air speed was about 250 to 300 miles per hour. I observed strikes in both wing roots and the cockpit area, and I claimed a damaged.

After hitting the second 190, I looked up to the right in time to see two 190s coming at us head-on. I fired a short burst at the leader, who was slightly to my left. The number-two man was also heading toward us from our left front. Stein, who was on my left wing, fired at the number-two man. As I turned to the left, I saw Stein's targeted 190 flip over onto its back. It was smoking very badly, and it exploded when it hit the ground. This was one of Stein's very first missions. I don't know how many he had flown, but he had not joined us until mid-August. (We lost Stein five days after this mission, during the Market-Garden operation.)

Stein was still on my left wing as I made a sharp right turn. He called, "Break right!" so I pulled into a sharp right break. The 190 that had been coming at me head-on was now returning in the final stages of a pursuit curve. He was at about my 5 o'clock and was firing his guns. He was very close—I estimate he was 150 yards away, maybe less—closing fast, and firing. I did not have the option of turning into him, as doing so would have set up an easy deflection shot for him. So I made an evasive maneuver that I had practiced to some degree, though never as violently as this. But I had this very situation in my mental drawer of things that might happen in combat.

The P-38 was slow to roll compared to many of the single-engine ships. One of the favorite maneuvers of 109 and 190 pilots against P-38s was the split-S. Because of the time required to react—that is, because the P-38 was a little slower to roll—it gave them a momentary lead time. They expected the P-38 to gain speed and dive, go into compressibility—where the controls freeze—and fly into the ground. It was one of their favorite maneuvers. (The P-38's compressibility problem was corrected in later P-38 models by adding dive flaps.)

I had no time at all to set up a turn. I hit full right rudder, chopped my right throttle, came back on the stick, and applied right elevator. I did this so violently that it just threw me all over the sky. But it was so quick, so sudden, that I may just have disappeared from 190 pilot's gunsight. As a matter of fact, after this mission, Lieutenant Stein asked me, "What happened? You just disappeared!" I'm convinced that, had I tried any other type of maneuver, the 190 would have hit me. But after I chopped the right throttle, along with all the other maneuvers, the torque of the left engine just threw me into a spin. I lost Stein in that maneuver, too.

When I recovered, I climbed to the right and another wingman joined me—2d Lieutenant Larry Baillargeon. As we were coming right over the main part of the action, a 190 that had been attacking one of our planes pulled up from below me. My airspeed at the time was about 250 miles per hour. I pulled up as he passed and gave him a three-second burst—20 degrees of deflection at about 300 yards. My tracers arched into him, and his left wing exploded. Larry confirmed this one as destroyed.

Next, I dropped into a right diving turn to gain airspeed. As I pulled up, Baillargeon pulled off to engage another 190. I pulled up and saw a 190 flying along, straight and level on a course from my left that put me on a converging course of about 30 degrees to him. He had about 100 feet of altitude on me, which put me at a slight disadvantage. If I had pulled up at that time, my angle of attack would have been bad. I didn't have enough altitude to get on his tail, and my trying to gain altitude would perhaps have set up a head-on confrontation.

I made an immediate sharp turn to the left, which set up a course away from him at about 45 degrees—and which would allow me to keep his cockpit area in sight. I also went to full throttle. First of all, I flew straight and level for a second or two to see if he was going to attack. When he didn't, I went into a dive to gain airspeed while I watched him over my right shoulder. And here he made a major error by continuing to fly straight and level. One of the biggest mistakes a pilot can make in a dogfight is to fly straight and level for any period of time. It only takes a matter of seconds for someone to come in and blow you away, so you had to constantly turn and clear the skies to see whether someone was coming in your tail.

I dived to hit his blind spot. I could tell that he wasn't going to try to engage me, so I kept diving in a shallow right turn, and then I turned more to the right, so I was almost on a course parallel to his. Now I was diving and looking up at him, so I gained all the speed I could. I dived down to where I was actually ahead of him, looking up and back at him. Then I pulled up under his blind spot. He was still failing to weave or take any other evasive action.

I pulled up into an Immelmann, keeping him in sight until I got my belly up. Then I rolled over and, altering my course just slightly, I pulled up into a chandelle. I fired a two- or three-second burst starting at 200 yards and closing to 150 yards or less, from about 45 to 30 degrees of deflection. I observed five or six 20mm hits right in both wing roots and the belly of the ship. I came up underneath him, and then, almost in a stall, I rolled out to the left and had to dive to gain airspeed. I lost sight of him and only claimed a damaged, but I'm fairly well convinced that, with all the hits that I'd gotten into his belly and cockpit area, it would have been almost impossible for him to have come out of it. I had now destroyed two and damaged two. I very possibly destroyed the two "damaged" fighters, but my gun camera had been loaded improperly, and I got no film of the action that day.

As I was circling to the left, Stein and Baillargeon joined up with me again. Then someone down on the deck called for help; he said he had some 190s on his tail. There were a number of smoke columns from planes that had gone down—mostly theirs. I don't think there were any of ours yet in that immediate vicinity. In one area, there were two columns of smoke where two planes had gone down very close together.

I called and asked the pilot of the P-38 with 190s on his tail, "Where are you? I can't see you, but where are you relative to the double column of smoke? If you can, fly towards the column of smoke, so we can locate you." I looked down, but I couldn't see a P-38. However, I did see three single-engine planes flying in a sort of V-formation. So with Baillargeon on my left and Stein on my right, I went diving down on those three 190s.

In my first dogfight, I had made a mistake. I had dived on a 190 that was strafing one of our pilots in his parachute. The 190 had split-essed to evade me and I had continued to dive at him. I came up behind him on the deck, but I was going so fast that I nearly overshot him. I had had to make a sharp climbing 360-degree left turn, or I would have gone by him and could have been dead meat. That Nazi chose to run. I chased him down and he eventually bailed out. But now I was a little more cautious on my dive.

As I started to level out on my dive, I was doing about 300 miles an hour. I hit the rear 190—a long-nosed model with an inline liquid-cooled engine—with scattered shots at about a 30-degree deflection and a range of about 200 yards. He twisted and turned a bit, then leveled out on the deck, where I hit him again with a short burst at 150 yards and no deflection. My airspeed was about 250 miles per hour. He started smoking—white smoke, indicating a coolant leak. As I fired that last burst, I saw a solid line of tracers from my .50-caliber guns, so I knew that I was about out of ammo. As I closed on the 190 ahead of me, firing those last bursts, the 190 on the left turned and made what I thought was to be a head-on pass at me. He was to my left, and I realized then that he was after Baillargeon, who took him on and shot him down. The 190 on the right evaded Stein.

I closed to fifty yards on the 190 ahead of me. By then, he was pouring out white smoke and flying level, twisting and turning slightly. I put the bead right on his tail and pulled the trigger, but nothing happened.

I called, "I've got one here down on the deck, but I'm out of ammo. Can anyone come down and finish him?" But I had to realize that there had been only eight of us at the start of the action—and twenty-five or thirty 190s. I didn't know it at the time, but we had lost two men—2d Lieutenant Robert Hazzard and 2d Lieutenant Herman Lane, who had reported being out of ammo. They were two of our finest pilots. That left six of us, and there wasn't anybody available to come down at take out this damaged 190.

I was still closing on the 190, because I had superior speed, so I pulled up to his left and flew formation off his left wing. I looked over at him and he looked over at me. Then he ducked his head, quickly looked over his instruments, and looked at me again.

This was a situation I had not prepared for. In a fraction of a second, I thought about what could I do. Could I flip up his wing? Could I ram him, or chew off his tail with a prop? Could I put my nose into his tail? I thought, "Well, what will happen if I wind down my right window and give him a few rounds from my .45?" But as these options flashed through my mind, I also thought, "Well, if I cripple my plane, I'll be a liability to the rest of the guys." Furthermore, even though he was smoking badly, he might still be able to put up a fight. So I had to pull up and let him go. The last I saw, he was flying straight away, pouring white smoke. Probably his engine seized in a hurry.

I went up and joined the others, and we flew back to Perrone. The tally for this engagement was Munger, two damaged; Baillargeon, one destroyed; Stein, one destroyed; 2d Lieutenant William Ryan, one damaged; and Milliken, two destroyed and three damaged. Hazzard and Lane might have accounted for others before they were shot down.

When I got back to base, I stood, helmet in hand, to look at the front of my ship. I was wondering what I would see there: fragments of enemy plane, or maybe fragments of an enemy pilot? As these thoughts flashed through my mind, I looked intently, but not a scratch was visible.

In the end, 2d Lieutenant Bob Milliken received official credit for destroying two FW-190s and damaging three others. His actions that day resulted in the award of a Silver Star. He shot down another FW-190 near Cologne on October 13.

First Lieutenant Bob Milliken's official tour of duty ended on November 11, 1944, but he volunteered to fly two sorties on December 18 in support of U.S. Army ground troops caught up in the Battle of the Bulge. It was on the last of these sorties that he achieved ace status when he downed a Bf-109 near Cologne. Milliken then served in Belgium and

Germany as an air-ground control officer with the IX Tactical Air Command and the U.S. XVIII Airborne Corps.

Bob Milliken returned to the United States in July 1945 and left the service in December.

HARD CHARGER

Captain DON STRAIT, USAAF
361st Fighter Squadron, 356th Fighter Group
Near Osnabruck, Germany—November 26, 1944

Donald Jackson Strait was born on April 28, 1918, in East Orange, New Jersey, and raised in Verona, New Jersey.

Since early high school, I have had a great interest in airplanes and flying. I rode my bicycle from my home in Verona, New Jersey, to Caldwell Airport, some ten miles away, to observe the flying activities and talk with the maintenance personnel and pilots. In 1937, it was the desire of my family that I accept a job with the Prudential Insurance Company. After two years, it was obvious to me that I had no interest in insurance or inside office work, so I reviewed my options for a career in aviation. An opportunity presented itself in early 1940, and I enlisted in the 119th Observation Squadron of the New Jersey Army National Guard.

As soon as I joined the 119th, I was assigned to the squadron armament section. In September 1940, the 119th was called to active duty for one year, and it operated out of its home base, Newark Airport. In early December, I was sent to aircraft armament school at Lowry Field in Denver, Colorado. Then I returned to Newark and went to work as an aircraft armorer, repairing machine guns and synchronizing them to fire through the spinning propeller of the BCI-A two-place training aircraft used by the squadron. During aerial gunnery practice missions, I became closely associated with a number of our pilots, who talked me into becoming an aerial gunner. This gave me an opportunity to fly in our two-seat O-46 and O-47 aircraft. I qualified as an expert aerial gunner and on numerous occasions the pilots also let me fly the aircraft from the back seat.

After one year of active duty, my squadron's tour was extended. In early 1942, I qualified as an aviation cadet and was assigned to Maxwell Field, Alabama, for Pre-Flight training and screening for single- or twin-engine flight school. During the screening process, I pushed hard for single-engine training, as I had a strong desire to be a fighter pilot.

My dream came true in March 1942. I was assigned to Union City, Tennessee, an Embree Riddle contract school, for Primary training in the PT-17. Basic Training took place in Greenville, Mississippi, in the BT-13; and I took the Advanced course at Marianna Field, Florida, in the AT-6. I received my wings and commission on January 14, 1943.

There was no way I wanted to fly anything but fighters. Assignment to a fighter squadron being trained for deployment to the Eighth Air Force in England was a goal that I had established for myself early in my flying career. On January 20, 1943, I was assigned to the 326th Fighter Group at Westover Field, Massachusetts, for training in the Republic P-47 Thunderbolt. I was thrilled.

At Westover, we went from light trainers with 450-horsepower engines to the seven-ton P-47 and its powerful 2,000-horsepower Pratt & Whitney engine. It was a real challenge. The cold weather and heavy accumulation of snow at Westover Field considerably complicated our training, but schedules had to be met. We flew at every opportunity so that our next phase, assignment to an operational group and squadron training in New England, could be accomplished without delay.

Typically, after sixty pilots had completed transition training and checked out in the Thunderbolt, a new fighter group would be formed and each of its three squadrons would be assigned to a training facility in New England. My group was designated the 356th, and I was assigned to the 361st Fighter Squadron, which trained at Bradley Field, near Hartford, Connecticut.

It was customary when reporting to your new unit to first visit the commanding officer. During this interview, I told my CO about my experiences in the 119th Observation Squadron and my duty as an aerial gunner. I also expressed a desire for additional duty in aircraft maintenance. He accepted my request and appointed me assistant engineering officer. This was a stroke of luck for me, as I was given the opportunity to undertake all aircraft test flights, thus adding to my flying experience. I worked daily with our engineering staff and our Republic Aviation P-47 factory representative. This experience gave me a jump over the other pilots, and I rapidly advanced to flight leader. I retained my engineering job until I became squadron operations officer in July 1944.

The 356th Fighter Group's P-47 training in New England was in preparation for assignment to the Eighth Air Force in England. We practiced long-range operations, aerial gunnery, ground gunnery, and instrument flying. Ultimately, the entire 356th Fighter Group completed its final phase of training at Grenier Field, New Hampshire, in early August 1943, and was commended by the I Fighter Command for having completed more training than any previous fighter group. This training, plus my additional work in maintenance and test flights, gave me more flight time and overall fighter experience than my contemporaries. My strong desire to excel had been recognized by my group commander; in just over one year, I had been promoted to the rank of captain and the position of flight commander.

At the time, we were preparing to fly our aircraft on the northern ferry route to England, but a test flight by eight aircraft proved to be unsuccessful because of bad weather, lack of alternate fields, and poor communication aids and rescue facilities along the route.

The air echelon of the 356th set sail aboard the HMS *Orion* on August 5, 1943, and after a rough and tough convoy crossing, we arrived in Glasgow, Scotland, on the fifteenth of that month. We were immediately assigned to Goxhill Airdrome in Lincolnshire for the purpose of receiving our aircraft from the depot in Burtonwood. This was a surprise, for prior to leaving Grenier Field for England, we had flown our P-47s to Newark Airport, where they were to be prepared for deck loading and sea delivery to England. These aircraft were new, and we had flown them approximately fifty hours to work out any maintenance problems. Our understanding was that they were to be delivered to us at our first base in England, so each pilot loaded every accessible area in his aircraft with fine Kentucky Bourbon, spare parts, music records, and assorted other goodies. After delivering these aircraft to Newark, we never saw them again. Somebody received some fine goodies upon receipt of our aircraft.

While stationed at Goxhill, we flew locally to work out any aircraft maintenance bugs and to receive some geographical and weather orientation. We also received operational briefings from combat pilots as to the type of air operations we would initially be involved with.

Our final destination was to be a Royal Air Force base called Martlesham Heath, which was located just east of Ipswich, in Suffolk. We were advised on September 5 that the runways were operational, and we relocated to the new base on September 9, 1943.

Facilities for housing officers of the fighter squadrons were extremely limited, but the 361st Fighter Squadron received a great break when we were quartered on the airfield, across from the officers club and within a short walk from our operations hut, maintenance facility, and flight line. Pilots from the other two squadrons were quartered off the base, in large country estates. Martlesham Heath was ideally located only five miles from the North Sea. This proved to be important, because the airfield was easy to locate in bad weather and reduced-visibility conditions. Many missions required letting down over the North Sea and flying to our base at tree-top level with low visibility; precision instrument landing systems were nonexistent at the time.

The group finally became operational on October 15, 1943, and flew a number of preparatory sweeps over northern France and the Dutch islands. Visual sightings of the *Luftwaffe* by our group were extremely limited. The group's first victories were not achieved until November 29, 1943, and air operations were routine through the remainder of 1943 and early 1944. Nevertheless, we were gaining experience at operating under extreme weather conditions and extended ranges over new operational areas.

I first experienced the thrill of combat on February 6, 1944, when my flight bounced a pair of FW-190s while we were escorting B-17s against the airdrome near Dreux, France. I immediately initiated an attack. When the two FW-190s split away from each other, I chased one to the deck, heading in a southerly direction. I scored hits on this aircraft and the pilot lost control and bailed out. My wingman and I headed north to England, and we were extremely low on fuel by the time we landed at an RAF base on the south coast. My first air engagement was successful, but it showed a lack of judgment in pressing an attack beyond the fuel reserves needed to return to home base. Fortunately, we had been able to pinpoint our location and successfully navigate 250 miles to a safe landing.

I scored single victories over Bf-109s during escort missions over Germany on February 10 and May 19. By June 1944, I had completed two twenty-five-hour extensions to my combat tour requirement of 200 hours. At that time, I was asked by Brigadier General Jesse Auton, the commander of the 65th Fighter Wing, whether I would be interested in flying another tour following a thirty-day leave in the United States. The purpose of this program was to retain a nucleus of experienced leaders in the VIII Fighter Command at a time when the number of those completing their tours and requesting return to the States was growing. I eagerly accepted on condition that I command the 361st Fighter Squadron upon my return. General Auton agreed and stated, "You can quit operational flying at any time and return to the States."

My home leave proved extremely beneficial; it gave me the opportunity to receive some rest and recreation, and most important, I got a chance to reflect on my operational experience and map a course of action for when I returned to England and assumed command of the 361st. I arrived back in England on September 19, 1944; became combat ready after a re-check in the P-47; and commenced operational flying on October 4. When Lieutenant Colonel James Cooper finished his combat tour on November 20, I became the squadron commander.

During my first tour, I had become interested in monitoring all phases of combat intelligence. Captain George May, an extremely innovative intelligence officer, and I developed a program in November 1944 for recording on a situation map the daily sightings and disposition of *Luftwaffe* aircraft. Thus, we were able to plan our strategy and brief the pilots on where we believed enemy aircraft might attack or be sighted during each mission. I invited Captain May to be my roommate, so he could continually keep me informed on everything of intelligence value that was important to me as a commander leading squadron and group missions.

On November 1, the first North American P-51 Mustangs arrived at Martlesham Heath and we began transition and maintenance training to convert the entire group as quickly as possible. Our first mission in the P-51s occurred on November 20, the same day I assumed command of the 361st Fighter Squadron. We escorted B-17s to targets in the area of Merseburg, Germany. The target was deep inside Germany, and the escort requirements were ideally suited for the P-51, with its outstanding range and low-fuel-consumption Rolls-Royce-Merlin engine.

As I reviewed the frag order for our November 26, 1944, mission, I became convinced that the enemy would attack the bomber force in considerable strength. Our route to the target passed over the Ruhr and just to the north of a number of airfields that based large numbers of FW-190 and Bf-109 fighters. Since I could schedule myself for any mission I wanted to fly, I decided to lead my squadron, whose call sign was "Chinwag." The group was to provide close penetration escort to the first two B-17 combat wings of the 1st Air Division, whose target was the Altenbeken railroad viaduct near Paderborn, Germany.

A little before 1100 hours, just after we made rendezvous with the bombers east of Zwolle in the Netherlands, MEW (Microwave Early Warning) called our group leader ("Lampshade Leader") and advised him that there were bandits forty miles to the south, heading northwest. Lampshade Leader asked Chinwag Squadron to investigate, because we were on the south side of the bomber force, closest to the bandits.

When my sixteen P-51s arrived in the Osnabruck area at 25,000 feet, I sighted forty-plus Bf-109s, also at 25,000 feet and coming head-on toward my squadron. I directed Chinwag Squadron to drop external fuel tanks and attack. Immediately thereafter, I spotted 150-plus FW-190s and Bf-109s, organized into four-plane flights and flying in gaggles of thirty to fifty aircraft stacked from 20,000 to 28,000 feet. They were clearly preparing to attack the bomber force. As I turned to attack a 109, I advised Lampshade Leader that we were in the middle of the "whole damn *Luftwaffe.*"

I closed to within about 350 yards of the enemy airplane, fired, and observed strikes along his wing root and fuselage. The 109 fell off into a steep dive, trailing smoke. My wingman, 2d Lieutenant James Bower, saw it crash.

Lampshade Leader arrived in our area with the rest of the group and initiated an attack. Meanwhile, I had pulled up and bounced a second 109. It went into a tight turn to the right. I tried to cut inside the 109's turn, but I went into a high-speed stall instead. My P-51 snapped to the right and lost considerable altitude before I recovered at 13,000 feet.

Lieutenant Bowers had lost me in the maneuver, but 2d Lieutenant Shelby Jett, whose call sign was Chinwag Blue-4, joined as my wingman. He had become separated from his element leader, but he spotted my aircraft on the way up from 13,000 feet.

I spotted another 109 in a dive, so I attacked it. As I closed to about 300 yards at 14,000 feet, I hit his wing area. The 109 flew into a cumulus cloud and I lost him for a moment, but Lieutenant Jett spotted him and fired, scoring more hits along the fuselage and right wing. The 109 went out of control, then crashed and exploded in a field—but I saw a parachute open before the aircraft blew up. Lieutenant Jett and I each received a half-credit for this 109.

Our fuel supply was becoming a concern, so we started a climb to the west in order to head for home, but I picked up three more 109s. Jett and I endeavored to engage the trio, but the 109s led us over a large city and evaded us underneath the clouds. By then, fuel was a major concern, so I initiated a westward climb to 18,000 feet and set course straight for home.

The November 26, 1944, engagement became the biggest day of the war for the 356th Fighter Group. We downed twenty-three enemy aircraft without losing a single American airplane. My squadron led the other two with a score of eleven victories, an accomplishment that made me extremely proud.

Captain Don Strait achieved ace status on December 5, 1944, when he shot down two FW-190s, near Eberswald, Germany; and on Christmas Day, he shot down a Bf-109 near Koblenz. Thereafter, Major Strait downed an FW-190 on January 14, 1945; another FW-190 on February 14; and three Fiesler Fi-156 Storch light reconnaissance planes on February 20. His 13.5 confirmed aerial victories made him the top ace of the 356th Fighter Group.

Major Don Strait took leave of the war zone in late April 1945 and arrived in New York by ship on May 8, the day the war in Europe ended. He rejoined the New Jersey Air National Guard in October 1946 and served on active duty during the Korean War, the Berlin Crisis, the Cuban Missile Crisis, and the Vietnam War. Though he had no formal education beyond high school, Don Strait worked in a succession of key jobs in the aircraft industry, graduated from the Air War College in 1955, and retired from the Air Force in 1978 with the rank of major general. He was inducted into the New Jersey Aviation Hall of Fame in 1989.

THREE FAST KILLS

1st Lieutenant DUERR SCHUH, USAAF
487th Fighter Squadron, 352d Fighter Group
Near Veldenbor, Belgium—December 26, 1944

Duerr "H" Schuh was born on December 25, 1916 in Douglas, Wyoming, and lived in several towns in the West and Midwest before the family settled in Denver in 1924, When Schuh enlisted in the Army Air Corps Flying Cadet program on January 16, 1942, he had completed three semesters of the mechanical engineering program at the University of Colorado in Boulder.

I had wanted to fly airplanes from the age of five, when I lived in Wheatland, Wyoming. The U.S. government flew mail to and from Cheyenne, Wyoming, and to Billings, Montana, and sometimes, adverse winds would cause the planes to run low on fuel, forcing them to land at Wheatland to get gas in order to continue on to their destination. My older brother and I would run out to these airplanes and tell the pilot we would keep the horses and cows that grazed at the edge of town away from licking holes in the fabric of the fuselage and lower wing. The animals would do that to get the salt taste from the dust on the fabric surfaces. When the pilot came back with the gasoline, he would put us in the cockpit while the plane was being fueled. Our eyes would bug out looking at all the instruments on the dash.

I graduated from Brooks Field in San Antonio, Texas, on November 11, 1942, as pilot and a second lieutenant. I was stationed at Key Field in Meridian, Mississippi, from December 1942 until January 1944, and then I went to the fighter school at Thomasville, Georgia, until April 1944. There I flew the P-39 Airacobra, the worst airplane the Army Air Forces ever had. I was shipped overseas from Tallahassee, Florida, in April 1944 and sent to the fighter replacement pool at Goxhill to await assignment to a combat group as a replacement pilot. In July, I joined the 487th Fighter Squadron of the 352d Fighter Group, a P-51 Mustang unit based at Bodney.

Most of the 352d Fighter Group's missions were escorting B-17 and B-24 heavy bombers. On a few missions, we were sent out to dive-bomb and strafe marshaling yards or strafe airdromes. Occasionally, we strafed truck convoys and trains, but only if we had enough fuel and ammunition enough after escorting the bombers back to friendly territory.

On my fifteenth combat mission, on September 11, 1944, I destroyed one Bf-109 at 27,000 feet near Einbeck, Germany. On my thirty-first mission, on November 2, 1944, I destroyed one Bf-109 at 30,000 feet over Merseburg, Germany.

I flew my forty-fifth combat mission on December 26, 1944. That day, the squadron dispatched four four-plane flights to sweep across eastern Belgium. The 487th Fighter Squadron always took off four ships at a time and formed up into a sixteen-ship stair-step formation—White Flight in the lead, then Blue Flight, Red Flight, and Yellow Flight trailing. If we had to climb out through overcast, we always went up in a very close formation, so we would all be together when we broke out of the overcast.

By about 1500 hours, the 487th Fighter Squadron was flying area cover over our assigned sector at 12,000 feet. The squadron commander, Lieutenant Colonel John Meyer, was leading Yellow and Red flights near Uxhein, and White and Blue flights were in the vicinity of Veldenbor. White Leader was Major William Halton, and I was White-3.

At about 1515 hours, White-2 called in 109s on the deck near Veldenbor. When I looked down, I could see approximately thirty Bf-109s organized in three waves of ten airplanes per wave. They were at very low altitude.

Major Halton dove down on the deck and pulled in behind the second wave of 109s, but apparently he did not see the third wave. I followed Halton and White-2 down, but I pulled in behind the third wave with White-4—1st Lieutenant William Miller—on my right wing. In order to keep from overshooting the 109s because of the speed I had accumulated in my dive, I had my flaps down about 20 degrees.

As I pulled in, I decided that I would first nail the 109 that was flying on the outer right of their formation. There wasn't a chance that any of the other 109s would throttle back and try to get on my tail. Besides, I believe we caught them by surprise.

I fired a three-second burst at the outer 109 from about 500 yards with a deflection of about 30 degrees, and I observed strikes to the right wing. The 109 burst into flames and plowed into the ground.

I immediately pulled over to the left and lined up on another 109. I'm sure the pilot didn't know I was back there; he made no attempt to evade. Once again, I fired from about 500 yards and at a deflection of 20 to 30 degrees, and I observed strikes at the right wing root and on the belly. This 109 spun in from about 200 feet and blew up.

At this point, several of the Germans led us into a tight Lufbery in which Lieutenant Miller overshot me and tacked onto two 109s. I flew his wing while he destroyed one of them with hits in the wing-root and cockpit areas. Miller apparently went on to damage the other 109, but by then I had had to break hard right, because I saw that four 109s were getting on my tail. I pulled around in a tight right turn and got one burst into the tail-end Charlie. I observed strikes on his right wing, and then he snapped to the right and plowed into the ground.

When I recovered, I was all alone. I had already called on the radio for help but had received none. By then, I was down to only one operable gun, so I flew back to base alone. When I got home, I had the radio checked. It was determined that my transmitter was not functioning, so no one heard me calling for help. Nevertheless, someone in Lieutenant Colonel Meyer's flight heard one of the other pilots call, and Meyer led his P-51s to the attack. Meyer and one of the other pilots each shot down a 109, bringing the squadron total in this melee to six 109s destroyed and one damaged.

First Lieutenant Duerr Schuh flew sixty-seven combat missions for a total of 271 combat hours. After returning to the United States in April 1945, he went through instrument instructor school at Bryan, Texas, and became an instrument instructor and check pilot. He left active duty in February 1947 with the rank of major in the Air Force Reserve. Schuh was promoted to lieutenant colonel in 1960 and stayed active in the reserves until he had twenty-six years' service. He then transferred to the Retired Reserve and was officially placed on retired status in 1976, at the age of sixty.

OVEREXCITED

1st Lieutenant DALE KARGER, USAAF
364th Fighter Squadron, 357th Fighter Group
Berlin, January 14, 1945

Dale Ernest Karger was born in Templeton, Pennsylvania, on February 14, 1925, and raised near Pittsburgh. In March 1943, several months before he graduated from high school, Karger entered flight training with Class 44-B at Maxwell Field, Alabama. He earned his wings at Spence, Field, Georgia, trained for overseas duty in P-40s, and was shipped to Goxhill Airdrome in England to polish his skills before moving into the pool of Eighth Air Force replacement fighter pilots. He was dispatched to the 357th Fighter Group in late August 1944 with all of twenty hours in P-51s under his belt. His first combat mission was a very rough bomber escort to Bremen on August 30, 1944.

First Lieutenant Karger's first victories were two FW-190s, which he downed while escorting bombers over Berlin on December 5, 1944. He downed a Bf-109 near Kassel on December 24.

On January 14, 1944, I was flying Greenhouse Green-4 position on a mission to Berlin with the 3d Bombardment Division. Our squadron was sweeping out in front of the bomber stream when 100-plus enemy fighters were spotted coming from at least two directions. The squadron was still in a fairly close formation and we still had our auxiliary fuel tanks on. I was in the tail-end-Charlie position in the formation.

When I looked to my starboard side, I was very much surprised to see an Me-262 jet aircraft opposite me up behind Greenhouse Green-2. The 262 was in so close in our formation that I was completely taken with excitement, and my thinking was a bit clouded, to say the least. Up until this time, we were maintaining radio silence, except for someone calling out the incoming bogeys. I yelled into the radio, "There's a jet job on your ass," which probably caused everyone in the group to quickly look behind. I was so excited, I couldn't think clearly enough to identify myself or the aircraft being trailed.

I have no idea why the German pilot didn't take out either the number-two man or myself at this time. One of the first things you are taught as a fighter pilot is to look more behind than ahead, but I think the reason for not doing that at this time was the fact that we were still in a pretty close formation which makes it rather difficult to look around.

The only thing I could think to do under the circumstances was swing my plane over and up behind the jet. The German must have anticipated this and immediately gave it full throttle straight ahead. By this time, I was directly behind him. And there I was, with fuel tanks on and gun switches in the Off position. Gun switches were kept off as a precautionary measure to keep you from accidentally pulling the trigger on the control stick and hitting one of your own people. Still caught up in the excitement of the moment, I looked at my controls and drew a blank as to which switch to turn on, even though they were all marked. In the meantime, because of his superior speed, the jet was pulling out of range fast. After smacking myself on the side of the head a couple of times, I regained enough composure to get the right switches on. I let go with a few quick bursts, but to no avail as he was too far out of range.

When I later told this story, I would say how lucky that guy was that I lost my cool, because there is no way he could have outrun the bullets from my six .50-caliber machine guns had the switches been on. The person I told the story to had another view of the whole thing; one that I never thought of; he said maybe I was the lucky one and that maybe that jet could have pulled up behind me and shot my ass off first. Needless to say, I pondered that one for a while.

Well, being as this thing was a fiasco from the start, you would think nothing else could go wrong! As fate would have it, while I was above and out to the side of the group after the jet, the whole bunch turned left, leaving me, as we would say later, fat, dumb, and happy—and all alone at 25,000 or 30,000 feet. I figured I would make the best of a bad situation, so I dropped my external tanks to get ready for whatever would come next. As I looked around, I could see a big dogfight starting about 5,000 feet below me. Everyone was turning left in a circle, and there was lots of shooting going on. My next mistake was that I thought I would dive right down into the middle of this mess and get me some. As I did this, I knew right away that it was a bad move; there were too many people shooting at each other. So I got out of there real fast and figured it would be better to sit on the outside and wait for a straggler to come out. In the meantime, Greenhouse-2, the guy that the jet was originally behind, joined up with me and became my wingman.

It wasn't long before a lone Bf-109 came along, heading for the deck. I think he had had his fill of what was happening and decided the easiest thing was to go home. As I got behind the 109 at about 20,000 feet, he started a slow decent to the east. While on his tail, I started closing very fast. I throttled back and even had to drop a few degrees of flaps to keep from overrunning him. At one time, I was almost flying beside him, wingtip to wingtip. When I dropped behind him to fire, I was so close that I think the bullets were going around both sides of the cockpit and converging in front. I couldn't see many hits. He may have been having engine trouble or some other problems, because he made no attempt at evasive maneuvers. When the 109 finally bellied into a field, I made one quick pass and fired, setting it on fire.

In spite of all the goofy things that happened to me on this particular mission, it ended up being pretty spectacular for the 357th Fighter Group. The sky was a perfect clear blue and any direction you looked you could see a couple of burning planes going down. The 357th was credited with shooting down fifty-six German aircraft on this one mission and we were awarded a Presidential Unit Citation and commendation by General Doolittle. Our losses for the day were kept to three or four.

Lieutenant Dale Karger got his jet—an Me-262—and achieved ace status near Munich on January 20, 1945. At nineteen years of age, he was also the youngest living ace in the Eighth Air Force. He subsequently shared in the downing of a Bf-109 on March 2, 1945, and he downed two more Bf-109s near Gutersloh on March 24, 1945. He returned to the United States in June 1945 and was on terminal leave when World War II ended on September.

RECON PATROL

2d Lieutenant LEE LARSON, USAAF
15th Tactical Reconnaissance Squadron
Dresden, Germany—April 8, 1945

Leland Alsen Larson was born on April 10, 1923, and raised in Whittemore, Michigan. He enlisted in the Army Air Forces in early 1943. After earning his wings in February 1944, he was posted to a fighter school, where he mastered the P-40 and P-51. Because of his extraordinary eyesight, Lieutenant Larson was selected for the Air Forces Tactical Reconnaissance School in Meridian, Mississippi, from which he graduated in July 1944. Upon his arrival in England in December 1944, Lee Larson was assigned to the Ninth Air Force's 10th Photographic Reconnaissance Group—just in time to take part as a novice pilot in the Battle of the Bulge. After getting a few shots into a German fighter on January 14, 1945, Lieutenant Larson received his first victory credit on March 21, when he downed a long-nosed FW-190 over Eisenach, Germany. Three days later, on March 24, he downed a Bf-109, also over Eisenach. Larson shared in the downing of a German fighter on March 27 and again on March 28. He received a half credit for each of these victories, bringing his total score to three. On April 4, 1945, Larson shared in the destruction of a Ju-188 medium bomber that went down over Wittenburg. In every aerial combat to that point, it was Lee Larson who had first spotted the enemy planes.

By April 8, 1945, I had been overseas for more than four months. At the time, I was a second lieutenant assigned to Flight B of the 15th Tactical Reconnaissance Squadron, a unit of the Ninth Air Force's XIX Tactical Air Command. The squadron was part of the 10th Photographic Reconnaissance Group. We flew in support of General George Patton's U.S. Third Army. At the time, the squadron was based at Trier, Germany; we were the first Air Forces squadron to fly off German soil. The runway was 2,900 feet long and paved, and it ran alongside the Moselle River.

Tactical reconnaissance missions were usually flown at 2,000 feet with two airplanes. The two planes usually flew well apart so that the wingman could provide good air coverage for the leader, who had to navigate and look for enemy positions and movement on the ground. Because my eyesight was especially good, I flew a lot of deep-route missions, checking railroad lines, highways, airfields, V-2 rocket installations, and any other important physical features. Eleven of these missions were flown with Captain Clyde East, who became an ace on March 27, 1945, while flying with me. By April 8, 1945, the 15th Tactical Reconnaissance Squadron had two other aces, Captain John Hoefker and 2d Lieutenant Joe Waits. Their success, and mine, was attributable to our good eyesight and the fact that we were out there all the time, flying low and looking for the enemy.

On April 8, 1945, I was again assigned to fly wing for Captain East. This was to be a deep-route mission to Dresden, Leipzig, and points in between. We were to check railroads, highways, airfields, and so forth.

We took off in two F-6Ds, which were P-51D Mustangs, each armed with six .50-caliber machine guns and equipped with a K-22 oblique camera mounted behind the seat armor plate and a K-24 vertical camera installed just behind the air scoop in the belly of the plane. The F-6D had a 1,520-horsepower Packard-Merlin-Rolls-Royce engine and a floating gunsight. In my opinion, it was the best damn airplane ever built. It took what I gave it.

Flying conditions and weather were excellent that morning. Northwest of Dresden, Germany, at 0800 hours, I spotted fifteen Ju-87 Stuka dive-bombers at 11 o'clock low, at approximately 500 feet of altitude. The Stuka formation was coming toward us from the east. I called the Stukas in to Captain East. I was hot to go after them, but East cautioned me that each had a 20mm cannon in the back seat that might be loaded for bear. This made sense to me, so I paused to see what East would do. But he was already zeroing in on the squadron leader. I followed and drew a bead on the number-three plane in the flight, which should have been flown by the second-in-command. Fortunately for us, the rear gunners had apparently expended their ammunition on some poor, hapless Russians. They were all turned around in their seats, probably listening to Axis Sally on the radio.

On the first pass we blew two of the Stukas out of the sky, just like that. Then we pulled up, just in case those rear gunners woke up and took action. To my amazement, all the remaining Stukas went from their stacked-right formation into a trail formation—one right behind the other. Now there was no way they could protect one another.

East went around again and pounced on one. I saw smoke and flames from that Stuka, and then I tried to "shoot the flock." I went straight along the formation from the rear to the front, firing short bursts at each Stuka in succession. I overshot every one of them until, finally, I was leading the German formation. East reminded me that I was going 125 miles per hour faster than the Stukas, which explained why I had overshot them.

I cut the throttle and dropped 20 degrees of flaps to slow down. That didn't do it, so I dropped 40 degrees of flaps. Finally, I had to drop 60 degrees of flaps to slow to their speed. Even then, I was coming up fast on the Stuka I had targeted. My floating gunsight settled on his fuselage and I started up the buzz saw. I saw pieces of the fuselage and left wing fly off, but at this point I had to pull up or collide with him. I'll bet it was the closest buzz job he ever saw. Frankly, I thought we were going to collide.

When I pulled up, I added a little throttle and pulled up 40 degrees of flaps, just in time to avoid a midair collision. When I looked down again, I saw that I was over a rail yard, where German troops on the ground were throwing the canvas off innumerable 20mm ack-ack cannon mounted on flatcars. I suddenly realized that being the hunted was not nearly as much fun as being the hunter. I pulled my flaps up all the way, threw the throttle past the emergency wire, and pulled straight up to 5,000 feet. When I got there, I looked for help from East. Just as I spotted him, my engine detonated and a ball of fire two feet in diameter came by the left side of the canopy. I had fed too much gas into the engine.

I was sure the German ack-ack gunners had me. It was the only time in seventy-seven combat missions that I panicked. I took hold of my bootstraps and rejoined East.

It couldn't have been a minute after I joined East that I spotted an He-111 twin-engine bomber underneath us, right on the deck. I called the Heinkel in to the East, and the team went to work. We'd been through this twin-engine bit on April 4, when we had shot down a Ju-188 near Wittenburg. As before, East took the left engine and I took the right. We shot the He-111 down in one easy pass from straight behind.

As we pulled out from the He-111, I spotted a Stuka that was attempting to land at a small airfield nearby. East took a chance that there wouldn't be any ack-ack at this field and rolled in to give the Stuka a burst. East wouldn't claim this one when we got back, but I saw the Stuka's left landing gear collapse. The Stuka hit the ground hard and I'll bet Hans at least get a headache from the impact.

As we flew on toward Leipzig, I spotted a Siebel Fh-104. This was a five-seat cabin monoplane the Germans used for hauling passengers. It was at 11 o'clock and level to us. I knew that I had expended my ammunition on the He-111. East thought he might be out, too, so at first we ignored the Siebel, which looked harmless. But, since the Siebel was going our direction anyway, East told me to cover him and he'd find out if there was a bullet and powder left in the old musket. I think I called East twenty-five or thirty times to tell him that he was clear, but East didn't acknowledge me once. If he wasn't clear, I didn't know what I could do with no bullets.

East kept getting closer and closer to the Siebel. I was beginning to think he was going to fly formation with the German, right into the Leipzig airport. Just then, however, I saw a string of tracers go into the Siebel's left wing. The German transport folded up like butterfly. Three men tried to parachute, but none made it as the transport went into tight spirals and crashed into a field.

Lee Larson was given full credit for one of the Stukas and a shared credit for the He-111. This brought his total to five, making him an ace. Exactly a month later, at 2000 hours on May 8, 1945, 2d Lieutenant Lee Larson was on his seventy-seventh combat mission of the war when he scored his sixth and final aerial victory, an FW-190 he downed near Radnitz, Germany. It was the last German airplane but one downed over Europe in World War II, the 7,503rd credited to a United States Army Air Forces fighter pilot in the European Theater of Operations. It was also the last German plane downed by an American fighter ace.

Lee Larson returned to Michigan as soon as he was demobilized from the service at the end of the war. He passed away in 1990.

Part III

In Combat Over Korea

DOGFIGHTING WITH A LOAD ON

Major PHIL DeLONG, USMC
VMF-312 (USS *Bataan*)
Off Hojong-do, North Korea—April 21, 1951

Phillip Cunliffe DeLong was born on July 9, 1919, in Jackson, Michigan. He attended the University of Michigan for two years, majoring in aeronautical engineering; he was also a member of the university's ROTC unit. His college education was put on hold when he enlisted in the Navy's V-5 flight program immediately after Pearl Harbor.

Cadet DeLong was called to active duty in March 1942 and began Pre-Flight training at the Dallas Naval Air Station. He graduated from Corpus Christi on December 16, 1942, and accepted a commission in the Marine Corps. From Corpus Christi, 2d Lieutenant DeLong went to Miami for advanced fighter training and then to Glenview, Illinois, for carrier qualifications. Then he was assigned to VMF-212, which was in the midst of retraining at the El Toro Marine Corps Air Station following its first combat tour on Guadalcanal. VMF-212 shipped out to the South Pacific again in April 1943 as a newly equipped F4U Corsair unit.

At the height of the Rabaul air offensive—between January 1, 1944, and February 15, 1944—1st Lieutenant Phil DeLong shot down seven Japanese fighters and three D3A Val dive-bombers, shared a Zero with another pilot, and shared two Zeros with two other pilots—for a tally of 11.166 enemy aircraft destroyed in World War II.

Captain DeLong returned to the United States with VMF-212 in May 1944 and next served for a year with a training squadron. Then he served a six-month occupation tour in Japan, followed by a tour with the U.S. Navy Bureau of Aeronautics. In July 1949, he began a one-year tour at the Quantico, Virginia, Marine Corps Air Station.

In July 1950, I went from Quantico to El Toro, where I joined VMF-312, the "Checkerboards." We went to Japan in September 1950 and shortly began flying operational missions from Kimpo, in South Korea. We moved to Wonsan, in North Korea, in October, and then north to Yonpo in December. We flew armed reconnaissance and tactical missions in support of the U.S. X Corps in the Chosin Reservoir area until December 14, when we were withdrawn to Itami, Japan. We flew missions over Korea from Itami until we were ordered to complete carrier qualifications aboard the escort carrier USS *Sicily* on January 20, 1951.

After completing our qualifications, VMF-312 went aboard the light carrier USS *Bataan* in March. As part of the Seventh Fleet's Task Force 95, we flew more reconnaissance and close air-support missions for U.S. Marine and U.S. Army ground forces all over Korea. Also, we took part in Task Force 95's mission to escort friendly ships and blockade enemy threats on the west coast of Korea.

On April 21, 1951, I led a four-plane flight off the *Bataan* at 0540. The task was an armed reconnaissance along the west coast of Korea. Our Corsairs were carrying full external loads—six 5-inch air-to-ground rockets apiece, plus 500-pound General Purpose and napalm bombs.

Around 0645, as we were coming opposite Chinnampo harbor, we heard a distress call from a pilot with another "Checkerboard" division, 1st Lieutenant William Godbey. He reported that he was bailing out of his Corsair because of engine trouble. I made radio contact with the *Bataan's* combat air patrol and relayed Godbey's request that a helicopter be dispatched to pick him up.

As Godbey's division orbited his position, my second section was detached to rendezvous with the helicopter, escort it to the rescue site, and then return with it to the Korean mainland. Meanwhile, my wingman, 1st Lieutenant Harold Daigh, and I continued on to our original target area.

We were climbing to altitude over Hojong-do and had reached about 2,000 feet when we both spotted four aircraft approaching from the northwest at 5,000 feet. At that moment, I had just pulled out my maps and had them spread all across my lap. Daigh called the approaching aircraft out to me as U.S. Air Force F-51s.

Believing the four fighters to be friendly, I didn't pay any attention to them as they made a right turn toward me from 10 o'clock in a loose right-echelon formation. I quickly became aware that they were *not* friendly aircraft when a 7.7mm bullet fired by one of them entered my cockpit and slightly damaged my radio. Other bullets also hit my airplane. It was then that I realized the four were in fact Communist piston-engine Yak-3, or maybe Yak-9, fighters.

While attacking me, the enemy pilots evidently had not spotted Daigh, who pulled in behind the last two Yaks. At this point, Daigh tried and failed to release his bombs.

Despite the heavy external load, he dived to the left and below the number-three Yak, made a climbing 360-degree turn, and opened fire on both of the rear enemy aircraft with unobserved results. Then he turned on another Yak that was at his 4 o'clock, opened fire, and hit it in the tail, fuselage, and wing. This Yak's starboard wing broke off and the aircraft crashed and burned.

Meanwhile, as soon as I was fired on, I executed a very quick split-S to pick up speed. I had a cockpit full of loose maps, which didn't help visibility, and I had to get rid of them before I could recover from the split-S. This was one of the more tense moments of the mission, considering that I had started the split-S at about 2,000 feet in a fully loaded F4U. I did collect the maps, did recover from the dive, and made a climbing turn to the left.

Two of the Yaks attacked me again from astern, but I was able to turn the tables. While I was still in my defensive turn, one of the enemy aircraft crossed in front of me from right to left. At this instant, I saw Daigh's first victim crash.

Returning my full attention to the Yak in front of me, I hit it with a solid burst of .50-caliber bullets and sent it streaming smoke to the ground. It crashed and burned about a half-mile from Daigh's kill. It was only then that I had an opportunity to jettison my bombs. I thought about salvoing the 5-inch rockets, too, but I decided against that; I thought I might be able to use them against the remaining Yaks.

I next turned to my left—eastward—and immediately spotted two Yaks in front of me, heading in the same direction. Daigh was pursuing one of them, but the second was behind Daigh, turning right onto his tail. I radioed a warning for Daigh to pull out, and he made a quick turn to the left and opened fire on the rear Yak as it overran him. It began smoking from the cockpit and wing areas.

As I came up on the lead Yak (the one Daigh had been trailing), I opened fire and started it smoking with the first burst of .50-caliber. It turned to the south, split-essed, and recovered to the west. I followed it through the split-S and continued to score hits. The Yak was smoking from its wings and fuselage, pieces of it were falling away, and the pilot stopped using evasion tactics. I knew I had him.

I still had my six 5-inch HVARs (high-velocity aviation rockets), which I thought might be effective as air-to-air missiles. I selected the rocket launchers, hit the switch . . . and nothing happened. So I gave the Yak another burst of .50-calibers, and more parts fell off. I reselected the rockets, hit the switch again . . . and nothing happened. I tried to salvo the whole load, but still nothing happened, so I gave the Yak another burst of .50-calibers.

Suddenly, papers flew from the Yak's cockpit as the pilot jettisoned his hood and bailed out. The Yak crashed into the ocean and its pilot descended much more slowly to the water, apparently unhurt.

Daigh and I joined up, climbed to about 6,000 feet, and orbited the enemy pilot's position. I called to the *Bataan's* combat air patrol that the helicopter sent to rescue Lieutenant Godbey should also pick up the enemy airman. It was my intention to wait for the rescue helicopter, but we had orbited for only about ten minutes when Daigh's plane developed a rough engine. I had smoke in my cockpit, so we headed south to find the *Bataan*.

They wouldn't let me aboard with six 5-inch rockets on my Corsair. The ordnance officer advised me by radio that they had rewired the rocket circuit on my F4U the night before and installed a new switch to activate the rockets. With this information, I was able to jettison the rockets and land aboard the *Bataan* at 0820. But think of the possibility I had had of shooting down an enemy aircraft with an air-to-ground rocket!

The fight had lasted about ten minutes, from about 0715 to 0725. Three Yaks were immediately confirmed as destroyed—two by me and one Lieutenant Daigh. These were the first Marine Corps kills of the Korean War, and the first by Corsairs in the Korean War. Daigh had badly damaged the fourth Yak, but neither of us saw it crash, so it was recorded as a probable until April 26, two days after a Yak fighter was located by United Nations forces in shallow waters off the coast. It was assumed to be Daigh's second victim, so his probable was officially upgraded. The pilot of the second Yak I shot down was not rescued; because of a communications foul-up between the *Bataan's* combat air patrol and the ship, the helicopter that was sent to pick up Lieutenant Godbey never got the word to pick up the enemy pilot. Nevertheless, several days later, a Chinese Yak pilot was pulled out of the water about twenty miles north of where our Yaks were shot down.

VMF-312 served on the Bataan *until June 1951, then rotated home to the United States. At that time, Phil DeLong was still the squadron's top gun, with two kills. He also had flown more missions during the Korean War than anyone else in the squadron—127 in all.*

Phil DeLong, who was awarded a Silver Star for his role in the April 21 dogfight, continued to serve in aviation flying and staff billets until he retired from the Marine Corps in 1965 with the rank of colonel.

TWO BOMBS AND YOU'RE OUT

MAJOR GEORGE LOVING, USAF
9th Fighter-Bomber Squadron, 49th Fighter-Bomber Group
Pyongyang Area, North Korea—Spring 1951

George Gilmer Loving was born on August 7, 1923, in Lynchburg, Virginia. When the United States entered World War II, he was a freshman at Lynchburg College, pursuing a plan to enlist in the Army's flying cadet program as soon as he met the two-year college requirement. As soon as the Army Air Corps' education requirement was changed to include high school graduates, Loving signed up and was accepted.

Cadet Loving entered the service in March 1942 and graduated with his wings and commission in March 1943. He was shipped overseas in October 1943 and joined the 31st Fighter Group in Naples, Italy. Lieutenant Loving flew 101 combat missions in Spitfires, mostly in support of U.S. Army and British ground forces.

On April 8, 1944, shortly after the 31st Fighter Group transitioned from Spitfires to P-51 Mustangs, 1st Lieutenant George Loving scored his first aerial victory, a Bf-109 he downed near Cervigano, Italy. Thereafter he downed four more German aircraft and became an ace with a double kill on July 31, 1944. He flew nine more missions over southern Europe—for a total of 101 Spitfire missions and 50 Mustang missions—before being rotated home.

Captain Loving trained P-47 pilots to the end of World War II and remained in the service after the war. As a major, he assumed command of the 49th Fighter-Bomber Group's 9th Fighter-Bomber Squadron in Korea on February 20, 1951.

Was it an ill omen? Two 500-pound bombs hurtled past us no more than fifty yards away, striking sparks as they bounded down the 5,000 foot, pierced steel-plank runway at Taegu Air Base.

Our mission was to take out a bridge serving the Chinese Communist Army east of Pyongyang. After completing that task, we would conduct an armed reconnaissance of a seventy-five-mile road segment, attacking any and all military elements we sighted—tanks, vehicles, artillery pieces, troops, and supplies. Our armament included two 500-pound General Purpose bombs, 5-inch high velocity aerial rockets, and a full load of .50-caliber machine gun ammunition. We were a flight of four Lockheed F-80 Shooting Stars, call sign Humdrum Red, taxiing down an inactive runway parallel to and a few yards from the active runway at Taegu. Humdrum Blue, another flight of four F-80s, had preceeded us by a few minutes.

Just as Humdrum Blue Leader's aircraft reached take-off speed, his bombs detached, giving us something to think about as they loped past us and continued their eerie and potentially deadly journey to the end of the runway, where they died in a cloud of dust, still unexploded. As the squadron commander, I would have to deal with the careless flight leader when I returned. For now, I had other things to do.

As we climbed to 25,000 feet, our route of flight took us from Taegu Air Base, in the mountainous south, on a northwesterly course. Seoul, the Republic of Korea's capital city that had been ravaged by the North Korean Peoples Army during the opening stage of the war and then mauled by U.S. forces during the city's recapture, was one of our checkpoints. We came to the front line thirty miles or so farther up the road. They were easy to delineate because vehicular traffic was heavy on the United Nations's side but completely absent on the Communist side. As we crossed, an artillery duel, silent to us, was in progress; it was marked by flashing explosions and clouds of smoke.

In the hands of a skillful pilot, the F-80 was an excellent dive-bombing platform. Easy to fly and highly stable in flight, it could deliver the goods if the pilot did his job. Accurate bomb delivery required a knowledge of wind direction and speed, and smooth handling of the flight controls. The challenge was to establish and maintain the right dive angle and airspeed while keeping the aiming cross (adjusted for wind direction and speed) on the target and releasing the bombs at the proper altitude. If all of these conditions were met, there was a good chance the bombs would hit the target.

Some two hundred miles from base, I began a descent to 8,000 feet and started looking for landmarks that would lead me to the target, still about forty miles ahead. As we leveled off, I picked up the river, then the bridge. There was nothing fancy about this hastily constructed overpass. Made of wood and wide enough for two lanes of military vehicles, it was perhaps seventy-five feet in length. Get a bomb near this structure and it would be history.

At this point, I had racked up approximately fifty dive-bombing missions. First Lieutenant Jim Haroldson,* flying as element leader in the number-three slot, had a couple dozen missions under his belt and was

---

* The name has been changed at General Loving's request out of respect and concern for the feelings of the man's family and loved ones.

marked as a future flight leader. An excellent pilot, he had demonstrated coolness under fire and maturity beyond his years. While the other two pilots in the flight were relatively new at combat flying, they were well trained and had perhaps a half-dozen missions each to their credit.

Intelligence had been vague about enemy defenses, but we always expected antiaircraft fire from almost any target worthy of attack. Surprise, a high attack airspeed, and a steep angle of approach, together with our brief time over the target, would provide good odds of surviving any enemy fire.

There wasn't a cloud in the sky, and smoke from a fire on the ground provided the clues we needed to judge wind velocity and direction. My gunsight was on and operating, and the bomb-selector control switch pointed to both. As the target slid toward the leading edge of my left wing, I flicked another switch to arm both bombs.

When the target reached the wing's leading edge, I did a wingover into a 45-degree dive, adjusted the throttle setting, opened the speed brakes, and maneuvered to place the gunsight's pipper on the upwind side of the target. At this point, smooth, coordinated flight was essential. At 4,000 feet, I punched the bomb-release button and began my pullout, registering four Gs on the meter as I zoomed back up out of the range of the small-arms fire that was coming at me. Both of my bombs struck the bridge's abutment on the south bank of the river, and my wingman's bombs, moments later, straddled the bridge's center section, creating two giant geysers as they struck the water and exploded.

We had not observed any antiaircraft fire during our attacks, so there wouldn't be that distraction for the last two pilots on target. As I leveled off at 6,000 feet, Jim Haroldson was well into his bomb run, and his wingman was just entering his dive. Although everything looked just fine, a catastrophic event was about to occur.

Those two out-of-control 500 pound bombs careening down the runway at Taegu had pointed up in a dramatic way the ever-present potential for deadly accidents in a combat theater. We all knew such accidents might occur at any time, but still the pressures of the moment could obscure the hovering threat.

Haroldson had observed where our bombs struck, and like any red-blooded fighter pilot, would do his best to do better by placing his bombs squarely on target. Competition has always played a strong role in fighter squadrons. In honing gunnery, rocketry, and bombing skills, careful count was kept during training sessions of the scores of every pilot. Status—one's standing with fellow pilots—depended on scoring well.

Down he came. I watched as he reached 3,000 feet, then 2,500 feet, and 2,000 feet. No bombs. "Oh, no," I muttered. "He's going too low." Then I saw the bombs release, and Haroldson started to pull up. A second or two later the bombs struck the center of the bridge, the twin explosions emitting ugly yellow flames and powerful shock waves. For a brief instant, I thought Haroldson would be all right. A close call, but okay. Then I saw flames spewing from his aircraft like a Fourth of July rocket. Instantly, I radioed, "Humdrum Red Three. Eject. You're on fire." He must have been incapacitated at that point, a victim of his own bomb blasts. Still streaming flames, the crippled aircraft slammed into a nearby hill.

The usual cause of such incidents is "target fixation"—a term used to describe a situation is which the pilot concentrates on the target to the exclusion of everything else, including a rapidly unwinding altimeter. It was a sad ending for an excellent pilot, well respected by his squadron mates.

We made one circuit of the crash site and then set course for the next phase of our mission. There was nothing more we could do for Haroldson, beyond filing a report detailing the circumstances of his tragic end.

I picked up the beginning point of our assigned road, eased down to fifty feet and set my throttle to maintain 350 miles per hour. The other two leveled off at 1,500 feet, trailing me by a quarter-mile, one on either side. Given our vulnerability to small-arms fire at low altitude, our usual tactic was to make a single pass on a target and not turn back unless it was something special.

United Nations Command had put out the word to the North Koreans that anybody and anything on the roads, waterways, and railroads would be considered a military target subject to attack. Regular fighter sweeps of transportation arteries during daylight hours were aimed at inhibiting enemy movement to the maximum. As a result, the enemy was forced to rely increasingly on night movement and use great care when on the roads during daylight hours. Targets were usually camouflaged and difficult to spot; sometimes they were concealed under trees or otherwise hidden from view.

By flying low, I could spot targets that couldn't be seen from higher altitude. Since I was flying too low and fast to attack them, I acted as a spotter, calling out targets to be attacked by the other two.

Out ahead, I sighted a half dozen vehicles parked beneath roadside trees at a slight curve in the road. As I flashed over them, I radioed, "Red Two. Six vehicles under tree line, left of road. Here." Red Two began a shallow dive, placed his gunsight pipper on the target area and began firing even before he could see the vehicles. The first of his .50-caliber rounds tore at the road some seventy-five feet short of the vehicles; then the stream of projectiles lunged forward, ripping the line of trucks from bumper to bumper.

Further along, I spotted a group of soldiers, perhaps fifty in number, and radioed, "Red Three. Troops. Right side of road, heading for the ditch. Here." He laced the area with .50-caliber rounds. As he flashed overhead at fifty feet, he could see the cringing soldiers sprawled out, face-down, in the ditch.

Although we were moving fast, almost six miles per minute, we made eight attacks along the seventy-five-mile route. Trucks, sedans, a couple of motorcyclists, small bands of troops, and a train of pack horses experienced the shock and surprise of our sudden and deadly out-of-nowhere attacks.

Near the end of our run, we happened upon three boxcars, empty and parked on a siding out in the middle of a rural area. What was this all about? Suspicious, I circled, looking for a clue to explain their presence. Suddenly, it became clear, explained by orderly rows of haystacks during a season when there was no hay. The rounds I fired into one of the stacks exploded hay in all directions. We had stumbled on an ammunition dump. We set to work, exploding one haystack after another, until the area looked like a tornado had touched down. It wasn't until my wingman radioed "Josephine" that we set course for Taegu. Josephine was the code word used to signal that an aircraft's fuel supply had reached the predetermined must-start-for-home-now level.

Confederate calvary general Jeb Stuart, who boldly led 1,200 troopers in circling McClellan's army during the Peninsula Campain of 1961, thus creating havoc in the rear areas, would have given us a thumbs-up for the commotion we stirred up along that seventy-five-mile stretch of the enemy's rear area. But there was a difference. Our incursion was a routine event, repeated day after day by flights of fighter-bombers. For the enemy's soldiers, the rear areas were as dangerous as the front lines.

Back at base, the flight leader whose bombs got everybody's attention was waiting for me. He was a likable fellow, mature and experienced, but from the day he joined the outfit there had been something about him that didn't quite fit the fighter-pilot mold. It was never clear to me whether his bomb release was accidental or intentional, but in any event he wanted out of combat. He had had enough, he said. We accommodated him. The last thing the Air Force needed was a fearful fighter pilot. Afterwards, I filed a report describing the sad end of a brave young fighter pilot.

Major George Loving commanded the 9th Fighter-Bomber Squadron until July 20, 1951, by which time he hads flown 113 combat missions over Korea. A career Air Force officer, he served on active duty thirty-seven years, and achieved the grade of lieutenant general by the time he retired in 1979.

MUDDER

1st Lieutenant JIM KASLER, USAF
335th Fighter Squadron, 4th Fighter-Interceptor Wing
Yalu River Area, China—May 15, 1952

James Helms Kasler was born in South Bend, Indiana, on May 26, 1926, and raised in Indianapolis. After graduating from high school in 1944, Kasler enlisted in the Army Air Forces and served as a B-29 gunner in combat over Japan near the end of the war. He left the service in May 1946 and attended Butler University for three years before entering the Air Force's pilot training program in January 1950. Second Lieutenant Kasler earned his commission and pinned on his silver wings at Williams Air Force Base, Arizona, in March 1951. Following gunnery training in F-84s, he was sent to Korea in November 1951.

First Lieutenant Jim Kasler downed a MiG-15 fighter over North Korea on April 1, another on April 21, and a third on May 5.

In May 1952, the 4th Fighter-Interceptor Wing was stationed at Kimpo Air Base, Korea. At that time, Colonel Harrison Thyng, our wing commander, decided that we should have a flight standing alert at dawn every day. Ours was one of the first flights to pull that duty.

My flight commander was Captain Philip Colman, a World War II ace with two MiGs credited so far. We called Phil "Casey," because he once slid an F-86 in on a railroad track after running out of fuel. Casey's wingman was 2d Lieutenant Jim Low, who had one MiG credited at the time. I was the element leader, with three MiGs credited; and my wingman was 1st Lieutenant Albert Smiley, who had one MiG credited so far.

We set up our aircraft and left Albert in a bunk in the ready Quonset hut to man the phone while we went out to try to get warm in the rising sun. Eventually, the phone rang several times, and Casey finally asked whether there was someone in the hut. I ran in and found Albert leaning on one elbow, looking at me. I asked, "Why in the hell didn't you answer the phone?" And he said, "I knew *someone* would."

I picked up the alert phone, and a voice asked, "Where in the hell have you been? Scramble! Scramble!" I hit the alarm and said to Albert, "I'll fix you when we get on the ground, you SOB."

We took off and headed straight for the Yalu River. As we got closer, the ground radar controllers kept directing us farther up the river, away from Antung, the huge MiG base in China, just across the Yalu. The controllers told us that the MiGs had turned, then a few minutes later they told us they had lost contact.

I had paid a visit to the radar site near Kimpo two days earlier, and they told me then that they could only pick up MiGs over Antung above 15,000 feet. With that in mind, I broke my element away from Casey's and dove toward Antung. I said, "Albert" into the radio, and when he looked over, I simply punched off my drop tanks. He did the same.

I caught the MiGs just as they were pitching out to land at Antung. I dropped my dive brakes and executed a split-S to get in behind the lead MiG. I opened fire from about 1,200 feet, and the MiG immediately started flying apart. When I pulled up on his left wing, the canopy was gone and the pilot was sitting in a pool of fire. The MiG then fell off to the right and scorched a wide, fiery trail across the air base.

Next, I looked out to the right and saw another MiG firing at Albert, who was intently watching another MiG he had just torched. I hollered for him to break as I went after the MiG on his tail. The MiG turned, dropped to the deck, and went right down the runway at Antung. The sky around my F-86 was black with flak.

I chased the MiG about fifty miles on the deck, until we reached the sea. At one time during the chase, Casey Colman dropped down between me and the MiG. I had just fired a burst that lit up the MiG. Casey bounced back up, out of the way, and said, "Come on, Kas, you have your five." I said, "Negative. Smiley got one of them."

When we reached the sea, the MiG pilot pulled up into an Immelmann. As he started down again, I scored with another burst. By this time I had closed to about 500 feet, and when we dove down we were over the coastal mud flats. The morning haze over the mud flats made forward visibility impossible, but I could still see straight down. I didn't realize I was in any danger until the MiG splashed into the mud. We were doing close to 500 knots and were both in a 60-degree dive when the MiG hit. When I saw the mud shoot up around the MiG, I dropped my dive brakes and grabbed the stick with both hands. I kept waiting for the impact, for I was certain I was going to join my opponent. The murk became darker and darker, then the sky ahead slowly started to become lighter. I pulled in my dive brakes and broke out into the sunlight at about 4,000 feet. I said over the radio, "Casey, I am an ace."

I don't know how close I came to the mud, but I don't think it could have been more than ten feet. About a month later, an intelligence officer in Tokyo told me that Mao Tse-tung's son had been shot down on May 15 and that the three MiGs Albert and I got were the only ones downed that day. Albert got off the hook for not answering the alert phone, because I was so thrilled about making ace.

First Lieutenant Jim Kasler shot down a sixth MiG-15 over North Korea on May 25. 1952. He remained in the Air Force after the Korean War, served in a rotation of staff and flying assignments, and received his bachelor's degree in 1963.

In February 1966, Major Jim Kasler was assigned to the 355th Tactical Fighter Wing's 354th Tactical Fighter Squadron, then based at Takhli Royal Thai Air Base. He was shot down while leading a strike over North Vietnam on August 8, 1966, and was not repatriated until 1973, at the conclusion of the Vietnam armistice negotiations. Thereafter Colonel Jim Kasler attended the Air University and served as a deputy fighter wing commander until he retired from the Air Force with the rank of colonel in May 1975.

ANTUNG AIR UNIVERSITY GRADUATE COURSE*

Major ROBBIE RISNER, USAF
336th Fighter Squadron, 4th Fighter Interceptor Wing
Yalu River Area—October 22, 1952

Robinson Risner was born on January 16, 1925, in Mammoth Springs, Arkansas. He graduated from high school in Tulsa in 1942 and enlisted in the Army Air Forces as an aviation cadet in April 1943. Upon completing his flight training, he was commissioned and awarded his wings in May 1944. He was then sent to Panama to fly P-38s and P-39s, and he was still there when the war ended.

First Lieutenant Risner left the Army Air Forces in 1946, but he was recalled to active duty in 1951 and trained to fly jets. In May 1952, Captain Robbie Risner arrived in Korea for a combat tour with the 4th Fighter Interceptor Wing, which was based at Kimpo.

Risner shot down his first MiG-15 on August 5, 1952; his second on September 9; his third on September 15; and his fourth and fifth on September 21. Shortly, he was promoted to the rank of major and continued to fly combat missions.

I saw a lot of great flying while in Korea, but the best pilot I came across was not an American. Our encounter happened while I was on close escort for fighter-bombers that were hitting a chemical plant in North Korea, right at the mouth of the Yalu River, the border between China

---

* Robinson Risner, *The Passing of the Night.* New York: Ballantine Books, 1973. Quoted with permission of the author.

and North Korea. Normally we did not go across the river into China, but on this day, as a part of my screen, I had to do a 360-degree turn between the bombers and potential MiG forces. This carried me right over mainland China, near Antung. Here was what we called the Antung Air University, a big MiG field.

We had not even made one orbit when I met four MiG-15s head-on. We saw one another about the same time. The MiGs carried bathtub-type fuel tanks, which sat up close to the belly, and we carried a tank under each wing. We dropped ours and they theirs. The MiGs were not eager to engage and made a 180-degree turn, heading toward Fen Chen, an airfield beyond Antung down the coast.

I was afraid that if I lost sight of them, they might make a descending turn and come back at the bombers, so I stayed with them. When they turned, my radar locked onto the tail-end Charlie. Although I was at maximum range, I fired a short burst. I knew I had hit him in the canopy because the glass began to fly. He made a hard turn into me, and the other three made a right descending turn away from me.

I told my number-three and -four men to go after the other three and I would take this one because I had already hit him. He came hard into me and I turned inside him. When I rolled out—I was not more than 1,500 feet from him—I leveled down on him again and gave a short burst. It sparkled him a little bit, and he did a half roll and hung upside down, then did a complete roll and ended upside down again.

Meanwhile, we were descending, almost at Mach-One, about as fast as we could go. We were getting real low when he rolled it the second time and started a split-S for the ground. He appeared to be much too low for this.

I did not think he would make it, so I widened my turn slightly to have a little more room between the ground and me. I said over the radio, "Two! This is going to be the easiest kill I ever had." I knew he was going to splatter.

But as I watched, he pulled out down a dry river bed! The dust billowed up and he stayed right on the deck. He was so low that he was throwing up small rocks. I dropped down to get him, but to hit him I had to get down behind him, in his jet wash. There was so much turbulence that I couldn't do anything in it. It bounced me around like a cork in a rough sea and then spit me out.

This guy was one fantastic pilot. When I did get down in his jet wash, he would chop his throttle and throw his speed brakes out so I would overshoot him. I would coast up right beside him—just wing-tip clearance—looking him right in the eye. When it looked as if I were going to overshoot him, I would have to pull up and do a hard roll over the top of him and come back around the other side behind him. When I did this, he would throw the coal to it and go into a hard turn, pulling all the Gs he could. About the time that I got my pipper on him, he would push the stick forward and go into an inverted turn, which is extremely difficult and hard on the body and eyes. He would turn right out of my windshield. I could not duplicate his maneuver. I had to do a half roll and start to catch him again.

One time, he actually flipped upside down, went up the side of a small mountain, over the top, and pulled it down on the other side. I was right side up, so when I went over the top of the mountain I had to do a half roll to go down the other side.

I was having a real difficult time, but I was hitting him occasionally. I had shot away part of his tail, his canopy was missing, and he was burning out of the left side. He was not in very good shape, but he was a great pilot—and he was fighting like a cornered rat!

We were down in the river bed again and Joe, my wingman, who'd been sticking with me all this time, was hollering, "Hit him, Lead. Get him, Lead." Believe me, I was doing my best.

Charlie (that's what we called the MiG pilots) chopped the throttle and threw his speed brakes out. I coasted up, afraid that I'd overshoot him. I did a roll over the top of him, and when I came down on the other side, I was right on his wing tip. We were both at Idle with our speed brakes out, just coasting.

He looked over at me, raised his hand, and shook his fist. I thought, "This is like a movie. This can't be happening!" He had on a leather helmet, and I could see the stitching in it. His oxygen mask had evidently been sucked off when I shot away his canopy.

Then he made a left 90-degree turn, then swung back to the right. Before I realized what was happening, he went between two hangar buildings. He had led me right onto Tak Tung Kau Airfield!

Joe began shouting, "Lead, they're shooting at us!" The flak was bursting all around. In fact, you could see the gun barrels flashing, because we were right on the deck, thirty-five miles inside China. He had gone up and down this river and taken me to the airfield, figuring the flak would chase me off. He made a turn and went down the runway.

He seemed to be trying to force his aircraft down for a landing, but he hadn't lowered his gear and was doing about 300 knots. He went so low that he was blowing dust off the runway. I was not down low enough to hit him, so I just stayed where I was, knowing that he was going to have to pull up or make a turn. When he pulled up, I really hammered him. I blew about four feet off his left wing. It just exploded. When that happened, he made a hard right chandelle, then a right turn back down, and paralleled the runway. He may have been aiming for the grass growing alongside. I fired all the rest of my ammunition into him. He leveled off, making about 350 knots. He touched the ground and came unglued. Little pieces flew everywhere.

As Joe and I started climbing out, we had to pass over Antung. We had been told they had about 250 radar-controlled heavy guns in this area. Joe's aircraft got hit in the belly and began losing fuel. When he was down to five minutes remaining, I told him to shut down and I would try to push him to Chodo Island, where we had a rescue operation. He made it with room to spare, but the nose of my plane was all boogered up. Just before he bailed out he said, "I'll see you at the base tonight."

I was in radio contact with the rescue helicopter. They told me Joe had landed close to shore. His parachute was still open and they decided to use the rotor to blow him into shore. The last word I caught was that he seemed to be in trouble and they were putting a man in the water.

Physically, Joe was the typical all-American boy. Six feet tall, blond, a fine swimmer, and, in fact, a former lifeguard. I was out of radio range, but I felt sure he was okay. That evening, we went to the rescue plane to meet him. When they opened the doors, Joe did not get off. They said he had drowned.

I was the twentieth pilot to shoot down five MIGs in air-to-air combat—the requirement to become an ace. We were required to fly 100 missions, but I flew a total of 109 and ultimately shot down eight MIGs.

Korea was probably the high point of my whole career, as far as real gratification is concerned. To be able to participate in air-to-air combat was a thrill. When you are in personal combat with another individual in a similar type of aircraft, the difference is going to be your training, your abilities, your motivation, and sometimes your guts. Then again, air-to-air warfare is a clean, impersonal type of thing. It's not dirty, like down in the trenches, and there is no hand-to-hand combat. When people die, you don't see it.

Major Robbie Risner downed his seventh MiG-15 on December 4, 1952; and his eighth and last on January 21, 1953. He remained on active duty with the Air Force after returning from Korea in mid-1953. He commanded another fighter squadron in Germany in 1954, and a fighter-interceptor squadron in the United States in 1955.

In 1964, Lieutenant Colonel Risner assumed command of the 67th Tactical Fighter Squadron in Okinawa. He was shot down over North Vietnam—and rescued—in April 1965; and then he was shot down—and captured—in North Vietnam in September 1965. For a large part of his incarceration in Hanoi, Colonel Risner was the senior ranking American officer, and he later became the vice commander of the 4th Allied POW Wing.

Robbie Risner was repatriated from North Vietnam in February 1973 and promoted to the rank of brigadier general. He later commanded an air division and retired from the Air Force on July 31, 1976, a little more than thirty-two years after earning his commission.

CAPTURED

Captain HAROLD FISCHER, USAF
39th Fighter Squadron, 51st Fighter-Interceptor Wing
Near Dapu, Manchuria—April 7, 1953

Harold E. Fischer was born May 8, 1925, in Lone Rock, Iowa, and grew up in Swea City, Iowa. He joined the U.S. Navy during World War II and became an aviation cadet in 1944, but he was discharged from the service at the end of the war, before he could complete flight training.

After completing two years of college at Iowa State University, Fischer persuaded the U.S. Army to commission him as a second lieutenant of infantry in February 1949. After completing an infantry course, Fischer simultaneously received orders sending him to Korea as an infantry platoon leader and *orders to begin flight training. Faced with alternatives, 2d Lieutenant Fischer did some "inventive paper wrangling" to transfer himself to the Air Force as a pilot trainee. He won his wings in December 1950 and made his way almost directly to the war zone in the Far East.*

Lieutenant Fischer's initial combat experience came as the pilot of an F-80 with the 8th Fighter Wing's 80th Fighter-Bomber Squadron. After completing an obligatory 105 missions in F-80s, Fischer served a stint as a staff officer at Far East Air Force headquarters. He then requested another combat tour. He was assigned to the 30th Fighter Squadron of the 51st Fighter-Interceptor Wing to fly F-86s. In the course of seventy missions with the 30th Squadron, he was credited with downing ten MiG-15s between November 26, 1952, and March 21, 1953.

Around the beginning of April 1953, there were reports that the Chinese were massing jet bombers in the Mukden area, and bombers had been seen on their airfields. These reports generated the fear that our own airfields might be attacked by the jet bombers. This caused us to remove a certain number of our aircraft to other airfields every evening. The basic reasoning for this was the protection of our aircraft from surprise attack. This was the United Nations reaction to the Chinese flying twin-engine medium bombers near the Yalu River. It caused the United Nations forces to expend tremendous resources and energy to ferry their aircraft to other bases every evening and return them to their home bases every morning.

It was my duty to lead a number of these flights to Taegu or Kunsan and there spend a short period of time before returning to our base at K-13 the next day. Ordinarily the quarters at the other bases were very inadequate; as a result, the ferry pilots were tired when they flew their combat missions.

On one of these flights to Kunsan, I led a flight of eight and spent a restless night. At Kunsan, I saw my old instructor from advanced flying school. It was good to talk to him, but he cautioned me about flying, particularly a bit from a recent news story about my ramming a MiG.

He opened the subject by mentioning that he thought my statement had been reported incorrectly, that the reporter had misinterpreted what I had said. During our conversation, I explained my theory on ramming as a combat tactic and, after some minutes at the bar, he began to see my point. Nevertheless, as he left, he cautioned me to be careful, and said that he had not taught me to fly like that.

The next day, fog blanketed the field at Kunsan, and we had to delay our takeoff until the weather cleared. While there, we talked to the crew chiefs, who told of an F-84 that had crash-landed just off the runway. When they got to the aircraft, the pilot was gone. They attributed the pilot's disappearance to guerrilla activity, which was rampant in the area around the field. There was also talk of aircraft that blew up on takeoff. All in all, the morale on the base was not the highest.

As soon as the fog lifted, we took off and climbed into the bright spring sun. It was April 7, 1953.

When I raised the gear handle into position, the gear didn't retract. I had neglected one of my pre-flight checks, which was repositioning the switch in the nose-gear compartment. This heralded the beginning of a very bad day.

Arriving at K-13 with my gear already down, I landed and spent some time at the base operations hut. Awaiting me was an application for a Regular Air Force commission that had been delivered by the commanding general's aide. It was to be filled out and hand carried by the general to USAF headquarters when he was relieved. It was a virtual assurance that I would get a regular commission, which was something I had wanted. But when the paperwork was in front of me, I experienced a certain reluctance to fill it out. Perhaps it was my way of rebelling against the military system, which I liked even though I was keenly aware of its many defects.

Our flight was scheduled for a mission later in the afternoon. I was to lead. We were briefed to break up into separate elements as soon as we arrived in the patrol area.

After we started up our engines, I taxied out to the end of the runway and waited for my number-two. He had somehow missed me when I taxied past him in the revetment, and he had to be told by the element leader to taxi out. This made us late for our group position, so we took off last. Meanwhile, precious fuel was wasted.

Climbing into the patrol area, we saw circling contrails in the center of Korea opposite Wonsan. Occasionally, two contrails would head north; they were obviously enemy aircraft. I called the number-three and requested that he investigate while I held my altitude. By the time three and four had approached the area, the distant aircraft had climbed up and disappeared from the contrail level.

Continuing our flight northward, I saw a flight of four aircraft—MiGs, all pulling contrails—as it came across the border. We attacked as they passed 2,000 feet beneath us. As we gained our position, the enemy flight began to zoom. Before the MiGs had the advantage, however, I fired my guns when they were 200 feet off to my right. I did so in order to compensate for the misaligment of my guns, which caused them to shoot wide of the mark. The guns were misaligned because they had not been boresighted since the mission before, when all the rounds had been expended on an enemy airplane. It was organizational policy to boresight the guns after every mission on which they were fired, specifically to prevent what my guns were doing now. This airplane had been given to me, and I had accepted it, because there were no spares, so I had no one but myself to blame for my gunnery problems. The only thing that I could do was curse, which I did vehemently. Before I could correct for the error in the guns by adjusting my sight pattern, we were attacked by four other MiGs that were above the contrail level.

There was nothing we could do except break off the attack. It was not a break in the true sense of the word; it was a turn and then a reversal of the turn, so we could attack the attackers. But it was no use, as the MiGs were traveling too fast. Rather than pursue the issue, which was hopeless, we set up our course for the mouth of the Yalu and then home again.

My wingman evidently had a tip tank that had not fed properly. He called to tell me that he was getting low on fuel. Just then, three aircraft came across our noses, heading north. It was an ideal situation. I called a bounce, but my wingman called that his fuel was getting lower. I made the wrong decision; I told him to head out, and that I would follow him. But I continued the attack.

There were three MiGs—two leading the way and one straggling behind. I chose the straggler. I dropped down and closed on him at a tremendous rate of speed. After getting off a shot, I made a gigantic roll around him and then fell in behind him. The MiG accelerated and was now even with his lead element, which I was rapidly overtaking. I rolled over on the number-two MiG in the formation and fired. This time I was on target, having properly adjusted my sight. I let him have a long burst. I hit this MiG and stopped his engine. He dropped back, which gave me an opportunity to hit the lead aircraft. From about 1,200 feet, all six .50s literally tore the aircraft apart. Large pieces of debris flew past my aircraft, and I unconsciously ducked as they went by.

I now had two choices—either go down under the next MiG, or go over it. I decided to go over the airplane, because I did not want to be in front of it, as I had been one time before.

At this time, the throttle came back into my hand. The instruments read that my engine was dying, and my speed fell off so rapidly that I was pushed forward against my shoulder straps. I thought of calling my wingman to let him know what was happening, but I did not because he might have been interpreted my message as a cry for help.

It was possible to reach the mouth of the Yalu, but I determined that I would be at zero altitude when I did. The characteristics of the F-86 in a ditching were not predictable. If one hit the surface just right, the airplane would not sink immediately, but the chances for this were slight. Nevertheless, I decided to risk it—until I smelled that bane of all pilots and saw that smoke was issuing into the cockpit. My airplane was on fire.

Now there was no decision to make if I wanted to live, for the aircraft would probably blow up in the next few seconds. I had to bail out. I reached down for the left handle and jettisoned the canopy. Then, with the right handle pulled up, I leaned back in the seat, put my feet in the stirrups, and squeezed the trigger. I was at 2,000 feet and my airspeed was 450 knots.

The 37mm shell that activated the ejection seat gave me a terrific impetus upward. It caused me to momentarily black out. When I recovered, the first sensation was a rushing of wind around me. I was rotating rapidly in space. I immediately pulled the ripcord and waited for a tremendous opening shock. There was none, which came to me as a great surprise. I had followed all the procedures that had been rehearsed so many times: first you unstrap your safety belt, then you step away from the seat, and the last action is the pulling of the ripcord. When the parachute opened, the first indication was a slight jar. I looked up and checked the panels. They were all there save one. Then I looked around for aircraft and to survey the vicinity.

I saw a MiG that appeared to be a derelict in the sky. It was trailing a long stream of flame, as long as the fuselage. It turned lazily toward me, and I thought for sure that it would fire upon me. The only thing I had was my chrome-plated .45; otherwise I was defenseless. The MiG was one I had fired on, and I figured the pilot must have had a desire for revenge. But he did not pursue it. As the MiG turned lazily away from me, I turned my attention to landing.

The terrain below was rocky and hilly, with scrub brush and trees growing on the side of the rocky crags. Where to land was a problem as I gradually drifted toward the side of a small hill.

The stillness around me was surprising. I could hear shouted voices from the ground. They seemed to come from all directions.

The next surprise was the landing itself. I expected to break a leg at the very least, but I drifted down and my landing was cushioned when the canopy of the parachute caught in the branches of a scrub tree. This really saved me from a bad landing and a roll down the hill.

After releasing the harness of the parachute, I lay back and took a moment to evaluate the situation. I saw a lot of blood on my scarf; it blended into the yellow cloth. I gingerly felt my ear. Evidently my helmet, when it came off, had torn my ear and caused it to bleed. My body was completely soaked with sweat, although it was fairly cold. A feeling of complete tiredness came over me. I attempted to climb up the hill, but I could not get up. The only way I could move up was to crawl. I checked my watch and found out it was 1720 hours. If I could hide until dark, there was a possibility that I could elude pursuers, whom I could hear all around me.

I dropped my life vest and began to move away from the vicinity of my landing. Before I left, I dragged my parachute down from the small tree so that it would not be so visible to those who would soon be seeking me. I still had my chrome-plated handgun.

I moved from the crest of the ridge on which I had landed and started to move away from the general vicinity. After crossing a small ravine,

I approached the crest of the hill adjacent to the hill on which I had landed. If there had been some place to hide, I would have gotten to it and dug myself into the side of the hill, but there was nothing in the area that offered good concealment.

I was just about to cross over the crest of the hill when I heard voices on the other side. I crouched down just below the crest and waited. Soon, a small, dark Chinese man dressed in typical farming attire came down the ravine that I had just crossed. He was unarmed and reminded me of a farmer who was out trying to track a cow or horse that had strayed. I had my .45 in my hand, but there was no cause for concern as to what he might do, for he posed no threat to me that I could see. I had heard that there were many friendly agents in this area, and the thought went through my mind that perhaps this individual was a friend, and not an enemy.

The man very carefully came to within twenty feet of me before he saw me, and then he gave no indication of being surprised. He made some motions, and I thought that this person was a friend. I made an instant decision—that he must be a friendly agent and that he could lead me to shelter, where I could hide. I put all my trust in him and followed him down the ravine. He in no way indicated that he was anything other than friendly to me. At the bottom of the ravine, we were suddenly confronted by a large group of peasants carrying every type of agricultural tool imaginable, and a few old rifles, too. I had had it.

The group of about thirty Chinese milled around and inspected me as if I were a creature from another planet. They were not in any way hostile. After taking away my weapon, which I had secreted in my immersion suit, they directed me to a small hut that was close by the bottom of the ravine. Inside, they directed me to lay down and rest. I saw evidence of confusion among them: was I an American or another of the white pilots who were flying from Chinese bases? I formed a plan based on their obvious indecision. I would make it as plain as I could that I wanted to go to the nearest air base, which was just a few miles away, at Dapu. I got up and started to walk in that direction. When they protested, I insisted in my language of sign and word. Using this stratagem, I was able to move ahead down the road and position myself about fifty or sixty feet ahead of the group. A number of children followed me more closely than the adults. I thought about running, but the immersion suit

I was forced to wear by regulation precluded this. The suit was good only for staying afloat, not running—and, according to some, it wasn't good for delaying hypothermia, either.

Another group, evidently of militia, then approached us, and there was an argument between the civilians and the militiamen. The civilians wanted me to go in the direction of the airfield, but the militiamen wanted me to go the other way. Both groups began to push with me in the center, and for a moment the issue was debated more violently than I desired. When one of the militiamen, evidently the leader, secured some wire, I thought that I was going to be strung up immediately, so I acquiesced and sat down by the side of the road. By this time, there were two guards with rifles, who were uncomfortably close. Escape was now out of the question.

Soon a jeep came roaring up the road. It was the standard military model used by our forces. Four Chinese soldiers were aboard it. With more force than was necessary, I was placed in the back seat—or rather, tossed into the back seat. The jeep turned around in the direction of the airfield to which I had been headed a few moments earlier. About a mile farther along, the road was blocked by the remains of my aircraft. The last time I had seen the plane, it was circling around me, but it had disappeared behind the hill when I landed. There, in front of me, lay the remains of about $700,000 worth of airplane, now merely scrap.

As the jeep rolled to a stop, a soldier who was evidently Russian came up alongside. This individual was extremely hostile. Behind him I could see a Russian truck and four other Russian soldiers, who were loading scrap from my F-86. I had some identification with me, and this evidently had been reported to the hostile soldier, for he came up to me and, with the four Chinese soldiers holding me down, grappled with me and took the identification. I have never seen so much hate in an individual as I saw in this one. When the Russian had my papers, we immediately moved around the wreck of the aircraft and drove directly to a small village. I was glad that the encounter was so brief.

The village must have been the headquarters of the Chinese army in this area. None of the soldiers wore stars on their caps, so they were evidently destined for the Korean theater. After stopping the jeep, the four guards took me into what appeared to be a large meeting hall. I was placed in the center of the room, on a chair that stood on a dirt floor. At one end of the room was a telephone, which I'm sure was going to be used by someone determine just what to do with me. All around, peering in the windows and doors, were Chinese soldiers of all shapes and sizes. One of the soldiers who was braver than the rest brought my portable oxygen cylinder to me and attempted to ask me what it was for. When I pulled the activating pin, he almost dropped from fright. He made frantic attempts to shut it off, but to no avail. I also saw my .45 on the hip of a Chinese soldier who probably was very proud of the weapon.

After innumerable telephone calls, a squad of Chinese soldiers indicated that I was to go with them, and we went out the door to another American army vehicle, a carryall. There, squeezed in between two soldiers, I was driven to various villages, so the population could view the American pilot who had been shot down. Conspicuous among these villages were the youth groups, the pioneers. I was already a political prisoner.

Our final destination was the airfield that I had attempted to reach on my own, Dapu. I had wanted to reach it for two reasons. First, if I could convince the Chinese that I was a MiG pilot, I might have been able to escape. Second, I had no desire to be a prisoner of a hostile, ungoverned mob.

We entered the confines of a large barracks area, where I was blindfolded. I was then taken to a large building and placed in a dormitory, where many soldiers in nondescript uniforms lay on beds or sat at tables. An individual who seemed to be in charge indicated to me that food was available and also that I would not be shot. This was somewhat of a relief to me. One individual who could speak a little English asked me the number of my airplane. I had no idea what the number was, but when they insisted I gave them a number that satisfied them. The food arrived shortly thereafter; it was an omelet, which even under these circumstances tasted very good. Whenever I turned around, there were individuals looking in through the windows, and finally the windows had to be covered up.

After what seemed like a long time, another individual came in and asked me to take off my undershirt. I did this with assistance from the guard, then I put it back on. I had no idea why they did this, except maybe to see whether or not I was armed.

Next, I was next taken across the street or driveway and put in a room with a bunk. The Chinese soldier or airman on the top bunk woke up and then went right back to sleep. I was given a blanket and told to go to bed. A guard sat up on a chair in the middle of the room. One would think that it would be impossible to sleep under these circumstances, but sleep can be a form of escape in many circumstances, and so it was in this one.

Because he was over Chinese territory at the time he was shot down, Captain Harold Fischer was eventually convicted of "violating the sacred territorial air of China." He was therefore incarcerated in Mukden, China, with three other U.S. Air Force pilots until June 1955. He spent the most of his captivity in solitary confinement.

Upon his return to the United States, Fischer earned a bachelor's degree in industrial administration and a master's degree in industrial psychology at Iowa State, where he remained for a tour of duty with the ROTC program. Thereafter, the majority of Fischer's assignments were in the intelligence and human factors fields. He served in Vietnam as chief of Air Force Advisory Team Three at Bien Hoa Air Base and flew Republic of Vietnam Air Force helicopters and jet and piston fighters on numerous combat missions. He retired with the rank of colonel in May 1978.

In April 1994, Fischer traveled to Ukraine to meet former Soviet Air Force pilots who had fought in the Korean War. During the reunion, he happened to meet one of those he engaged on April 7, 1953. The former Soviet pilot told Fischer that his bullets hit the MiG-15 piloted by Senior Lieutenant Konstantin Ugramov twenty-two times in the rudder, right wing root, and fuselage. Ugramov managed to land (though with great difficulty), but the number of hits cited were enough to count as a kill under the U.S. Air Force rules in force at the time of the engagement. Fischer also learned that he was shot down by Captain Gregory Berelidze, a six-victory ace who was himself shot down and killed before the end of the Korean War. Based on information Fischer obtained from his former adversaries and other sources, it appears that on his last mission he downed one of the three MiGs he encountered and severely damaged another.

Epilogue

A FRIEND, NEVER MET

1st Lieutenant BOB GOEBEL, USAAF
308th Fighter Squadron, 31st Fighter Group
Ploesti, Romania—August 18, 1944, and 1994

Following his graduation from high school, Robert John Goebel, a native of Racine, Wisconsin, enlisted in the Army Air Forces as an aviation cadet. He was called to active duty on April 4, 1942, and commissioned at twenty years of age on May 23, 1943. After six months' service in the Panama Canal Zone, 2d Lieutenant Goebel was transferred to the Twelfth Air Force and assigned to the 31st Fighter Group, then about to transition from Spitfires to P-51s.

Goebel's first aerial victory was a Bf-109 he downed over Wallersdorf, Austria, on May 29, 1944. Thereafter, in little more than two months, he downed four more Bf-109s and an Me-110, and was credited with a Bf-109 probable. He rose steadily in the admiration of his peers, and his superiors gave him more responsibility despite his tender years and relative inexperience.

♦

I finally admitted it. I didn't kill him deliberately, with malice and intent, but kill him I did. At least I was responsible for his death.

Strange it was that I even remembered something that happened more than fifty years ago. It wasn't a particularly singular occurrence; at least in those times it wasn't. It happened back during World War II, on August 18, 1944, to be exact. With the first burst of machine-gun fire I saw the bright flashes of the armor-piercing incendiary projectiles tear into his aircraft, saw the canopy fly off and his body come hurtling out—all in far less time than it takes to tell.

The 31st Fighter Group had been equipped with Spitfires, one of two such American groups in the Mediterranean, and had provided support and air cover for the ground forces through North Africa, Sicily and the early Italian campaign. Nevertheless, the Fifteenth Air Force, formed in late 1943, needed additional escort fighters for its heavy bombers, in order to attack targets in such well-defended places as Ploesti, Munich, Budapest, western Czechoslovakia, and even up into southern Poland. At the end of March 1944, the 31st was ordered to turn in its Spitfires, accept delivery of new P-51s, and move to San Severo on the eastern side of Italy as part of the Fifteenth Air Force.

I joined the group just as the transition was taking effect. By mid-August, I had already flown fifty-five combat missions and had been in enough fights with German and other Axis fighters to believe that I was one of the hunters rather than one of the hunted. I had shot down six Bf-109s in the process. Of course, by *Luftwaffe* standards, I was a neophyte. Many of their pilots, those who still survived, had been in combat for several years and had flown hundreds of sorties. But I didn't feel like a new type, exhibiting the excessive confidence so often associated with fighter pilots.

Although we pilots in the 31st Fighter Group did not realize it at the time, the *Luftwaffe* had been worn down to the point where shortages of pilots and materiel had seriously affected their ability to engage the formations of bombers and fighters that appeared often and unrelentingly over southern European targets. By late summer of 1944, the defense of the German industrial targets had become an impossible task for the *Luftwaffe*. We still lost aircraft and pilots to the German fighters—there was no mistaking the fact that the Bf-109G, in the hands of an experienced pilot, was a formidable opponent—but the fighter opposition was definitely weakening.

At that time, my squadron commander was Captain Tommy Molland, an old hand from the group's Spitfire days in North Africa and Sicily, and a close friend. He told me that he had gotten permission to put up four extra aircraft on an upcoming mission. Unlike the sixteen aircraft of the normal squadron formation, the extra flight would have no close-escort responsibility but would be free to roam about the skies in the vicinity of the target looking for enemy fighters. His idea was that German fighters were avoiding the Mustangs and were using their remaining strength to attack the bomber formations where the escort was thin or nonexistent. If one could loiter in the target area long enough, Tommy's reasoning went, the chances were good that enemy fighters could be found and engaged. He said that he was going to lead the extra flight himself, and offered me the number-three, or element lead, slot. I jumped at the chance. Besides being a great opportunity for some air action, I was pleased that he had seen fit to choose me to participate in his experiment.

The mission he picked was on August1 18, another trip to the oil fields of Romania. The task of the group on that day was to provide close escort for B-24s of the 55th Heavy Bombardment Wing attacking oil refineries near Ploesti.

We had our usual powdered eggs and coffee, but I went easy on the coffee. Ploesti was a long way—five and a half hours all told—and the relief tube, as a means of processing slightly used coffee, was absolutely useless. At the briefing, the tail markings of the 55th Bomb Wing were described and other mission details were covered, but Tommy and I couldn't have cared less. We had no intention of staying with our squadron and their bombers once we reached the Ploesti-Bucharest area. Takeoff was set for 0814 hours, all the data was duly inked onto palms or backs of hands, and watches were synchronized. Then it was time to go, so everyone headed for their transportation to the airdrome, located some six miles to the west.

Tommy and I had scheduled two of the newer pilots to fly our wings, and so the four of us piled into Tommy's jeep for the trip to the field. We were in no hurry since we were going to take off last and tag along behind our squadron, the 308th, as it climbed up to its assigned altitude of 26,000 feet.

The bomber rendezvous was made at 1000 hours between Craiova and Pitesti, and the squadron immediately took up its assigned escort duty over the bombers. Tommy stayed with the formation for a short time, but when I saw some tiny, fast-moving dots to the east and called them out, he made a slight turn to the right and off we went to investigate. But we lost visual contact with the planes, so after loitering beyond the Ploesti-Bucharest area for a bit, Tommy turned back toward the target area. We weren't straight and level for thirty seconds when I happened to look back. What I saw really shocked me. Very close—far too close—and slightly above us was a formation of Bf-109s. I called a break immediately, and the fight was on. The initial stages of the fight are a blur. The first gut-wrenching, graying-out turns are all instinctive, as are the moves inside the cockpit; tanks away, mixture Full Rich, full throttle, full RPM, gun switch on.

Now I am behind a 109, in range. I open fire. The six .50s immediately come to life. A half-second later, the burst produces a series of sudden flashes on his fuselage and wing roots. His canopy is off, and he's over the side, falling away from my view to a lower altitude where his chute can be opened in safety. I snap a quick look around, spot another 109 at my 11 o'clock and well below me, diving at high speed. A sharp turn to check my tail, and then I'm closing on him, still at max throttle. He takes evasive action. It is a zero-deflection shot. He rapidly fills the sight. Pipper in the middle of the fuselage. *Now!* My aircraft seems to tremble as the machine guns begin firing. Again, a split-second later, the strikes begin to play upon the 109's fuselage, but this time I hold the trigger down. The canopy flies away . . . two, three seconds. It's a long burst. In the midst of this furious fusillade, a black figure separates from the doomed aircraft. Now I stop firing and follow this falling figure, turning steeply to keep him in sight, waiting for his chute to blossom. He falls and falls, but still no chute. Now it's too late. He hits in an open field, where a Romanian farmer has stopped his horse-drawn plow to watch the deadly game played out over his field.

I have never seen anything like this before, and I am momentarily stunned. Incredibly, I wonder half-aloud if I hit him as he left his machine, but in another second the sense of peril returns and I am again the hunter, reducing power, checking instruments, calling on the radio, and searching every bit of sky in my vicinity. No 109s. No Tommy. No wingman. Nothing.

I was not yet finished for the day. On my climb, I was bounced by two more 109s, but I succeeded in getting one of them. Then it was over and I was finally out of the target area, homeward bound. It was then that I began the introspection that was to last for more than fifty years. Why did I hold the trigger down? Could I have stopped firing sooner? Absolute nonsense, of course, trying to examine reflex actions that occurred in a span of a few split seconds. Still, the fact that there wasn't and couldn't be an answer did not stop the questioning.

The latent doubts over the years finally evolved into a desire to identify the unknown warrior-victim. But it was only recently that I began seriously to act on this compulsion. From a fellow aviation writer, I secured the address of a Belgian, Eric Mombeek, who specialized in World War II *Luftwaffe* history. I wrote to Mombeek to give the particulars of the fight and a request to determine, if possible, the name of the German pilot. About two weeks later, I received his reply. He said that only two *Geschwaders* (wings, like our groups) could have been involved and only one, the 1st *Gruppe* of *Jagdgeschwader* 53 (JG, for fighter wing) was in action on the day in question. He further stated that, fortunately, a very complete and scholarly history of JG-53 (which was nicknamed the *Pik As,* or Ace of Spades, *Jagdgeschwader)* had just been published. When he consulted it, he discovered that there was indeed a reference to a pilot shot down on that day whose parachute did not open. It resulted from an action with a P-51 near Gazanesti, Romania, exactly where I had placed the encounter. There was no doubt about it; we both were certain it was the correct aircraft. The pilot's name was Herbert Franke, a veteran *Feldwebel* (sergeant) who had recently been promoted to *Leutnant*. Included in the letter was a photocopy of a picture from the book of the 3d *Staffel* (flight) taken at Maniago, Italy, in the spring of 1944. A red arrow drawn above the group pointed to Herbert Franke. I studied the small image as it stared back at me, and it was an emotional moment.

I finally managed to locate and purchase a copy of the history, and painstakingly translated the text. Gradually, bits and pieces of the military career of Herbert Franke began to emerge.

He first appears as an *Obergefreiter* (corporal) flying with I/JG 53 on the Russian Front. On June 6, 1942, he crashed a Bf-109F near Voronezh, but no details were given other than the aircraft was totally destroyed. He next shows up a year later. The date is July 13, 1943, and his *Gruppe* had earlier been withdrawn from Sicily to Vibo Valentia, on the extreme southwest coast of Italy. On this day, the *Gruppe* was being transferred farther east to Lecce, because Vibo was being pummeled mercilessly by Allied bombers. Several of the pilots, including Herbert Franke, had flown their aircraft to Lecce, but since there were more aircraft than available pilots at Vibo, seven of them boarded General Adolf Galland's He-111 at Lecce to be ferried back to Vibo. The bomber arrived just at the end of a bombing raid, and the excited pilot overshot the landing field and wound up ditching 50 meters beyond the shore in the Tyrrhenian Sea, wrecking the aircraft and injuring all of the passengers. Herbert was taken to the hospital in Naples and did not return to duty until February 1944. The 3d *Staffel* of I/JG 53, of which he was a member, was then based at Maniago, in northern Italy. The Fifteenth Air Force had been attacking rail targets in northern Italy and sallying farther north into Hungary and Austria, so his unit, sitting astride the pathway northward, was in a position to intercept the American bombers and fighter escort.

On April 5, 1944, on one such intercept mission, his *Gruppe* engaged a formation of B-24s and their accompanying P-38 escorts. Even as Franke shot down a P-38, he fell victim to another P-38. He was wounded and forced to bail out of his "Yellow 5" just west of Treviso, landing him in the hospital again. When he rejoined the *Gruppe,* it had been transferred to Romania to assist in the defense of the Ploesti oil complex. During the month of June 1944, he succeeded in shooting down two B-24s, one on June 6 and the other on June 24.

On August 2, he wrote a letter to his friend, Ernst Pausinger, who was in the hospital in Vienna with wounds to his face and left eye suffered when he was shot down by a B-24 gunner. Up until now, all of the information I had gleaned about Herbert consisted of facts—dates, units, and locations. Now, for the first time I hear him speak. Not to me, of course, but still I hear him expressing himself in his own words. It is a poignant letter indeed, obviously written in haste, in response to a letter he had received from Pausinger.

Dear Ernst,

I received your letter from Vienna with thanks. Please excuse me for first answering it today. Things are again rather mad. Deadly dogfights with large numbers of greatly superior Mustangs. We can scarcely get close to the bombers.

Hauptmann Bauer has fallen, *Unteroffizier* Zemper was shot while hanging in his parachute. Many that you don't even know have not returned. I wouldn't like to mention numbers, or else it would look very bad to you. Only now and then is one of the Tommies still shot down. At the present time, only Kornatz, Burggraf, and I (of the people you knew) are still flying in the *Staffel*.

But, little friend, how can one be upset if he has to lie in bed? Man, sleep away until you are completely rested! I could sleep day and night!!! And with your eye, it will heal good. I hold both my thumbs. [I'm pulling for you.] Only don't give up.

The only happy news: *Unteroffizier* Janietz was promoted to *Feldwebel*. That is, however, the only good news. We have become just a young pile [motley crew].

Herbert Franke was to live only sixteen days after he wrote this letter. Our paths were inexorably drawing together now, resulting in his death on August 18.

I wrote to several of his *Staffel*mates who survived the war, hoping to learn more about Herbert, but I had no success. I had just about resigned myself to being satisfied with what I had when Fate intervened again.

One day in the Spring of 1994, I was leafing through a copy of *Jager*

Blatt, which a friend had given me. *Jager Blatt* is a bimonthly news booklet put out by the *Gemeinschaft der Jagdflieger,* the German Association of Fighter Pilots. I was looking at pictures, picking out words I recognized, when I was electrified by one in particular. It was a picture of two older men, one presenting a painting to the other. They were identified as Edu Neumann, commander of Axis fighter forces in Romania during World War II, and *Ernst Pausinger!* Surely there could not be two Ernst Pausingers; this had to be the friend of Herbert to whom he had written his last letter. When my astonishment wore off, I called my friend, Kurt Schulze, himself an ex-*Luftwaffe* pilot, and asked whether he could get the address of Pausinger for me.

A few days later, Kurt telephoned with the news that Pausinger had indeed been in the I/JG 53 and today lived in Bavaria, in the tiny town of Herrngiersdorf. Armed with this news and the address, I wrote to Pausinger to explain who I was and ask for any additional information that he might have. Six weeks went by, and I had begun to think that he wanted nothing to do with me. Then a letter arrived from Herrngiersdorf. It was from Ernst Pausinger, and he volunteered the information that he had been in Italy on holiday and had only seen my letter a short time before. He seemed genuinely interested in my request and in continuing the correspondence. Many of the details he offered I already had from the *Pik As* history, but he did provide some new information:

> On 11 June 1944 I myself was wounded, shot down by a Liberator, and was taken to a hospital near Bucharest. I saw Herbert Franke there for the last time.
>
> I first learned of his death in October 1944, after I had come back to the unit. Afterward I was told that *Hauptmann* Seiz, who led the honor guard at the burial for Franke, became a Russian POW [after Romania had gone over to the Allies] and first came home in 1949. Franke was, as far as I can remember and after discussion with Mr. Seiz, a charming, friendly, reserved comrade. But we still have not been able to get his home address.

I have since exchanged many letters with Ernst. To my question about where Herbert is buried, he replied that the return of fallen soldiers to

Germany was not permitted in "Socialist Times," and to his knowledge, Herbert and all of his comrades still lie in the cemetery in Bucharest.

Ernst and I finally met face to face in October 1994 in Geisenheim, Germany. He is himself a "charming, friendly, reserved comrade," and despite the language difficulty, we got on famously. While withdrawing several bottles of beer from a small bag that he brought, he explained that the small brewery which produced them had only been in the family for a hundred years, but otherwise had been in continuous production for 850 years, since 1131. And so, arms around each other's shoulders, we drank the beer, except for one bottle that I saved and brought home with me. When will I drink the last bottle? I don't know. Perhaps never. I might just keep it to look at, to help me remember other times and places.

While I have found no surviving trace of Herbert Franke, I have found his friend, and his friend has become my friend.

In all, during the course of sixty-one combat missions flown over southern, central, and eastern Europe in under six months, Captain Bob Goebel ended his combat career with credits for ten Bf-109s and one Me-110 shot down, plus one Bf-109 probable. He went on reserve status at the end of the war and completed a degree in physics on the GI Bill in time to return to active career status during the Korean War. Lieutenant Colonel Bob Goebel retired from the Air Force in 1966 following many years of service with the NASA Manned Space Program.

Bibliography

Belote, James H., and William M. Belote. *Titans of the Seas: The Development and Operations of Japanese and American Carrier Task Forces During World War II.* New York: Harper & Row, 1975.

Carter, Kit C., and Robert Mueller. *The Army Air Forces in World War II: Combat Chronology, 1941-1945*. Washington, D.C.: Office of Air Force History, 1973.

Craven, Wesley F., and James L. Cate (eds.). *The Army Air Forces in World War II,* Vol. I, *Plans and Early Operations, January 1939 to August 1942*. Chicago: University of Chicago Press, 1948.

_______________. *The Army Air Forces in World War II,* Vol. IV, *The Pacific: Guadalcanal to Saipan, August 1942 to July 1944*. Chicago: University of Chicago Press, 1950.

_______________. *The Army Air Forces in World War II,* Vol. V, *The Pacific: Matterhorn to Nagasaki, June 1944 to August 1945.* Chicago: University of Chicago Press, 1953.

Dull, Paul S. *The Imperial Japanese Navy (1941-1945).* Annapolis: Naval Institute Press, 1978.

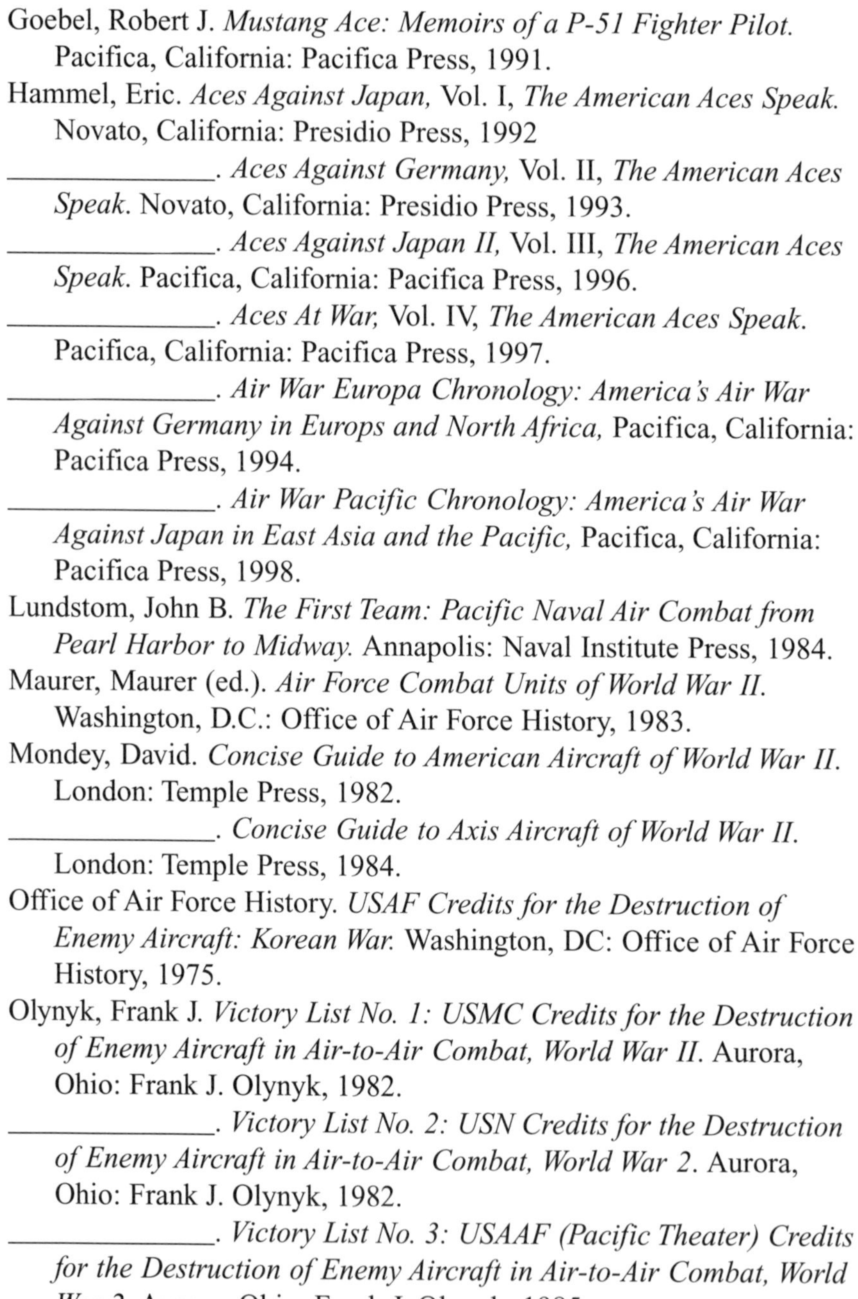

Goebel, Robert J. *Mustang Ace: Memoirs of a P-51 Fighter Pilot.* Pacifica, California: Pacifica Press, 1991.

Hammel, Eric. *Aces Against Japan,* Vol. I, *The American Aces Speak.* Novato, California: Presidio Press, 1992

______________. *Aces Against Germany,* Vol. II, *The American Aces Speak.* Novato, California: Presidio Press, 1993.

______________. *Aces Against Japan II,* Vol. III, *The American Aces Speak.* Pacifica, California: Pacifica Press, 1996.

______________. *Aces At War,* Vol. IV, *The American Aces Speak.* Pacifica, California: Pacifica Press, 1997.

______________. *Air War Europa Chronology: America's Air War Against Germany in Europs and North Africa,* Pacifica, California: Pacifica Press, 1994.

______________. *Air War Pacific Chronology: America's Air War Against Japan in East Asia and the Pacific,* Pacifica, California: Pacifica Press, 1998.

Lundstom, John B. *The First Team: Pacific Naval Air Combat from Pearl Harbor to Midway.* Annapolis: Naval Institute Press, 1984.

Maurer, Maurer (ed.). *Air Force Combat Units of World War II.* Washington, D.C.: Office of Air Force History, 1983.

Mondey, David. *Concise Guide to American Aircraft of World War II.* London: Temple Press, 1982.

______________. *Concise Guide to Axis Aircraft of World War II.* London: Temple Press, 1984.

Office of Air Force History. *USAF Credits for the Destruction of Enemy Aircraft: Korean War.* Washington, DC: Office of Air Force History, 1975.

Olynyk, Frank J. *Victory List No. 1: USMC Credits for the Destruction of Enemy Aircraft in Air-to-Air Combat, World War II.* Aurora, Ohio: Frank J. Olynyk, 1982.

______________. *Victory List No. 2: USN Credits for the Destruction of Enemy Aircraft in Air-to-Air Combat, World War 2.* Aurora, Ohio: Frank J. Olynyk, 1982.

______________. *Victory List No. 3: USAAF (Pacific Theater) Credits for the Destruction of Enemy Aircraft in Air-to-Air Combat, World War 2.* Aurora, Ohio: Frank J. Olynyk, 1985.

____________. *Victory List No. 4: AVG & USAAF (China-Burma-India Theater) Credits for the Destruction of Enemy Aircraft in Air-to-Air Combat, World War 2*. Aurora, Ohio: Frank J. Olynyk, 1986.

____________. *Victory List No. 5: USAAF (European Theater) Credits for the Destruction of Enemy Aircraft in Air-to-Air-Combat, World War 2*. Aurora, Ohio: Frank J. Olynyk, 1987.

____________. *Victory List No. 6: USAAF (Mediterranean Theater) Credits for the Destruction of Enemy Aircraft in Air-to-Air Combat, World War II*. Aurora, Ohio: Frank J. Olynyk, 1987.

Risner, Robinson. *The Passing of the Night.* New York: Ballantine Books, 1973.

Sherrod, Robert. *History of Marine Corps Aviation in World War II.* Novato, California: Presidio Press, 1980.

Stafford, Commander Edward P., USN. *The Big E.* New York: Ballantine Books, 1974.

Tillman, Barrett. *Corsair: The F4U in World War II and Korea*. Annapolis: Naval Institute Press, 1979.

______________. *Hellcat: The F6F in World War II*. Annapolis, Naval Institute Press, 1979.

______________. *The Wildcat in WWII*. Annapolis: Nautical & Aviation Publishing, 1983.

Toliver, Raymond F., and Trevor J. Constable. *Fighter Aces of the U.S.A.* Fallbrook, California: Aero Publishers, Inc., 1979.

Williams, Mary H. *U.S. Army in World War II*: Special Studies, *Chronology: 1941-1945*. Washington, D.C.: Center of Military History, 1984.

Index

♦